Betty Crocker

Cookies

Irresistibly Easy Recipes for Any Occasion

WITHDRAWN

Houghton Mifflin Harcourt
Boston • New York • 2019

GENERAL MILLS

Global Business Solutions Director:
Heather Polen

Global Business Solutions Manager:
Andrea Kleinschmit

Executive Editor: Cathy
Swanson Wheaton

Recipe Development and Testing:
Betty Crocker Kitchens

Photography: General Mills
Photography Studios and
Image Library

HOUGHTON MIFFLIN HARCOURT

Editorial Director: Deb Brody

Executive Editor: Anne Ficklen

Associate Editor: Sarah Kwak

Senior Managing Editor: Marina
Padakis Lowry

Art Director: Tai Blanche

Cover and Interior Design: Tai Blanche

Senior Production Coordinator:
Kimberly Kiefer

hmhbooks.com

Library of Congress Cataloging-in-Publication Data

Names: Crocker, Betty, author. | Betty Crocker Kitchens.
Title: Betty Crocker cookies : irresistibly easy recipes for any occasion. Other titles: Cookies
Description: Boston : Houghton Mifflin Harcourt, 2019. | Series: Betty Crocker cooking | Includes index.
Identifiers: LCCN 2019002546 (print) | LCCN 2019003101 (ebook) | ISBN 9780358118152 (ebook) |
ISBN 9780358118190 (paper over board)
Subjects: LCSH: Cookies. | LCGFT: Cookbooks.
Classification: LCC TX772 (ebook) | LCC TX772 .C695 2019 (print) | DDC 641.86/54—dc23
LC record available at https://lccn.loc.gov/2019002546

Manufactured in China

C&C 10 9 8 7 6 5 4 3 2 1

Cover photo: Gingerdoodle Cookies, page 136

Find more great ideas at BettyCrocker.com

Dear Cookie Lover,

Baking cookies is magical! It's amazing how the aroma of freshly baked cookies draws those we love to the kitchen and keeps them there a little longer or sends them off with a delicious, heartwarming, edible hug.

Inside you'll find recipes for every occasion, whether you want to add a sweet surprise to a lunchbox, are baking for the holidays or want a yummy treat when it's too hot to turn on the oven. From simple to decadent, these delicious cookies will be devoured.

We'll show you how to **have fun baking with kids,** creating special times together while keeping the mess and stress at bay! Try our tips and tricks for throwing a low-key, **memorable cookie exchange** or enjoy all the clever places you can use cookies for other uses, as well as creative ways to **show your cookie cutters some love** beyond the holidays.

Look for these special recipes:

Start with a Mix Slash time in the kitchen by jump-starting your prep with a mix

Big Batch Recipes making 4 or more dozen; perfect for cookie swaps or cookie monsters

All our recipes are tested in the Betty Crocker Kitchens, so you know you'll have success every time. We've packed this book with all our best tips and tricks to make you a cookie-baking champion! Enjoy our "Fun Look Back at Cookies," since our first *Cooky Book* was published and how cookies have changed in our "Cookie Goes Round" feature, sprinkled throughout the book.

Let's Bake Up Some Magic!

Betty Crocker

Contents

Cookie and Bar Know-How

Baking cookies isn't rocket science, but knowing the essential tips and tricks can ensure baking success so that no matter what little bites of heaven you bake, you'll be proud to serve them. Small, yes, but cookies still require attention to achieve a big kitchen victory. Read on to find all the info you need to be a cookie-baking rock star, straight from the Betty Crocker Kitchens.

INGREDIENTS

FLOUR All-purpose flour is recommended for making cookies and bars. It's what we've used to test all our recipes, unless otherwise noted. Whole wheat flour can be used if substituted for up to one-third of the all-purpose flour called for in a recipe. If a larger proportion of whole wheat flour is used (and the recipe wasn't specifically developed with it), the cookies could be too dry and crumbly.

SWEETENERS In addition to adding sweetness, sugar also helps to add tenderness to the cookies and helps them brown.

LEAVENINGS Cookies usually call for one or both of baking powder or baking soda to help lighten cookie dough by making it rise. Sometimes cream of tartar is used as a leavening as well as to impart a slightly sour flavor to the cookies.

> *Be sure to check the use-by date of your leavenings. If your cookies aren't performing, this could be the culprit!*

FATS AND OILS These add tenderness and flavor to cookies and bars. For best results, use the ingredient called for in the recipe, and do not substitute another ingredient unless the recipe gives an alternate. We use salted butter (not margarine) for most cookies for the best results. Margarine usually contains water, which can affect the spread of the cookie. Spreads that are at least 65 percent fat will work; however, the flavor may be compromised.

BEST METHOD FOR EVENLY SOFTENED BUTTER Soften it at room temperature for 30 to 40 minutes.

QUICK METHOD FOR SOFTENING BUTTER

Microwave unwrapped butter in a glass bowl on Low 30% power. It will take 30 seconds to 1 minute for ½ cup to 1 cup. (Watch carefully, as butter can soften unevenly, causing parts of it to quickly melt.)

EGGS Eggs add structure, moisture and richness to cookies and bars. All recipes in this book have been tested with large eggs. Egg product substitutes, made of egg whites, can be substituted for whole eggs, but the cookies and bars may have a more dry, crumbly texture.

OATS In some recipes, either quick-cooking or old-fashioned oats would work, but sometimes the variety matters. Use what is called for in the recipe. Instant oatmeal products are not the same as quick-cooking oats and should not be used for baking.

NUTS, PEANUTS AND ALMOND BRICKLE CHIPS When a recipe calls for nuts, feel free to substitute any variety of nut or peanuts. Nuts and almond brickle chips can easily become rancid, giving your cookies an off flavor. Check these ingredients by tasting them before adding them to your cookies. Prevent rancidity by storing nuts and peanuts in a tightly covered container in the refrigerator or freezer up to 2 years. Do not freeze cashews—they don't freeze well.

MIXING

Most recipes in this book call for using either an electric mixer or spoon, depending on the ingredients used and how hard it is to mix.

Note the specific directions for the recipe you are making. Sugars, fats and liquids are usually beaten together first until well mixed, to incorporate air into the dough and disperse the fat. Flour and other ingredients are almost always added afterward to avoid overmixing the dough, which can result in tough cookies.

CHOOSING PANS
COOKIE SHEETS

SHINY ALUMINUM COOKIE SHEETS These are our recommendation for perfectly baked cookies. Choose sheets with a smooth surface. They reflect heat, letting cookies bake evenly and brown properly. We used these pans to test cookies in this book.

INSULATED COOKIE SHEETS These pans help cookies from becoming too dark on the bottom, but cookies baked on these sheets may take longer to bake, and they may not brown as nicely overall. Cookies can be difficult to remove from these cookie sheets because the bottoms are more tender.

NONSTICK AND DARK COOKIE SHEETS Cookies baked on these pans may be smaller in diameter and more rounded. The tops and especially the bottoms will be more browned, and the bottoms will be hard. Follow manufacturer's directions; some recommend reducing the oven temperature by 25°F.

- Choose cookie sheets that are at least 2 inches smaller than the inside of your oven to allow air to circulate while baking.

- Cookie sheets may be open on one to three sides. There are four sides on 15x10-inch pans. If used for cookies, the cookies may not brown as easily and can be harder to remove without damaging their shape.

- Owning at least two cookie sheets is helpful. While one batch bakes, you can prepare the next batch.

Softening Butter

If your recipe calls for softened butter, it's important to soften it to the correct stage or your cookies will either spread too much (with overly softened butter) or not enough (with butter that's not softened enough).

Perfectly Softened: Butter is soft (leaves a slight indentation when touched lightly), yet still holds its shape.

Too Soft: Butter is overly softened and doesn't hold its shape.

Partially Melted: Butter is overly softened and has started to melt.

Cookie Scoop Sizes

Use the appropriate-size scoop to make cookies these common sizes:

Amount of Cookie Dough	Scoop Size	Dough Ball Size
¼ cup dough	16	
Rounded tablespoon	50	1¼-inch
Level tablespoon	70	1-inch
Rounded teaspoon	100	¾-inch

- For even baking, bake one cookie sheet at a time in the middle of the oven. If you do bake two cookie sheets at once, position the oven racks as close to the middle as possible, and rotate the position of the cookie sheets halfway through baking.

- Use completely cooled cookie sheets, as cookies will spread too much if placed and baked on a warm cookie sheet.

- Check cookies and bars at the minimum bake time given in the recipe, adding a minute or two, if necessary, until the baking doneness described in the recipe is achieved.

- Cool cookies as directed. Use a flat, thin metal spatula to remove them from the baking sheet.

- Cool bars and brownies in the pan on a cooling rack.

- Use a plastic knife to cut brownies and soft, sticky bars.

Measuring Correctly

Spoon brown sugar into measuring cup; firmly pack with back of spoon.

Dip measuring spoon into food; level off (if dry) or fill to rim (if liquid).

Spoon in dry ingredients, then level off top using a flat-edged utensil such as the back of a knife or metal spatula.

Check amount of liquid by looking at it at eye level while cup sits steady on counter.

BAKING PANS Shiny metal pans are recommended for baking bars for the same reason we recommend this finish for cookie sheets. They reflect heat and prevent the bottoms of the bars from getting too brown and hard. Follow the same guidelines as for nonstick and dark cookie sheets (above).

Use the exact size of pan called for in the bar recipe. Bars made in pans that are too big can easily get overcooked or become hard, and those made in pans that are too small can be doughy and raw in the center and hard on the edges.

GREASING PANS

Grease cookie sheets or pans for bars only as directed in recipe. We love the convenience of cooking spray for most recipes, but you can use shortening, if you like, unless otherwise noted in recipe. Do not use butter to grease the pans unless specifically called for, because the areas between cookies can burn. We sometimes call for cooking parchment paper and may also give directions to grease the paper to help delicate cookies or sticky bars release better.

- Avoid greasing nonstick cookie sheets, as cookies will spread too much.

- As an alternative to greasing, line cookie sheets or pans with cooking parchment paper or line with a silicone mat.

TIPS FOR PERFECT COOKIES OR BARS

- To see how the dough bakes, bake a test cookie before baking an entire batch. If the cookie spreads too much, add a tablespoon or two of flour to the remaining dough. If the cookie is too round or not soft enough, stir 1 or 2 tablespoons of milk into the remaining dough.

- Make cookies all the same size so they will bake evenly. Using a spring-loaded scoop can ensure the same size cookies. See the chart on page 8 for scoop sizes. If dough is sticky, you may need to lightly spray the scoop with cooking spray before scooping, so that the dough doesn't stick to and clog the spring mechanism. Also, clean out the scoop as needed.

STORING COOKIES AND BARS

See specific guidelines in the *How to Store* tips with each recipe or use these general guidelines. Store only one type of cookie in a container to keep the texture and flavors intact. If different cookies are stored in the same container, they can transfer moisture to one another, making crisp cookies soft, and they can pick up flavors from each other.

CRISP COOKIES Store at room temperature in loosely covered containers.

CHEWY COOKIES Store at room temperature in resealable food-storage plastic bags or tightly covered containers.

FROSTED OR DECORATED COOKIES Let frosting harden or set before storing; then store by placing between layers of cooking parchment or waxed paper, plastic wrap or foil. Store in tightly covered containers.

BARS Most bars can be stored tightly covered, but follow specific recipe directions, as some may need to be stored loosely covered or may need to be refrigerated.

Pictured clockwise from top left are Snickerdoodles, page 18; Oatmeal-Raisin Cookies, page 17; and Lemon Bars, page 34.

Bake Up
a Classic

Favorite Chocolate Chip Cookies

PREP TIME: 1 Hour 25 Minutes • **START TO FINISH: 1 Hour 40 Minutes** • **About 6 dozen cookies**

1½ cups butter, softened
1¼ cups granulated sugar
1¼ cups packed brown sugar
1 tablespoon vanilla
2 eggs

4 cups all-purpose flour
2 teaspoons baking soda
½ teaspoon salt
1 bag (24 oz) semisweet chocolate chips (4 cups)

1 Heat oven to 350°F. In large bowl, beat butter, granulated sugar, brown sugar, vanilla and eggs with electric mixer on medium speed or with spoon until light and fluffy. Stir in flour, baking soda and salt (dough will be stiff). Stir in chocolate chips.

2 Onto ungreased cookie sheets, drop dough by tablespoonfuls 2 inches apart; flatten slightly.

3 Bake 11 to 13 minutes or until light brown (centers will be soft). Cool 1 to 2 minutes; remove from cookie sheets to cooling racks.

Peanut Butter Chocolate Chip Cookies

Transform these cookies into Peanut Butter Chocolate Chip Cookies by substituting 2 cups of candy-coated peanut butter milk chocolate chips or peanut butter baking chips for 2 cups of the chocolate chips.

how to store: Store these cookies covered at room temperature.

1 Cookie: Calories 140; Total Fat 7g (Saturated Fat 4g, Trans Fat 0g); Cholesterol 15mg; Sodium 85mg; Total Carbohydrate 18g (Dietary Fiber 0g, Sugars 12g); Protein 1g
Exchanges: ½ Starch, ½ Other Carbohydrate, 1½ Fat
Carbohydrate Choices: 1

14

BAKE
UP
A
CLASSIC

The Cookie Goes Round

FROM *BETTY CROCKER COOKY BOOK*: CHOCOLATE CHIP COOKIES— LATE 1930s

"NEW COOKY SWEEPS THE NATION . . . from the New England Toll House, Whitman, Mass. Enjoyed immediate and continuing popularity. It was introduced to homemakers in 1939 on our radio series, 'Famous Foods from Famous Places.'"

TODAY: CHOCOLATE CHIP COOKIES

Chocolate chip cookies are still all the rage. We love this version, as they have a little more body and the perfect ratio of brown sugar to white sugar, which makes the flavor and texture amazing!

Oatmeal-Raisin Cookies

PREP TIME: 45 Minutes • **START TO FINISH: 45 Minutes** • **About 3 dozen cookies**

⅔ cup granulated sugar
⅔ cup packed brown sugar
½ cup butter, softened
½ cup shortening
1 teaspoon vanilla
2 eggs
1 teaspoon baking soda
1 teaspoon ground cinnamon

½ teaspoon baking powder
½ teaspoon salt
3 cups quick-cooking or old-fashioned oats
1 cup all-purpose flour
1 cup raisins
½ cup chopped nuts, if desired

ingredient info:

This classic oatmeal cookie can be tailored to your personal tastes. If you like, substitute 1 cup semisweet chocolate chips for the raisins, or you can use sweetened dried cranberries for the raisins.

how to store:

Store these cookies in a tightly covered container.

1   Heat oven to 375°F. In large bowl, beat granulated sugar, brown sugar, butter, shortening, vanilla and eggs with electric mixer on medium speed or with spoon until well blended. Beat or stir in baking soda, cinnamon, baking powder and salt. Stir in oats, flour, raisins and nuts.

2   Onto ungreased cookie sheets, drop dough by rounded tablespoonfuls about 2 inches apart.

3   Bake 9 to 11 minutes or until light brown. Immediately remove from cookie sheets to cooling racks.

1 Cookie: Calories 140; Total Fat 6g (Saturated Fat 2g, Trans Fat 0g); Cholesterol 15mg; Sodium 105mg; Total Carbohydrate 18g (Dietary Fiber 1g, Sugars 10g); Protein 1g
Exchanges: 1 Starch, 1 Fat
Carbohydrate Choices: 1

17

BAKE
UP
A
CLASSIC

Snickerdoodles

PREP TIME: 40 Minutes • **START TO FINISH: 50 Minutes** • **About 4 dozen cookies**

1¾ cups sugar
½ cup butter, softened
½ cup shortening
2 eggs
2¾ cups all-purpose flour

2 teaspoons cream of tartar
1 teaspoon baking soda
¼ teaspoon salt
2 teaspoons ground cinnamon

1 Cookie: Calories 90; Total Fat 4g (Saturated Fat 2g, Trans Fat 0g); Cholesterol 15mg; Sodium 55mg; Total Carbohydrate 13g (Dietary Fiber 0g, Sugars 7g); Protein 1g
Exchanges: 1 Other Carbohydrate, 1 Fat
Carbohydrate Choices: 1

1 Heat oven to 400°F. In large bowl, mix 1 ½ cups of the sugar, the butter, shortening and eggs. Stir in flour, cream of tartar, baking soda and salt.

2 Shape dough into 1¼-inch balls. In small bowl, mix the remaining ¼ cup sugar and the cinnamon. Roll balls in cinnamon-sugar mixture. On ungreased cookie sheets, place balls 2 inches apart.

3 Bake 8 to 10 minutes or until set. Remove from cookie sheets to cooking racks.

Peanut Butter Cookies

PREP TIME: 25 Minutes • **START TO FINISH: 2 Hours 35 Minutes** • **About 2½ dozen cookies**

½ cup granulated sugar
½ cup packed brown sugar
½ cup peanut butter
¼ cup shortening
¼ cup butter, softened

1 egg
1¼ cups all-purpose flour
¾ teaspoon baking soda
½ teaspoon baking powder
¼ teaspoon salt

1 In large bowl, mix granulated sugar, brown sugar, peanut butter, shortening, butter and egg. Stir in remaining ingredients. Cover and refrigerate about 2 hours or until firm.

2 Heat oven to 375ºF. Shape dough into 1¼-inch balls. On ungreased cookie sheets, place balls about 3 inches apart. Flatten in crisscross pattern with fork dipped into sugar.

3 Bake 9 to 10 minutes or until light golden brown. Cool 5 minutes; remove from cookie sheets to cooling racks.

why it works:

Want the perfect bumpy top on your cookies? Wipe off any excess dough and sugar that may collect between the tines of the fork.

how to store:

Store these peanutty cookies in a tightly covered container. For a special treat, sandwich two of these all-time favorites together with a scoop of chocolate ice cream. Roll the edge in chopped candy bar or nuts. Store in a tightly covered container in the freezer.

1 Cookie: Calories 110; Total Fat 6g (Saturated Fat 2g, Trans Fat 0g); Cholesterol 10mg; Sodium 470mg; Total Carbohydrate 13g (Dietary Fiber 0g, Sugars 7g); Protein 1g
Exchanges: ½ Starch, ½ Other Carbohydrate, 1 Fat
Carbohydrate Choices: 1

Peanut Butter Blossom Cookies

PREP TIME: 1 Hour • **START TO FINISH: 1 Hour** • **About 3 dozen cookies**

½ cup granulated sugar
½ cup packed brown sugar
½ cup creamy peanut butter
½ cup butter, softened
1 egg
1½ cups all-purpose flour

¾ teaspoon baking soda
½ teaspoon baking powder
Additional granulated sugar
About 36 milk chocolate candy drops or pieces, unwrapped

1 Heat oven to 375°F. In large bowl, beat ½ cup granulated sugar, the brown sugar, peanut butter, butter and egg with electric mixer on medium speed or with spoon until well blended. Stir in flour, baking soda and baking powder until dough forms.

2 Shape dough into 1-inch balls; roll in additional granulated sugar. On ungreased cookie sheets, place balls about 2 inches apart.

3 Bake 8 to 10 minutes or until edges are light golden brown. Immediately press 1 milk chocolate candy in center of each cookie; remove from cookie sheets to cooling rack.

ingredient info:

You can use any type of granulated sugar to roll these balls in: coarse sugar, colored sugars or sparkling sugar, each for a different look.

how to store:

Store these cookies in a single layer in a covered container.

1 Cookie: Calories 120; Total Fat 6g (Saturated Fat 3g, Trans Fat 0g); Cholesterol 15mg; Sodium 75mg; Total Carbohydrate 14g (Dietary Fiber 0g, Sugars 10g); Protein 2g
Exchanges: 1 Starch, 1 Fat
Carbohydrate Choices: 1

Chocolate Crinkles

PREP TIME: 1 Hour 45 Minutes • **START TO FINISH: 3 Hours 45 Minutes** • **About 6 dozen cookies**

2 cups granulated sugar	4 eggs
½ cup vegetable oil	2 cups all-purpose flour
2 teaspoons vanilla	2 teaspoons baking powder
4 oz unsweetened baking chocolate, melted, cooled	½ teaspoon salt
	½ cup powdered sugar

1 In large bowl, mix granulated sugar, oil, vanilla and chocolate. Stir in eggs, one at a time. Stir in flour, baking powder and salt. Cover; refrigerate at least 3 hours.

2 Heat oven to 350°F. Spray cookie sheets with cooking spray.

3 Drop dough by teaspoonfuls into powdered sugar; roll around to coat and shape into balls. On cookie sheets, place balls about 2 inches apart.

4 Bake 10 to 12 minutes or until almost no imprint remains when touched lightly in center. Immediately remove from cookie sheets to cooling racks.

kitchen secret:

To save time in cleaning up, line your cookie sheet with a piece of cooking parchment paper. Simply bake cookies as directed, spraying the parchment with cooking spray as you would the cookie sheet if directed.

how to store:

Store these cookies in a tightly covered container.

1 Cookie: Calories 70; Total Fat 2g (Saturated Fat 1g, Trans Fat 0g); Cholesterol 10mg; Sodium 35mg; Total Carbohydrate 10g (Dietary Fiber 0g, Sugars 6g); Protein 1g
Exchanges: ½ Starch, ½ Fat
Carbohydrate Choices: ½

25

BAKE
UP
A
CLASSIC

An Amusing Look Back at Cookies

Or is it "cookys"? Whatever the spelling, cookies have had a fun place in our families, memories and gatherings. Here's a look back on the cookie scene since Betty Crocker's first *Cooky Book* was published. Enjoy drooling (or giggling) over these popular cookies of the past.

1963

Betty Crocker's Cooky Book introduced

The letter from Betty Crocker stated, "remembering the motto 'happy the home with the full cooky jar,' we hope you'll turn to this book often." This book is still sold as a facsimile today as cookie lovers enjoy a nostalgic look back at cookies from yesteryear.
But why "cooky"? We think the spelling was chosen because it was an approachable and casual version of the word, in the day. The spelling still makes us chuckle!

1965

Magic Cookie Bars at every gathering

Also known as Hello Dolly Bars or 7-Layer Bars, these very popular bars showed up at potlucks everywhere; partly for the easy preparation and partly for the tasty combination of nuts, chocolate, graham and coconut. Try our sophisticated twist on the original: Dark Chocolate–Cherry Macadamia Bars (page 233) are fabulous.

1970s

Sneaky Hippie Food

Brunch was introduced as an entirely new meal. Green gelatin salads, cheese from a can and TV dinners were in vogue. Granola, the hippie favorite of the 1960s, found its way into cookies and bars and it's been a love-affair ever since. Chewy Chocolate-Drizzled Granola Bars (page 284) will fuel any fixation you may have.

1980s

Biscotti Are Big

Those delightfully slender, crisp cookies were popular alongside coffee and tea as dunkers. Better yet, they made it perfectly acceptable to eat cookies for breakfast! Look for cookie versions of a breakfast quick bread as well as trail mix bars in this book, making homemade breakfast fun and convenient (and still making cookies a breakfast food).

1990s

Dip and Dunk

Dunkaroos™, an iconic lunch box staple, were a Betty Crocker product consisting of cookies and frosting packaged side by side for dunking. They offered a fun, engaging way to enjoy frosted cookies. Who wouldn't want a lunch box treat that's also something to play with? Today, we've got more sophisticated dips for cookies. Check out the irresistible recipes, starting on page 258.

1994
Indoor S'mores

Golden Grahams™ cereal, melted marshmallow and chocolate made into bars meant you could enjoy s'mores anytime and without the need of a fire! Our Stuffed S'more Cookies (page 153) are a delicious, on-the-go way to have the flavors of s'mores without getting your fingers sticky.

2000
Ahead of the Pumpkin Craze?

Betty Crocker's 9th edition of "Big Red" debuted—with a recipe for homemade Pumpkin Spice Bars. Could this be what started American's obsession with everything pumpkin spice? Pumpkin-Turmeric Bars (page 250) add a global twist to the typical pumpkin spice flavor with the addition of turmeric.

2009
Whoopie Pie Madness

Legend has it that happy kids and husbands would exclaim, "whoopie!" if they found one of these cream-filled, soft sandwich cookies packed in their lunch. Maine and Pennsylvania are supposedly still fighting over rights to the invention of the yummy cookie. Popularity had been steadily heating up to boiling, when in 2009, they showed up everywhere . . . bakeries, restaurants and even at weddings! The Betty Crocker Kitchens developed easy-to-follow recipes for intriguing flavors such as Triple Chocolate Stout, Cookies and Cream and Mini Rainbow Whoopie Pies.

2011
Red Velvet Everything

At first it started with red velvet cake and then red velvet cupcakes . . . but then things started getting interesting. Betty Crocker was on the scene with Red Velvet Cookie Bars, Red Velvet Whoopie Pie, Red Velvet Torte and Red Velvet Wedding cake recipes.

2016
Hazelnut Spread Swoon

Anything with hazelnut spread was irresistible, and frankly, the addiction hasn't really faded! Sure, you can eat spoonfuls right out of the jar, but putting it in recipes, such as Hazelnut Chocolate Cookie Balls (page 68), is so much more satisfying!

TODAY
New Flavors

We get excited about trying new global flavors or unique combinations of ingredients, and everything must be camera-worthy, as well! Cranberry, Rosemary and Blue Cheese Drop Cookies (page 41) and Sparkling Orange Ricotta Sandwich Cookies (page 160) are right here for you and your taste cravings.

Betty Crocker Cookies

It has a cookie for every occasion. From the holidays and classics to totable treats and no-bake cookies, every recipe is carefully created in the Betty Crocker Kitchens with tips and tricks to help you bake up successful treats any time you have a cookie craving.

Classic Sugar Cookies

PREP TIME: 2 Hours • **START TO FINISH: 4 Hours 30 Minutes** • **About 8 dozen cookies**

COOKIES

3	cups powdered sugar
2	cups butter, softened
2	teaspoons vanilla
1	teaspoon almond extract
2	eggs
5	cups all-purpose flour
2	teaspoons baking soda
2	teaspoons cream of tartar

DECORATOR'S GLAZE

4	cups powdered sugar
¼	cup water
¼	cup light corn syrup
1	teaspoon almond extract
	Food colors, as desired

DECORATIONS

Decorating gel, colored sugar and/or decors, if desired

Decorating icing, if desired

Flaked coconut, if desired

1 In large bowl, beat 3 cups powdered sugar, the butter, vanilla, 1 teaspoon almond extract and eggs with electric mixer on medium speed or with spoon until blended. Stir in flour, baking soda and cream of tartar. Cover and refrigerate at least 2 hours.

2 Heat oven to 375°F. Spray cookie sheet with cooking spray. Divide dough in half. On lightly floured surface, roll each half ⅛ inch thick. Cut into desired shapes with 3-inch cookie cutters. On cookie sheet, place cutouts about 2 inches apart.

3 Bake 5 to 7 minutes or until edges are light brown. Remove from cookie sheet to wire rack. Cool completely, about 30 minutes.

4 In small bowl, beat 4 cups powdered sugar, water, corn syrup and 1 teaspoon almond extract on low speed until smooth. Divide among several small bowls. Stir desired food color, one drop at a time, into each until desired color is reached. Decorate cookies with glaze and other decorations.

kitchen secret:

You can divide this recipe in half for a smaller batch of cookies.

kitchen secret:

Roll dough to an even thickness by rolling it between two wooden sticks or rulers of the desired thickness. Place the sticks just wide enough apart that the rolling pin can roll over both of them at the same time. The dough will become the right thickness as you roll it thinner and the rolling pin hits the sticks.

how to store:

Store these cookies in a tightly covered container at room temperature.

1 Cookie: Calories 100; Total Fat 4g (Saturated Fat 2g, Trans Fat 0g); Cholesterol 15mg; Sodium 60mg; Total Carbohydrate 14g (Dietary Fiber 0g, Sugars 9g); Protein 1g
Exchanges: 1 Other Carbohydrate, 1 Fat
Carbohydrate Choices: 1

Gingerbread Cutouts

PREP TIME: 1 Hour 30 Minutes • **START TO FINISH: 2 Hours 40 Minutes** • **About 10 dozen cookies**

1½ cups granulated sugar
1 cup butter, softened
3 tablespoons molasses
2 tablespoons water or milk
1 egg
3¼ cups all-purpose flour
2 teaspoons baking soda
2 teaspoons ground cinnamon

1½ teaspoons ground ginger
½ teaspoon salt
½ teaspoon ground cardamom
½ teaspoon ground cloves
Currants or assorted candies, if desired
Colored sugar or additional sugar, if desired

kitchen secret:
Place the tiny candies or sprinkles onto the unbaked cookies with clean tweezers.

how to store:
Store these gingerbread cookies in a covered container.

1 Cookie: Calories 40; Total Fat 1.5g (Saturated Fat 1g, Trans Fat 0g); Cholesterol 5mg; Sodium 45mg; Total Carbohydrate 6g (Dietary Fiber 0g, Sugars 3g); Protein 0g
Exchanges: ½ Other Carbohydrate, ½ Fat
Carbohydrate Choices: ½

1 In large bowl, beat granulated sugar, butter and molasses with electric mixer on medium speed or with spoon until well mixed. Beat in water and egg until blended. Stir in flour, baking soda, cinnamon, ginger, salt, cardamom and cloves. Cover and refrigerate about 1 hour or until firm.

2 Heat oven to 350°F. Roll one-third of dough at a time on floured surface to ⅛-inch thickness. (Keep remaining dough refrigerated until ready to roll.) Cut with floured 2½-inch gingerbread boy or girl cookie cutter. On ungreased cookie sheets, place cutouts 1 inch apart. Decorate with currants or candies. Sprinkle with colored sugar.

3 Bake 6 to 7 minutes or until set. Remove from cookie sheet to cooling rack; cool.

31

BAKE
UP
A
CLASSIC

Gingersnaps

PREP TIME: 45 Minutes • START TO FINISH: **45 Minutes** • **About 4 dozen cookies**

1 cup packed brown sugar	1 teaspoon ground cinnamon
¾ cup shortening	1 teaspoon ground ginger
¼ cup molasses	½ teaspoon ground cloves
1 egg	¼ teaspoon salt
2¼ cups all-purpose flour	Granulated sugar
2 teaspoons baking soda	

1 Heat oven to 375°F. Lightly spray cookie sheets with cooking spray or line with cooking parchment paper.

2 In large bowl, beat brown sugar, shortening, molasses and egg with electric mixer on medium speed or with spoon until well blended. Stir in remaining ingredients except granulated sugar.

3 Shape dough by rounded teaspoonfuls into balls. Dip tops into granulated sugar. On cookie sheets, place balls, sugared sides up, about 3 inches apart.

4 Bake 10 to 12 minutes or just until set. Immediately remove from cookie sheets to cooling rack.

ingredient info:

Molasses is a thick, sticky, dark brown syrup that comes from the refining process of raw sugar. Molasses can be light, dark or blackstrap. Light molasses has the lightest color and mildest flavor. Dark molasses is darker and has a more pronounced full flavor than light molasses. These two can be interchanged in baking. Blackstrap molasses is very dark with a bitter flavor and should not be used in baking unless the recipe indicates blackstrap molasses.

how to store:

Store these spiced cookies in a tightly covered container.

1 Cookie: Calories 50; Total Fat 2g (Saturated Fat 0g, Trans Fat 0g); Cholesterol 0mg; Sodium 45mg; Total Carbohydrate 8g (Dietary Fiber 0g, Sugars 4g); Protein 0g
Exchanges: ½ Other Carbohydrate, ½ Fat
Carbohydrate Choices: ½

Double Chocolate Brownies

PREP TIME: 15 Minutes • **START TO FINISH:** 3 Hours • **32 brownies**

2 oz unsweetened baking chocolate, chopped
2 oz semisweet baking chocolate, chopped
2 cups sugar
1 cup butter, softened
4 eggs

1 cup all-purpose flour
½ teaspoon salt
1 teaspoon vanilla
¾ cup chopped pecans, toasted
¾ cup semisweet chocolate chips

1 Heat oven to 350°F. Spray 13x9-inch pan with cooking spray; lightly flour. In small microwavable bowl, microwave baking chocolate on Medium (50%) 1 minute to 1 minute 30 seconds, stirring every 30 seconds, until softened and chocolate can be stirred smooth.

2 In medium bowl, beat sugar and butter with electric mixer on medium speed until light and fluffy. Add eggs, one at a time, beating after each addition just until blended. Add melted chocolate; beat just until blended. On low speed, beat in flour and salt just until blended. Stir in vanilla and ½ cup each of the pecans and chocolate chips. Spread batter in pan. Sprinkle with remaining ¼ cup each pecans and chocolate chips.

3 Bake 40 minutes or until set. Cool completely in pan on cooling rack, about 2 hours. For brownies, cut into 8 rows by 4 rows.

ingredient info: Unsweetened baking chocolate is dark and bitter because no sugar has been added. This type of chocolate is used primarily in baking where other sweeteners are used. Semisweet chocolate, most commonly found in chip form, has cocoa butter and sugar added and is used for both baking and eating.

how to store: These brownies can be stored in a tightly covered container.

1 Brownie: Calories 190; Total Fat 11g (Saturated Fat 6g, Trans Fat 0g); Cholesterol 40mg; Sodium 90mg; Total Carbohydrate 20g (Dietary Fiber 1g); Protein 2g
Exchanges: 1 Starch, ½ Other Carbohydrate, 2 Fat
Carbohydrate Choices: 1

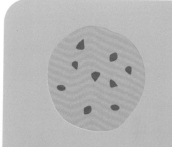

The Cookie Goes Round

FROM *BETTY CROCKER COOKY BOOK*: BROWNIES —1920S–1930S

"MUCH REQUESTED IN THE ROARING 20s—Legend has it that the first brownies were a fallen chocolate cake. However it happened, brownies are the first choice for picnic baskets, carried lunches, and boxes from home. They still head the cooky 'hit parade' today."

TODAY: BROWNIES

Brownies never go out of style. We love this recipe because it's twice as decadent—two types of chocolate for an even richer, more chocolatey experience. Because . . . can you ever have too much chocolate?

Lemon Bars

PREP TIME: **10 Minutes** • START TO FINISH: **2 Hours** • **25 bars**

1 cup all-purpose flour
½ cup butter, softened
¼ cup powdered sugar
1 cup granulated sugar
2 teaspoons grated lemon zest

2 tablespoons lemon juice
½ teaspoon baking powder
¼ teaspoon salt
2 eggs
Additional powdered sugar

1 Heat oven to 350°F. In medium bowl, mix flour, butter and ¼ cup powdered sugar with spoon until well mixed. Press in ungreased 8- or 9-inch square pan, building up ½-inch edges.

2 Bake crust 20 minutes; remove from oven.

3 In medium bowl, beat remaining ingredients except additional powdered sugar with electric mixer on high speed about 3 minutes or until light and fluffy. Pour over hot crust.

4 Bake 25 to 30 minutes or until no indentation remains when touched lightly in center. Cool completely in pan on cooling rack, about 1 hour. Sprinkle with powdered sugar. For bars, cut into 5 rows by 5 rows.

ingredient info:
If you like, substitute lime zest and lime juice for the lemon zest and juice. Fans of coconut may want to stir ½ cup coconut into the egg mixture in Step 3.

how to store:
Store these bars in a single layer in a tightly covered container.

1 Bar: Calories 100; Total Fat 4g (Saturated Fat 2g, Trans Fat 0g); Cholesterol 25mg; Sodium 70mg; Total Carbohydrate 13g (Dietary Fiber 0g, Sugars 10g); Protein 1g
Exchanges: 1 Other Carbohydrate, 1 Fat
Carbohydrate Choices: 1

Pictured clockwise from left are Cherry-Chocolate Buffalo Plaid Cookies, page 83; Chocolate Peanut Butter Hi Hat Cookies, page 58; and Cranberry, Rosemary and Blue Cheese Drop Cookies, page 41.

Baking Spirits Bright

Peppermint–Chocolate Cake Mix Sandwich Cookies

PREP TIME: 45 Minutes • **START TO FINISH: 1 Hour 15 Minutes** • **18 sandwich cookies**

COOKIES

- 1 box Betty Crocker™ Super Moist™ devil's food cake mix with pudding
- ⅓ cup vegetable oil
- 2 eggs

MARSHMALLOW FROSTING

- 1 cup butter, softened
- 1 jar (7 oz) marshmallow creme
- 2 cups powdered sugar
- 1 teaspoon vanilla

GARNISH

- ⅓ cup finely crushed peppermint candies

1 Heat oven to 350°F. Line 2 cookie sheets with cooking parchment paper.

2 In large bowl, mix Cookie ingredients with electric mixer on low speed until soft dough forms. Scoop dough by level tablespoonfuls onto cookie sheets.

3 Bake 8 to 10 minutes or until edges are set and slightly crispy. Cool 5 minutes on cookie sheets; remove to cooling racks. Cool completely, about 15 minutes.

4 To make Frosting, in large bowl, beat butter and marshmallow creme with electric mixer on medium speed until smooth. Beat in powdered sugar and vanilla until smooth. Spoon 2 tablespoons frosting onto each of half of the cookies; top with remaining cookies.

5 Roll edges of cookies in crushed peppermint candies.

ingredient info:

Use crushed toffee candy bars in place of the peppermint for a chocolate-caramel twist.

why it works:

Think small! You can easily go bite size with these cookies if you like. Spoon dough by rounded teaspoons instead of tablespoons, and bake 6 to 9 minutes. Fill with frosting and roll in crushed peppermint candies.

how to store:

Store these cookies in a single layer in a tightly covered container.

1 Sandwich Cookie: Calories 340; Total Fat 16g (Saturated Fat 8g, Trans Fat 0g); Cholesterol 50mg; Sodium 310mg; Total Carbohydrate 49g (Dietary Fiber 0g, Sugars 23g); Protein 2g
Exchanges: ½ Starch, 3 Other Carbohydrate, 3 Fat
Carbohydrate Choices: 3

Cranberry, Rosemary *and* Blue Cheese Drop Cookies

PREP TIME: **35 Minutes** • START TO FINISH: **55 Minutes** • **About 3½ dozen cookies**

½ cup granulated sugar
½ cup packed brown sugar
½ cup butter, softened
1 egg
1½ cups all-purpose flour
½ teaspoon salt
½ teaspoon baking soda

1 cup sweetened dried cranberries
1 tablespoon chopped fresh rosemary
½ cup blue cheese crumbles (from 4- or 5-oz container)

1 Heat oven to 350°F. Line cookie sheets with cooking parchment paper.

2 In large bowl, stir granulated sugar, brown sugar and butter with spoon until well mixed. Add egg; beat until well mixed. Stir in flour, salt and baking soda. Stir in cranberries and rosemary. Stir in blue cheese. Onto ungreased cookie sheets, drop dough by level tablespoonfuls about 2 inches apart.

3 Bake 10 to 13 minutes or until light golden brown. Cool 5 minutes; remove from cookie sheets to cooling racks. Cool completely, about 20 minutes.

1 Cookie: Calories 80; Total Fat 3g (Saturated Fat 1.5g, Trans Fat 0g); Cholesterol 10mg; Sodium 80mg; Total Carbohydrate 12g (Dietary Fiber 0g, Sugars 8g); Protein 1g
Exchanges: ½ Starch, ½ Other Carbohydrate, ½ Fat
Carbohydrate Choices: 1

ingredient info:
Purchasing blue cheese that has already been broken apart into "crumbles" makes it easy to evenly mix it into the dough and gives the cookie the best appearance and flavor.

why it works:
Using a combination of granulated sugar and brown sugar gives this cookie the perfect soft and chewy texture. The slight caramel-like flavor and color contrasts the cranberries, cheese crumbles and rosemary nicely.

kitchen secret:
Add this unique sweet-savory cookie to a cheese board, or pair them with a glass of wine. The unique flavor combination makes it a great cookie to bring to a cookie exchange party as well.

how to store:
Store these cookies tightly covered in the refrigerator.

41

BAKING
SPIRITS
BRIGHT

Buckeye Cookies

PREP TIME: 25 Minutes • **START TO FINISH: 2 Hours** • **About 2½ dozen cookies**

1 pouch Betty Crocker double chocolate chunk cookie mix
¼ cup vegetable oil
2 tablespoons water
1 egg

½ cup creamy peanut butter
¼ cup powdered sugar
½ teaspoon vanilla
¾ cup semisweet chocolate chips
¼ cup heavy whipping cream

1 Heat oven to 375°F. In large bowl, stir cookie mix, oil, water and egg until soft dough forms.

2 Onto ungreased cookie sheets, drop dough by slightly rounded tablespoonfuls 2 inches apart.

3 Bake 8 to 10 minutes or until edges are set. Cool 1 minute; remove from cookie sheets to cooling racks.

4 Meanwhile, in small bowl, mix peanut butter, powdered sugar and vanilla until well blended. Spread about 1 teaspoon mixture on top center of each cooled cookie.

5 In small microwavable bowl, microwave chocolate chips and cream uncovered on High 30 to 45 seconds; stir until smooth. Spoon a generous teaspoonful on each cookie; spread gently over peanut butter layer. Allow chocolate to set until firm, about 1 hour.

kitchen secret: A trick for making drop cookies all the same size: use a spring-handled cookie or ice cream scoop. (See "Cookie Scoop Sizes," page 8.)

how to store: Store these cookies in a covered container at room temperature.

1 Cookie: Calories 150; Total Fat 8g (Saturated Fat 3g, Trans Fat 0g); Cholesterol 10mg; Sodium 95mg; Total Carbohydrate 17g (Dietary Fiber 0g, Sugars 12g); Protein 2g
Exchanges: 1 Starch, 1½ Fat
Carbohydrate Choices: 1

42

BAKING
SPIRITS
BRIGHT

The Cookie Goes Round

FROM *BETTY CROCKER COOKY BOOK*: BONBON COOKIES—FROM THE LATE 1950s

"CANDY-LIKE COOKIES IN VOGUE—Women were fascinated by these beautiful and delicious cookies which were baked as cookies, served and eaten as candies." Bonbon Cookies were little round cookies with their tops dipped in a glaze, to look like candies.

TODAY: BUCKEYE COOKIES

Our Buckeye Cookies take the flavors and appearance of buckeye candies but are in a cookie form. Appropriately named, since they resemble the nut from the Ohio buckeye tree, these chocolate and peanut butter confections are loved for their flavor!

Peppermint Pattie Snowdrifts

PREP TIME: **35 Minutes** • START TO FINISH: **2 Hours 15 Minutes** • **About 3½ dozen cookies**

1 pouch Betty Crocker double chocolate chunk cookie mix
¼ cup butter, softened
2 tablespoons water
1 egg

About 42 chocolate-covered peppermint patties, unwrapped (from two 12-oz bags)
1¼ cups dark chocolate chips
½ cup heavy whipping cream
1 tablespoon holiday candy sprinkles, if desired

why it works:
For even baking, make sure cookies are the same shape and size.

how to store:
Store these cookies covered in a tightly covered container at room temperature with waxed paper between layers.

1 Heat oven to 375°F. In large bowl, mix cookie mix, butter, water and egg with spoon until soft dough forms. On ungreased cookie sheets, drop dough by rounded teaspoonfuls 2 inches apart.

2 Bake 6 to 8 minutes or until edges are set. Press 1 peppermint pattie on each cookie. Cool 2 minutes; remove from cookie sheets to cooling racks. Cool completely, at least 1 hour.

3 In medium microwavable bowl, microwave chocolate chips and whipping cream uncovered on High 60 seconds, stirring once, until chips are softened and can be stirred smooth. Spoon generous teaspoonful on top of each peppermint pattie on cookie; spread to cover candy. Sprinkle with candy sprinkles. Refrigerate cookies until set, about 15 minutes.

1 Cookie: Calories 150; Total Fat 6g (Saturated Fat 4g, Trans Fat 0g); Cholesterol 10mg; Sodium 65mg; Total Carbohydrate 23g (Dietary Fiber 0g, Sugars 17g); Protein 1g
Exchanges: ½ Starch, 1 Other Carbohydrate, 1 Fat
Carbohydrate Choices: 1½

45

BAKING
SPIRITS
BRIGHT

Easy Peanut Butter Cookie Cups

PREP TIME: **20 Minutes** • START TO FINISH: **50 Minutes** • **About 3 dozen cookies**

1 pouch Betty Crocker peanut butter cookie mix

3 tablespoons vegetable oil

1 tablespoon water

1 egg

¼ cup chopped cocktail peanuts

¼ cup peanut butter chips

1½ tablespoons coarse sparkling sugar

36 miniature chocolate-covered peanut butter cup candies, unwrapped

1 Heat oven to 375°F. Place mini paper baking cup in each of 36 mini muffin cups.

2 In large bowl, stir cookie mix, oil, water and egg until soft dough forms. Stir in peanuts and peanut butter chips.

3 Shape dough into 1-inch balls. Dip top half of each ball into sugar. Place 1 ball, sugar side up, into each muffin cup.

4 Bake 8 to 10 minutes or until edges are light golden brown. Immediately press 1 peanut butter cup into center of each cookie. Cool in pan 5 minutes; remove to cooling rack. Cool completely.

kitchen secret:

Have only one mini muffin pan? Refrigerate the rest of the dough while baking the first batch. Cool the pan about 10 minutes, then bake the rest of the dough, adding 1 to 2 minutes to the bake time.

how to store:

Store these cookie cups in a tightly covered container.

1 Cookie: Calories 130; Total Fat 6g (Saturated Fat 2g, Trans Fat 0g); Cholesterol 5mg; Sodium 110mg; Total Carbohydrate 16g (Dietary Fiber 0g, Sugars 11g); Protein 2g **Exchanges:** 1 Starch, 1 Fat **Carbohydrate Choices:** 1

Caramel-Rum Eggnog Cups

PREP TIME: **35 Minutes** • START TO FINISH: **55 Minutes** • **2 dozen cookies**

FILLING
- ½ cup white vanilla baking chips
- ¼ cup dairy eggnog (do not use canned)

COOKIES
- ½ cup butter, softened
- ⅔ cup packed brown sugar
- 1 egg
- 1¼ cups all-purpose flour
- ¼ cup unsweetened baking cocoa
- ½ teaspoon baking soda
- ¼ teaspoon ground nutmeg

TOPPING
- 2 tablespoons salted caramel or caramel topping (from 15-oz jar)
- 1 or 2 drops rum extract
  Coarse (kosher or sea) salt, if desired

1 Heat oven to 350°F. Spray 24 mini muffin cups with cooking spray.

2 In small bowl, place vanilla baking chips. In 1-quart saucepan, heat eggnog just until hot; pour over baking chips. Let stand 3 to 5 minutes. Stir until chips are melted and smooth.

3 In medium bowl, beat butter, brown sugar and egg with electric mixer on medium speed until well mixed. Beat in remaining Cookie ingredients until well mixed. Shape dough by rounded tablespoonfuls into 1¼-inch balls (dough will be slightly sticky). Press 1 ball in bottom and up the sides of each muffin cup.

4 Bake 9 to 11 minutes or until set. Using handle end of wooden spoon or rounded back of measuring teaspoon, make indentation in center of each cookie cup. Cool completely in pan on cooling racks, about 15 minutes. Remove cookie cups from muffin cups. Cool completely, about 15 minutes.

5 Fill each cookie with 1 teaspoon filling. In small bowl, mix salted caramel topping and rum extract; drizzle over cups. Sprinkle with coarse salt.

ingredient info:
Eggnog is a seasonal drink popular around the Christmas holidays. If you like to have a sip year-round or to make this recipe when it's out of season, purchase extra at the holidays and freeze. Or you can make homemade eggnog.

why it works:
Dusting your fingers lightly with flour will help make it easier to mold the cups, since the dough is a little sticky.

how to store:
Refrigerate these cups in a single layer in a tightly covered container.

1 Cookie Cup: Calories 110; Total Fat 5g (Saturated Fat 3.5g, Trans Fat 0g); Cholesterol 20mg; Sodium 80mg; Total Carbohydrate 15g (Dietary Fiber 0g, Sugars 9g); Protein 1g
Exchanges: ½ Starch, ½ Other Carbohydrate, 1 Fat
Carbohydrate Choices: 1

Bourbon Old-Fashioned Cups

PREP TIME: **20 Minutes** • START TO FINISH: **1 Hour 5 Minutes** • **24 cookie cups**

COOKIE CUPS

1	cup packed brown sugar
½	cup butter, softened
1	teaspoon vanilla
1	egg
1½	cups all-purpose flour
¼	teaspoon baking soda
¼	teaspoon salt

BOURBON OLD-FASHIONED CREAM

2	cups powdered sugar
¼	cup butter, softened
½	teaspoon grated orange zest
3	to 4 drops Angostura bitters
1	to 2 tablespoons bourbon
6	maraschino cherries, drained and quartered

1 Heat oven to 350°F. In medium bowl, beat brown sugar, ½ cup butter, the vanilla and egg with electric mixer on medium speed or with spoon until well blended. Stir in flour, baking soda and salt.

2 Shape dough into 24 balls, using about 1 rounded tablespoon dough for each. Place balls into 24 ungreased mini muffin cups.

3 Bake 12 to 14 minutes or until edges are set. Immediately press indentation into each with end of wooden spoon. Cool in pan 15 minutes. Remove cups from pan to cooling rack. Cool completely, about 15 minutes.

4 In medium bowl, beat powdered sugar, ¼ cup butter and the orange zest with electric mixer on low speed until blended. Gradually beat in bitters and enough bourbon, 1 teaspoon at a time, until the consistency of pudding.

5 Spoon mixture in quart-size resealable plastic food-storage bag. Cut off small corner of bag. Pipe mixture into indentation of each cooled cookie cup. Garnish with maraschino cherry slice.

ingredient info:

Created in the early 1800s for medicinal treatment, Angostura bitters gained popularity with bartenders to add complexity and balance to cocktails. The name comes from a small town in Venezuela where the inventor experimented with local herbs and plants.

why it works:

Testing shows that 15 minutes is the optimal time to lift the cookie cups from the pans. This gives the cookies time to firm up and release from the side of the pan. If cookies cool completely, they will be more difficult to remove from the pan.

how to store:

Store these cookie cups in single layer in a tightly covered container at room temperature.

1 Cookie Cup: Calories 160; Total Fat 6g (Saturated Fat 3.5g, Trans Fat 0g); Cholesterol 25mg; Sodium 90mg; Total Carbohydrate 25g (Dietary Fiber 0g); Protein 1g
Carbohydrate Choices: 1½

Gumdrop Cookies

PREP TIME: **50 Minutes** • START TO FINISH: **2 Hours 10 Minutes** • **About 5 dozen cookies**

2½ cups all-purpose flour
1 teaspoon baking powder
½ teaspoon baking soda
¼ teaspoon salt
1½ cups granulated sugar
1 cup butter, softened

1 egg
1 teaspoon vanilla
1½ cups quartered green, red and white spice-flavored gumdrops
2 tablespoons coarse white sparkling sugar

1 Heat oven to 350°F. In medium bowl, mix flour, baking powder, baking soda and salt; set aside.

2 In large bowl, beat sugar and butter with electric mixer on medium speed until fluffy; scrape side of bowl. Beat in egg just until smooth. Beat in vanilla. On low speed, beat flour mixture into sugar mixture until well blended. Stir in ¾ cup of the quartered gumdrops.

3 Shape dough into 1-inch balls. On ungreased cookie sheets, place balls 2 inches apart; flatten each ball to 1½-inch circle. On each dough round, sprinkle sparkling sugar and place 3 quartered gumdrops.

4 Bake 9 to 11 minutes or until edges are set and light brown. Cool 2 minutes; remove from cookie sheets to cooling racks. Cool completely, about 20 minutes.

ingredient info: Gumdrops can be fruity or spice-flavored. Fruit gumdrops are larger than the spice-flavored gumdrops. For this recipe, we tested with spice-flavored gumdrops.

ingredient info: Coarse sparkling sugar adds extra sparkle to holiday cookies and can be found in the cake decorating section at most grocery stores.

why it works: Make cutting spice drops easier by spraying kitchen scissors with cooking spray to help prevent spice drops from sticking. For best results, make sure gumdrop pieces remain separate when stirring into dough so there are some in every cookie!

how to store: Store these cookies at room temperature in a covered container.

1 Cookie: Calories 80; Total Fat 3g (Saturated Fat 2g, Trans Fat 0g); Cholesterol 10mg; Sodium 55mg; Total Carbohydrate 13g (Dietary Fiber 0g, Sugars 8g); Protein 0g
Exchanges: 1 Other Carbohydrate, ½ Fat **Carbohydrate Choices:** 1½

The Cookie Goes Round

FROM *BETTY CROCKER COOKY BOOK*: HOLIDAY FRUIT DROPS —FROM THE LATE 1940s

"NATION ENJOYS POST-WAR BOOM—With the boys back home and sugar no longer rationed, Christmas holidays were happy indeed. Rich, colorful cookies like these were perfect for all types of holiday hospitality." Holiday Fruit Drops were made with soured milk, broken pecans and candied cherries.

TODAY: GUMDROP COOKIES

Gumdrop Cookies, with their color coming from the jewel-like tones of chopped gumdrops, are still perfect for any kind of holiday hospitality! They're as pretty to look at as they are to eat.

Candy-Kissed Snowman Cookies

PREP TIME: 50 Minutes • START TO FINISH: 2 Hours 10 Minutes • About 2½ dozen cookies

1	pouch (17.5 oz) Betty Crocker sugar cookie mix
½	cup butter, melted
3	tablespoons all-purpose flour
1	egg
¼	cup coarse white sparkling sugar
30	thin pretzel sticks (2¼ inches), broken in half
60	red cinnamon candies

30	milk chocolate candy drops, unwrapped
60	miniature semisweet chocolate chips
1	candied orange slice, flattened, cut into small triangles
2	tablespoons white creamy ready-to-spread or white fluffy whipped frosting
5	drops red or green food color

1 Heat oven to 375°F. In medium bowl, stir cookie mix, butter, flour and egg until soft dough forms.

2 Shape dough into 30 (1-inch) and 60 (¾-inch) balls. Roll in sugar.

3 For each snowman, on ungreased cookie sheets, place 1 (1-inch) ball and 2 (¾-inch) balls, with edges just touching, 2 inches apart. Insert 2 pretzel sticks for arms and 2 cinnamon candies for buttons.

4 Bake 7 to 8 minutes or until light golden brown. Immediately place 1 candy drop for hat, 2 miniature chocolate chips for eyes and 1 orange triangle for nose.

5 Cool 5 minutes; carefully remove from cookie sheets to cooling racks. Cool 30 minutes.

6 Stir frosting and food color until well blended. Place in small resealable freezer plastic bag; seal bag. Cut small tip from one corner; squeeze to pipe scarf.

why it works:
Use two different-size cookie scoops to make portioning cookie dough even faster and more consistent.

why it works:
Making and baking snowmen in batches of six gives time to complete the decorating process easily.

why it works:
Place milk chocolate candy drops on top of snowman, and let melt into cookie. Make sure the candy is attached before moving snowman! If not, let cool a few minutes longer.

how to store:
Store these snowmen in a single layer in a tightly covered container. You can place waxed paper between layers to fill each container.

1 Cookie: Calories 140; Total Fat 6g (Saturated Fat 4g, Trans Fat 0g); Cholesterol 15mg; Sodium 90mg; Total Carbohydrate 19g (Dietary Fiber 0g, Sugars 12g); Protein 1g
Exchanges: ½ Starch, 1 Other Carbohydrate, 1 Fat
Carbohydrate Choices: 1

55

BAKING
SPIRITS
BRIGHT

Coconut and Almond Fluff-Topped Chocolate Cookies

PREP TIME: 1 Hour 15 Minutes • **START TO FINISH: 2 Hours 50 Minutes** • **About 4 dozen cookies**

COOKIES

2¼	cups sugar
½	cup butter, softened
½	teaspoon almond extract
4	eggs
2½	cups all-purpose flour
½	cup unsweetened baking cocoa
1½	teaspoons baking powder
¼	teaspoon salt
1	cup semisweet chocolate chips

FLUFF AND GARNISH

½	cup coconut, toasted
⅓	cup toasted chopped almonds
2	envelopes (0.25 oz each) unflavored gelatin (from 1-oz box)
⅓	cup cold water
½	cup sugar
⅔	cup light corn syrup
⅛	teaspoon almond extract

1 Heat oven to 350°F. Lightly spray large cookie sheets with cooking spray.

2 In large bowl, beat 2 cups of the sugar, butter, ½ teaspoon almond extract and eggs with electric mixer on medium speed until creamy. Add flour, cocoa, baking powder and salt; beat on low speed until well mixed. Stir in chocolate chips. Cover with plastic wrap; refrigerate 1 hour or until slightly firm.

3 In small bowl, place remaining ¼ cup of the sugar. For each cookie, drop a tablespoonful of dough into sugar; roll dough in sugar and shape into 1¼-inch ball. Repeat with remaining dough and sugar. On cookie sheets, place balls 2 inches apart. Press bottom of drinking glass on each ball until about ¼ inch thick.

4 Bake 8 to 10 minutes or until edges are set. Cool 2 minutes; remove from cookie sheets to cooling racks. Cool completely, about 30 minutes.

5 Meanwhile, in small bowl, stir coconut and almonds until blended; set aside. In heavy 1-quart saucepan, stir gelatin and cold water until gelatin is dissolved. Add ½ cup sugar. Cook over medium-low heat, stirring constantly, 5 to 8 minutes or until sugar is dissolved. Remove from heat. In same saucepan, beat gelatin mixture, corn syrup and ⅛ teaspoon almond extract with electric mixer on high speed 8 to 10 minutes or until fluffy and soft peaks form.

6 Spoon about 1 tablespoonful fluff onto each cookie. Immediately sprinkle each cookie with about ½ teaspoon coconut mixture.

why it works:

How long to beat the fluff? Beating to soft peaks means you beat it only until a peak forms when the beaters are pulled out of the mixture but folds over immediately. If the peak stands up and doesn't fold over, the mixture has been beaten too long—and you've made marshmallows!

why it works:

It's important to refrigerate the dough in this recipe for 1 hour to reduce the stickiness and make it easier to work with. You can also lightly spray your measuring spoon with cooking spray to help it release.

how to store:

Store these cookies in a tightly covered container.

1 Cookie: Calories 140; Total Fat 4.5g (Saturated Fat 2.5g, Trans Fat 0g); Cholesterol 20mg; Sodium 55mg; Total Carbohydrate 24g (Dietary Fiber 1g); Protein 2g **Exchanges:** 1 Starch, ½ Other Carbohydrate, 1 Fat **Carbohydrate Choices:** 1½

Chocolate Peanut Butter Hi Hat Cookies

PREP TIME: 50 Minutes • **START TO FINISH:** 2 Hours • **About 3 dozen cookies**

COOKIES

- 1 pouch Betty Crocker peanut butter cookie mix
- 3 tablespoons vegetable oil
- 1 tablespoon water
- 1 egg

  About 36 miniature chocolate-covered peanut butter cup candies, unwrapped

PEANUT BUTTER FROSTING

- ⅓ cup butter, softened
- ¼ cup creamy peanut butter
- 3 cups powdered sugar
- ¼ cup milk
- 1½ teaspoons vanilla

CHOCOLATE COATING

- 1¼ cups semisweet chocolate chips (10 oz)
- 2 tablespoons vegetable oil

  About 36 mini marshmallows (from 10-oz bag)

1 Heat oven to 375°F. Make and bake cookies as directed on pouch using oil, water and egg, but do not press with fork. Cool 2 minutes on cookie sheets; remove to cooling rack. Cool another 3 minutes, then place 1 peanut butter cup in center of each cookie. Cool completely on cooling rack, about 45 minutes.

2 In medium bowl, beat butter and peanut butter with electric mixer on medium speed until well blended. Beat in powdered sugar, milk and vanilla until smooth. Place frosting in decorating bag fitted with tip.

3 On top of each cookie, pipe frosting around peanut butter cup in concentric circles of decreasing size, getting as much height as possible, ending with cone shape with peak in center. Place cookies in refrigerator while making Chocolate Coating, about 15 minutes.

4 In small microwavable bowl, microwave chocolate chips and oil uncovered on High 30 seconds, then 10 to 15 seconds, stirring after each interval, until mixture is smooth.

5 Dip cone-shaped frosting on each cookie into chocolate coating to within ¼ inch from cookie, allowing a rim of peanut butter frosting to show and letting excess chocolate drip off.

6 Between palms of hands, roll mini marshmallows, one at a time, into balls. Attach to tops of hats while chocolate is still wet to look like hat pom-poms.

ingredient info:

If the chocolate coating is too thick, add additional oil a teaspoon at a time, stirring until smooth. Reheat in microwave 10 seconds, stirring until smooth, if needed.

how to store:

Store these cookies in a single layer in a tightly covered container.

1 Cookie: Calories 230; Total Fat 11g (Saturated Fat 4g, Trans Fat 0g); Cholesterol 10mg; Sodium 130mg; Total Carbohydrate 30g (Dietary Fiber 1g, Sugars 24g); Protein 2g
Exchanges: 1 Starch, 1 Other Carbohydrate, 2 Fat
Carbohydrate Choices: 2

Photo appears on page 37.

Holiday Lime Cooler Cookies

PREP TIME: 1 Hour 25 Minutes • **START TO FINISH: 1 Hour 55 Minutes** • **About 6 dozen cookies**

COOKIES

2	cups butter, softened
1	cup powdered sugar
3½	cups all-purpose flour
½	cup cornstarch
2	tablespoons grated lime zest
1	teaspoon vanilla

Granulated sugar

LIME GLAZE AND DECORATION

1	cup powdered sugar
2	tablespoons Key lime or regular lime juice
2	tubes (0.68 oz each) green decorating gel, if desired

1 Heat oven to 350°F. In large bowl, beat butter and 1 cup powdered sugar with electric mixer on medium speed or mix with spoon. Stir in flour, cornstarch, lime zest and vanilla until well blended.

2 Shape dough into ¾-inch balls. On ungreased cookie sheets, place balls about 2 inches apart. Press bottom of glass into dough to grease, then dip into granulated sugar; press on dough balls until ¼ inch thick.

3 Bake 9 to 11 minutes or until edges are light golden brown. Remove from cookie sheets to cooling racks. Cool completely, about 30 minutes.

4 In small bowl, stir together 1 cup powdered sugar and the lime juice. Stir in additional juice if necessary. Spread glaze over cookies. Squeeze drops of decorating gel on glazed cookies; drag toothpick through gel for marbled design.

ingredient info:

When grating peel, or zest, from a lime or any citrus fruit, grate just the colored part; the white part will be bitter.

why it works:

Powdered sugar and cornstarch create the melt-in-your-mouth quality of these cookies.

why it works:

If you like using a cookie press, make lime ribbon cookies. Prepare dough as directed, but do not shape it into balls. Place dough in a cookie press with a ribbon tip, and form long ribbons of dough on ungreased cookie sheet; cut ribbons into 3-inch lengths. Continue as directed for baking.

how to store:

Store these cookies in a tightly covered container.

59

BAKING
SPIRITS
BRIGHT

1 Cookie: Calories 90; Total Fat 5g (Saturated Fat 3g, Trans Fat 0g); Cholesterol 15mg; Sodium 40mg; Total Carbohydrate 9g (Dietary Fiber 0g, Sugars 4g); Protein 0g
Exchanges: ½ Other Carbohydrate, 1 Fat
Carbohydrate Choices: ½

Italian Christmas Cookies

PREP TIME: **40 Minutes** • START TO FINISH: **2 Hours 45 Minutes** • **About 4½ dozen cookies**

COOKIES
- 2½ cups all-purpose flour
- 2 teaspoons baking powder
- ½ teaspoon salt
- 1¼ cups granulated sugar
- ½ cup butter, softened
- ⅓ cup whole milk ricotta cheese (from 15-oz container)
- 2 teaspoons grated lemon zest
- 2 eggs
- 1 teaspoon vanilla

FROSTING
- 2¼ cups powdered sugar
- 3 to 4 tablespoons lemon juice
- Gel food colors, as desired
- Candy sprinkles, as desired

1 Heat oven to 350°F. In small bowl, stir flour, baking powder and salt.

2 In large bowl, beat granulated sugar, butter, ricotta cheese and lemon zest with electric mixer on medium speed about 1 minute or until fluffy; scrape side of bowl. Beat in eggs, one at a time, just until smooth. Stir in vanilla. On low speed, beat flour mixture into sugar mixture until well blended. Cover and refrigerate 30 minutes.

3 Using floured fingers, shape dough into 1-inch balls. On ungreased cookie sheets, place balls 2 inches apart.

4 Bake 9 to 11 minutes or until set but not brown. Cool 2 minutes; remove from cookie sheets to cooling racks. Cool completely, about 15 minutes.

5 In small bowl, beat powdered sugar and 3 tablespoons lemon juice with spoon until smooth and spreadable. If frosting is too stiff to spread, add additional lemon juice, 1 teaspoon at a time. Tint with food color. Using knife, spread ½ teaspoon frosting on each cooled cookie; immediately top with sprinkles. Let stand about 30 minutes or until frosting is set.

ingredient info:
Whole milk ricotta is recommended for success of this recipe.

why it works:
For even baking, make sure cookies are the same shape and size.

how to store:
Store these cookies covered in a tightly covered container at room temperature.

1 Cookie: Calories 80; Total Fat 2g (Saturated Fat 2g, Trans Fat 0g); Cholesterol 10mg; Sodium 55mg; Total Carbohydrate 14g (Dietary Fiber 0g, Sugars 10g); Protein 1g
Exchanges: 1 Other Carbohydrate, ½ Fat
Carbohydrate Choices: 1

61

BAKING
SPIRITS
BRIGHT

Butterscotch Pretzel Cookies

¾ cup butterscotch chips
(from a 12-oz bag)
⅔ cup sugar
½ cup butter, softened
1 teaspoon vanilla
1 egg

2 cups all-purpose flour
½ teaspoon baking powder
¼ teaspoon baking soda
1½ cups coarsely crushed mini
pretzel twists

1 Heat oven to 350°F. In small microwaveable bowl, microwave butterscotch chips on 50% power for 1 to 1½ minutes; stirring every 30 seconds or until chips can be stirred smooth; set aside.

2 In large bowl, beat sugar and butter with electric mixer on medium speed until light and fluffy. Add melted butterscotch chips, vanilla and egg; beat until well mixed. Beat in flour, baking powder and baking soda. Stir in ¼ cup of the pretzels.

3 Divide dough into quarters. Roll each quarter into a 12-inch log. Carefully roll and press each log into remaining 1¼ cups crushed pretzels. Press logs to 1¼ inches wide; cut dough logs into 2-inch pieces. On ungreased cookie sheets, place pieces at least 2 inches apart.

4 Bake 7 to 10 minutes or until edges are set. Cool 2 minutes; remove from cookie sheets to cooling racks. Cool completely, about 15 minutes.

ingredient info:

Butterscotch chips melt differently than other chips. It's important to melt them on 50% power and stir every 30 seconds to avoid scorching. When melted, they will be thicker than chocolate chips when stirred smooth.

why it works:

Place pretzels into a gallon-size resealable food-storage bag and seal. Use a rolling pin or meat mallet to coarsely crush. The pretzels will stick to the dough the best if the fine crumbs are discarded before rolling: place the pretzels into a fine mesh strainer and tap the sides to sift the fine crumbs and discard. The pieces left will stick more easily to the dough.

how to store:

Store these cookies at room temperature in a tightly covered container.

1 Cookie: Calories 140; Total Fat 6g (Saturated Fat 4g, Trans Fat 0g); Cholesterol 20mg; Sodium 110mg; Total Carbohydrate 20g (Dietary Fiber 0g); Protein 2g
Exchanges: 1 Starch, ½ Other Carbohydrate, 1 Fat
Carbohydrate Choices: 1

Host an Easy Cookie Exchange

What could be better than bringing friends together for an evening of fun and laughter . . . and then getting a variety of delicious cookies to take home when it's over? Cookie swaps may be daunting to some, but we'll show you how to throw together one that keeps the focus on fun!

GREAT TIPS FOR A COOKIE EXCHANGE

1. **INVITE EARLY** The month of December fills up fast for most folks . . . invite people early so they'll be free to say "yes"! Consider using free online invitations that also keep track of guest RSVPs. Limit the number of guests to no more than 10 to keep the gathering intimate and manageable. It's easier to plan for 10 different types of cookies than it is for 20. (Could you *really* eat 20 dozen cookies, anyway?)

2. **SET EXPECTATIONS** Ask your guests to let you know what type of cookie they will be bringing so that there will be all different kinds at the party. If you use the online invitations, guests can see what types have already been claimed, which helps eliminate duplicates.

   Have guests bring a dozen cookies for each of the guests, an additional half dozen for serving at the party and enough copies of the recipes on recipe cards for each guest. But most of all, let your guests know that this is about having fun and getting together . . . and not about making the perfect cookies!

3. **PLAN FOR SUCCESS** Have a large surface space available, such as a table, counter or sideboard, for the guests to put out their cookies, each with a name tag near it, marked with the name of their cookies. Have a large platter or two available for them to arrange their cookies for enjoying at the party. You can have guests bring their own containers to bring their cookies home in or provide containers for them. Look for inexpensive containers at your nearby party or dollar store or online. If you like, punch a hole in the recipe cards and string together sets with a ribbon, or provide small recipe card holders for the guests to put the recipes in to take home.

4. **PROVIDE FUN FOOD** Set out a few savory appetizers to balance the sweetness of the cookies you'll be nibbling. They can be as easy as cheese and crackers and a dish of olives, if you wish. Offer a few beverages, such as fruit-infused water and wine or a signature holiday cocktail, to really make it festive.

5. **ENJOY** Guests can go around the table, gathering a dozen of each type of cookie provided, to take home to enjoy during the holiday season. It's also a great way to catch up, giggle and have fun—that's what will create a memorable party. If you're relaxed and having fun, chances are your guests will, too!

Look for recipes with this icon: BIG BATCH

These large-quantity cookies are perfect for cookie exchanges.

Thumbprint Cookies

Classic Spritz

Snickerdoodles

Chocolate Buffalo Plaid Cookies

butter, softened
cups powdered sugar
teaspoons cherry extract or vanilla
egg
2½ cups all-purpose flour
⅛ teaspoon red gel food color
2 tablespoons unsweetened baking cocoa
3½ inch marzipan (from 7 oz package)
Decorator frosting, if desired

Christmas Snickerdoodles

PREP TIME: 20 Minutes • START TO FINISH: **1 Hour 50 Minutes** • **About 6 dozen cookies**

2 tablespoons red sugar
1 tablespoon ground cinnamon
2 tablespoons green sugar
1½ cups granulated sugar
½ cup shortening

½ cup butter, softened
2 eggs
2¾ cups all-purpose flour
2 teaspoons cream of tartar
1 teaspoon baking soda
¼ teaspoon salt

1 Heat oven to 400ºF. In small bowl, mix red sugar and 1½ teaspoons of the cinnamon; set aside. In another small bowl, mix green sugar and remaining 1½ teaspoons cinnamon; set aside.

2 In large bowl, beat granulated sugar, shortening, butter and eggs with electric mixer on medium speed, or mix with spoon. Stir in flour, cream of tartar, baking soda and salt.

3 Shape dough into ¾-inch balls. Roll in sugar-cinnamon mixtures. On ungreased cookie sheets, place balls about 2 inches apart.

4 Bake 8 to 10 minutes or until centers are almost set. Cool 1 minute; remove from cookie sheets to cooling racks. Cool completely, about 30 minutes.

why it works:

These are a terrific cookie to make in stages because the dough can be covered and refrigerated for up to 24 hours before baking. If it's too firm, let stand at room temperature for 30 minutes.

how to store:

Store these cookies in a covered container.

1 Cookie: Calories 60; Total Fat 3g (Saturated Fat 1g, Trans Fat 0g); Cholesterol 10mg; Sodium 40mg; Total Carbohydrate 9g (Dietary Fiber 0g, Sugars 5g); Protein 0g
Exchanges: ½ Other Carbohydrate, ½ Fat
Carbohydrate Choices: ½

67

BAKING
SPIRITS
BRIGHT

Hazelnut Chocolate Cookie Balls

PREP TIME: **1 Hour 15 Minutes** • START TO FINISH: **1 Hour 45 Minutes** • **About 4 dozen cookie balls**

COOKIES

- 1 cup butter, softened
- 1 cup powdered sugar
- 2 tablespoons hazelnut spread with cocoa (from 13-oz jar)
- 1 teaspoon vanilla
- ¼ teaspoon salt
- 1½ cups all-purpose flour
- ¾ cup unsweetened baking cocoa
- ¾ cup hazelnuts (filberts), toasted, skins removed

CHOCOLATE ICING

- 1 cup semisweet chocolate chips
- 1 teaspoon vegetable oil

1 Heat oven to 350°F. In large bowl, mix butter, powdered sugar, hazelnut spread, vanilla and salt with a spoon until well mixed. Stir in flour and cocoa until well mixed.

2 Shape about 1½ teaspoonfuls dough around 1 hazelnut, covering completely, into 1-inch balls. On ungreased cookie sheets, place balls 1 inch apart. Finely chop remaining hazelnuts; set aside.

3 Bake 8 to 10 minutes or until set. Cool 2 minutes; remove from cookie sheets to cooling racks. Cool completely, about 15 minutes.

4 In small microwavable bowl, microwave chocolate icing ingredients uncovered on High 30 to 60 seconds, stirring once, or until chips are softened and can be stirred smooth. Spoon about 1 teaspoon chocolate onto each cookie; sprinkle with about ½ teaspoon chopped hazelnuts. Let stand about 30 minutes or until icing is set.

68

BAKING
SPIRITS
BRIGHT

ingredient info:

Toasting hazelnuts not only enhances the flavor but loosens their skins, making it a breeze to remove them. To toast hazelnuts, heat oven to 350°F. Spread nuts on 15x10x1-inch baking pan. Bake uncovered 8 to 10 minutes, stirring occasionally, until golden brown. Place nuts between 2 sheets of paper towels and rub vigorously to remove peels.

ingredient info:

For the hazelnut lovers, substitute about 1 cup hazelnut spread with cocoa for the Ganache.

how to store:

Store these cookie balls at room temperature in a tightly covered container.

1 Cookie Ball: Calories 100; Total Fat 7g (Saturated Fat 3½g, Trans Fat 0g); Cholesterol 10mg; Sodium 45mg; Total Carbohydrate 9g (Dietary Fiber 1g); Protein 1g
Exchanges: ½ Starch, 1½ Fat
Carbohydrate Choices: ½

Mexican Wedding Cakes

PREP TIME: 1 Hour 40 Minutes • START TO FINISH: **2 Hours 10 Minutes** • **About 6 dozen cookies**

2 cups butter, softened	1 cup finely chopped nuts
1 cup powdered sugar	½ teaspoon salt
2 teaspoons vanilla	Additional powdered sugar
4½ cups all-purpose flour	

how to store:

Store these cookies in a tightly covered container.

1 Cookie: Calories 90; Total Fat 6g (Saturated Fat 4g, Trans Fat 0g); Cholesterol 15mg; Sodium 55mg; Total Carbohydrate 8g (Dietary Fiber 0g, Sugars 2g); Protein 1g
Exchanges: ½ Starch, 1 Fat
Carbohydrate Choices: ½

1 Heat oven to 400°F. In large bowl, mix butter, 1 cup powdered sugar and the vanilla. Stir in flour, nuts and salt until dough holds together.

2 Shape dough into 1-inch balls. On ungreased cookie sheets, place balls about 1 inch apart.

3 Bake 10 to 12 minutes or until set but not brown. Remove from cookie sheet, and roll in additional powdered sugar while warm. Cool completely on cooling rack, about 30 minutes. Roll in powdered sugar again.

71

BAKING
SPIRITS
BRIGHT

Cream Cheese Sugar Cookies

PREP TIME: 50 Minutes • START TO FINISH: 1 Hour 40 Minutes • About 5 dozen cookies

COOKIES

- 2½ cups all-purpose flour
- 1 teaspoon baking powder
- ½ teaspoon baking soda
- ½ teaspoon salt
- 1½ cups granulated sugar
- ½ cup butter, softened
- 1 package (8 oz) cream cheese, softened
- 1 egg
- 2 teaspoons vanilla

FROSTING

- 2½ cups powdered sugar
- ¼ cup butter, softened
- 2 to 4 tablespoons milk
- ½ teaspoon vanilla
  Gel food colors, as desired
  Candy sprinkles, as desired

1 Heat oven to 350°F. In small bowl, mix flour, baking powder, baking soda and salt; set aside.

2 In large bowl, beat granulated sugar, ½ cup butter and the cream cheese with electric mixer on medium speed about 1 minute or until fluffy; scrape side of bowl. Beat in egg just until smooth. Stir in 2 teaspoons vanilla. On low speed, beat flour mixture into sugar mixture until well blended. Cover and refrigerate 15 minutes.

3 Shape dough into 1-inch balls. On ungreased cookie sheets, place balls 2 inches apart.

4 Bake 10 to 12 minutes or until edges are set. Cool 2 minutes; remove from cookie sheets to cooling racks. Cool completely, about 15 minutes.

5 Meanwhile, in medium bowl, beat powdered sugar, butter, milk and vanilla with spoon until smooth and fluffy. If frosting is too stiff to spread, add more milk, 1 teaspoon at a time. Tint with food color. Using knife, spread slightly less than 1 teaspoon frosting on each cooled cookie; top with sprinkles.

ingredient info:

If you're looking for a shortcut, use vanilla creamy ready-to-spread frosting instead of the homemade frosting.

why it works:

It's helpful to have at least 2 cookie sheets; when one batch of cookies is finished baking, another batch is ready to go into the oven.

how to store:

Store these cookies in a tightly covered container at room temperature.

1 Cookie: Calories 90; Total Fat 4g (Saturated Fat 2g, Trans Fat 0g); Cholesterol 15mg; Sodium 70mg; Total Carbohydrate 14g (Dietary Fiber 0g, Sugars 10g); Protein 1g
Exchanges: 1 Other Carbohydrate, ½ Fat
Carbohydrate Choices: 1

Candy Cane Cookies

PREP TIME: 40 Minutes • **START TO FINISH: 6 Hours** • **About 4½ dozen cookies**

1 cup sugar	3½ cups all-purpose flour
1 cup butter, softened	1 teaspoon baking powder
½ cup milk	¼ teaspoon salt
1 teaspoon vanilla	½ teaspoon red food color
1 teaspoon peppermint extract	2 tablespoons finely crushed peppermint candies
1 egg	2 tablespoons sugar

1 In large bowl, stir together 1 cup sugar, the butter, milk, vanilla, peppermint extract and egg. Stir in flour, baking powder and salt. Divide dough in half. Stir food color into half. Cover and refrigerate at least 4 hours.

2 Heat oven to 375°F. In small bowl, stir together peppermint candy and 2 tablespoons sugar; set aside.

3 For each candy cane, shape 1 rounded teaspoon dough from each half into 4-inch rope by rolling back and forth on floured surface. Place 1 red and white rope side by side; press together lightly and twist. On ungreased cookie sheets, place rope; curve top of cookie down to form handle of cane.

4 Bake 9 to 12 minutes or until set and very light brown. Immediately sprinkle candy mixture over cookies. Remove from cookie sheets to cooling racks. Cool completely, about 30 minutes.

why it works:

To make cookies about the same size, measure dough for one cookie with a ruler, and then use that dough to measure all the rest.

how to store:

Store these cookies in a tightly covered container.

1 Cookie: Calories 80; Total Fat 4g (Saturated Fat 2g, Trans Fat 0g); Cholesterol 15mg; Sodium 50mg; Total Carbohydrate 11g (Dietary Fiber 0g, Sugars 5g); Protein 1g
Exchanges: ½ Starch, ½ Other Carbohydrate, ½ Fat
Carbohydrate Choices: 1

75

BAKING
SPIRITS
BRIGHT

Cookie Ball Christmas Tree

PREP TIME: 1 Hour 25 Minutes • **START TO FINISH:** 3 Hours 10 Minutes • **40 cookie balls**

COOKIE BALLS

1½	cups sugar
⅓	cup butter, melted
1	tablespoon milk
2	teaspoons vanilla
1	egg
6	oz cream cheese, softened
2¼	cups all-purpose flour
½	cup chopped pistachio nuts
1	teaspoon baking powder
½	teaspoon baking soda
¼	teaspoon salt

COATING AND DECORATIONS

3	cups green candy melts (from two 12-oz bags)
1	square vanilla-flavored candy coating (from 14-oz package)
1	teaspoon red, white and green candy sprinkles
1	bar (1.55 oz) milk chocolate candy
1	large yellow gumdrop

1 Heat oven to 350°F. In large bowl, beat sugar, butter, milk, vanilla, egg and 2 oz of the cream cheese with electric mixer on medium speed for 1 to 2 minutes or until well mixed. Stir in flour, pistachio nuts, baking powder, baking soda and salt until well mixed.

2 On large ungreased cookie sheets, drop dough by tablespoonfuls 2 inches apart.

3 Bake 9 to 11 minutes or until edges are set. Cool 2 minutes; remove from cookie sheets to cooling racks. Cool completely, about 30 minutes.

4 Line large cookie sheets with waxed paper. In food processor bowl with metal blade, place one-third of the cookies. Cover; process to fine crumbs. Remove and set aside; continue to process remaining cookies to fine crumbs. Place all cookie crumbs in food processor. Add remaining 4 oz of the cream cheese. Process 3 to 4 minutes or until well mixed and can be pressed together. Roll rounded tablespoonfuls of cookie mixture into 40 (1¼-inch) balls; place on cookie sheets. Cover loosely, and refrigerate 15 minutes or until firm.

5 In medium bowl, microwave green candy melts uncovered on High 1 to 2 minutes; stir. Continue microwaving and stirring every 15 seconds until melts are softened and can be stirred smooth.

6 Remove one-fourth of the cookie balls from refrigerator. Using 2 forks, dip and roll cookie balls, one at a time, in green candy melts, shaking off excess melt. Place balls on waxed paper–lined cookie sheets. Continue with remaining candy melt and cookie balls. Let stand 15 minutes or until candy is set.

7 On serving tray, arrange 21 balls into triangle shape, starting with 6 balls as base of triangle. Continue arranging descending rows until all the balls have been used. Arrange another 10 balls in a second layer on top of balls on platter, starting with 4 balls as base of triangle and arranging in descending rows until all 10 balls have been used. Reserve remaining balls for another use.

8 In small microwavable bowl, microwave vanilla-flavored candy coating uncovered on High 30 to 60 seconds, stirring once, or until coating is softened and can be stirred smooth. Spoon melted candy coating into a 1-quart resealable food-storage plastic bag. Cut a tiny corner from bag. Pipe onto balls for garland. Immediately sprinkle white coating with sprinkles.

9 Break candy bar into 4 equal pieces of 3 squares each. Stack and place at base of tree to resemble tree trunk. Flatten gumdrop to ¼-inch thickness. Using 1¼-inch star cookie cutter or paring knife, cut star from gumdrop. Insert one end of a toothpick into bottom edge of star. Press other end of toothpick into top ball of tree. Cover loosely and refrigerate until serving time.

ingredient info:
You can decorate the remaining cookie balls as desired and place around Christmas tree on platter or add to your holiday cookie tray.

why it works:
Using a plastic fork with the center tines removed makes it easier to dip balls in the candy melts. Tap sides of bowl to remove any excess candy melt. If the candy melts begin to harden while dipping, microwave on High about 15 seconds or until it thins and becomes of coating consistency.

how to store:
Cover tree on serving platter with plastic wrap and store in the refrigerator.

1 Cookie Ball: Calories 160; Total Fat 8g (Saturated Fat 5g, Trans Fat 0g); Cholesterol 15mg; Sodium 85mg; Total Carbohydrate 22g (Dietary Fiber 0g); Protein 1g
Exchanges: ½ Starch, 1 Other Carbohydrate, 1 ½ Fat
Carbohydrate Choices: 1.5

Easy Holiday Cutout Cookies

PREP TIME: 20 Minutes • **START TO FINISH: 1 Hour 30 Minutes** • **About 2 dozen cookies**

1   pouch (17.5 oz) Betty Crocker sugar cookie mix
⅓   cup butter, melted
2   tablespoons all-purpose flour
1   egg
1¼   cups fluffy white whipped frosting (from 12-oz container)

Decorating icing (assorted colors, as desired)
Decorating gels (assorted colors, as desired)
Decorator sugar crystals (assorted colors, as desired)

1   Heat oven to 375°F. In large bowl, stir cookie mix, butter, flour and egg with a spoon until soft dough forms. On floured surface, roll dough to ¼-inch thickness. Cut with floured cookie cutters in desired shapes. On ungreased cookie sheets, place cutouts 1 inch apart.

2   Bake 7 to 9 minutes or until lightly browned. Cool 1 minute; remove from cookie sheets to cooling racks. Cool completely, about 30 minutes.

3   Spread frosting on cookies. Decorate as desired with remaining ingredients. Let stand until set.

why it works:

Transfer cookies to cookie sheet with a metal spatula at least as wide as the cookie so the dough doesn't lose its shape.

how to store:

Be sure the icing is set, and then store these cookies in a tightly covered container.

1 Cookie: Calories 160; Total Fat 7g (Saturated Fat 2g, Trans Fat 2g); Cholesterol 15mg; Sodium 80mg; Total Carbohydrate 23g (Dietary Fiber 0g, Sugars 15g); Protein 1g
Exchanges: ½ Starch, 1 Other Carbohydrate, 1½ Fat
Carbohydrate Choices: 1½

79

BAKING
SPIRITS
BRIGHT

Vegan Sugar Cookies

PREP TIME: 1 Hour 15 Minutes • **START TO FINISH:** 3 Hours 15 Minutes • **About 5 dozen cookies**

COOKIES
- 1½ cups powdered sugar
- 1 cup vegan margarine, softened
- ¼ cup vanilla soymilk
- 1 teaspoon vanilla
- ½ teaspoon almond extract
- 2½ cups all-purpose flour
- 2 tablespoons cornstarch
- 1 teaspoon baking soda
- 1 teaspoon cream of tartar

ICING
- 4 cups powdered sugar
- 4 tablespoons vanilla soymilk
- ½ teaspoon vanilla

1 In large bowl, beat 1½ cups powdered sugar, the margarine, ¼ cup soymilk, 1 teaspoon vanilla and the almond extract with electric mixer on medium speed. Stir in flour, cornstarch, baking soda and cream of tartar until blended. Cover and refrigerate at least 2 hours.

2 Heat oven to 375° F. Spray cookie sheets with cooking spray. Divide dough in half. Roll each half on generously floured surface to a ½ to ¼-inch thickness. Cut into desired shapes with 2- to 2½-inch cookie cutters. On cookie sheets, place cutouts about 2 inches apart.

3 Bake 7 to 8 minutes or until edges are light brown. Remove from cookie sheets to cooling racks.

4 In large mixing bowl, beat Icing ingredients with fork or whisk until smooth. If icing is too thick, beat in 1 additional teaspoon soymilk. Frost cookies. Sprinkle with colored sugar, if desired.

1 Cookie: Calories 90; Total Fat 3g (Saturated Fat 1g, Trans Fat 0g); Cholesterol 0mg; Sodium 55mg; Total Carbohydrate 15g (Dietary Fiber 0g, Sugars 11g); Protein 0g
Exchanges: 1 Other Carbohydrate, 1 Fat
Carbohydrate Choices: 1

ingredient info:
You can tint this icing to several different colors. Divide it among small bowls, and tint each one a different color, evenly blending in food color with fork or whisk.

ingredient info:
If you are baking vegan, always read labels to make sure each recipe ingredient is vegan. If unsure about an ingredient or product, check with the manufacturer.

how to store:
Store these cookies covered at room temperature.

why it works:
To make the leaf veins as shown in the photo, sprinkle dark green-colored sugar with a baby spoon onto frosted cookie. Then sprinkle a lighter green-colored sugar over the entire cookie.

Cherry-Chocolate Buffalo Plaid Cookies

PREP TIME: **1 Hour** • START TO FINISH: **3 Hours** • About 2½ dozen cookies

1	cup butter, softened	⅛	teaspoon red gel food color
1½	cups powdered sugar	2	tablespoons unsweetened baking cocoa
1½	teaspoons cherry extract or vanilla	3½	-inch piece marzipan (from 7-oz package)
1	egg		Decorator frosting and candy decors, if desired
2½	cups all-purpose flour		

1 In large bowl, beat butter and powdered sugar with electric mixer on medium speed until blended. Add cherry extract and egg; beat until well mixed. On low speed, gradually beat in flour. Divide dough in half. Beat food color into one-half of dough until desired color. Stir cocoa into other half of dough. Divide both doughs in half. Wrap each of the 4 pieces in plastic wrap, and refrigerate at least 30 minutes.

2 On lightly floured surface, roll each dough piece into 9½x3½-inch rectangle. Trim edges if necessary. Cut each rectangle crosswise in half. From the long side of each rectangle, cut each rectangle into six ½-inch strips.

3 Alternate placing 1 red strip, 1 chocolate strip and 1 red strip beside each other, pressing together lightly. Brush top of dough lightly with water. Make another layer of dough, alternating 1 chocolate strip, 1 red strip and 1 chocolate strip. Repeat, making two more layers of dough and brushing each layer with water. Stack the 4 layers, alternating colors of dough; lightly press together. Repeat with remaining dough strips to form another stack of 4 layers of alternating dough colors. Wrap each log in plastic wrap. Refrigerate at least 30 minutes.

4 Heat oven to 350°F. Unwrap dough; trim ends. On a lightly floured surface, cut 1 log into about ¾-inch slices. For each cookie, using fingers, gently press each slice into a rectangle 3½x2½ inches, about ¼ inch thick. Cut with floured 3-inch stocking cookie cutter. On ungreased cookie sheets, place cutouts about 2 inches apart. Repeat with remaining log.

5 Bake 6 to 8 minutes or until cookies are set. Cool 5 minutes; remove from cookie sheets to cooling racks. Cool completely, about 15 minutes.

6 To form stocking cuffs, cut marzipan into ¼-inch slices; cut each slice in half. Press each piece into 2x1-inch rectangle. Place each piece on top of stocking, firmly pressing around the top and sides of the cookie to cover and attach to cookie. Pipe names on cuffs with frosting, or decorate with candy decors, using a tiny amount of frosting for glue. Let cookies stand until frosting has set.

why it works:

For cookies with a smoother surface, after pressing the dough into rectangles with your fingers, turn it over before cutting with the cookie cutter.

how to store:

Store these cookies in a tightly covered container at room temperature.

1 Cookie: Calories 130; Total Fat 7g (Saturated Fat 4g, Trans Fat 0g); Cholesterol 20mg; Sodium 50mg; Total Carbohydrate 15g (Dietary Fiber 0g); Protein 1g
Exchanges: ½ Starch, ½ Other Carbohydrate, 1 ½ Fat
Carbohydrate Choices: 1

BAKING
SPIRITS
BRIGHT

Easy Reindeer Cookie Bars

PREP TIME: 35 Minutes • **START TO FINISH: 2 Hours** • **27 cookie bars**

1 pouch (17.5 oz) Betty Crocker sugar cookie mix

½ cup butter, softened

4 oz (half of 8-oz package) cream cheese, softened

1 egg

1 container chocolate creamy ready-to-spread frosting

27 miniature pretzel twists, broken in half

54 candy eyeballs

27 brown candy-coated milk chocolate candies

1 Heat oven to 350°F. Line 13x9-inch pan with foil, leaving foil overhanging at 2 opposite sides of pan; spray with cooking spray.

2 In large bowl, mix cookie mix, butter, cream cheese and egg with spoon until soft dough forms. Spread dough in bottom of pan.

3 Bake 19 to 23 minutes or until golden brown. Cool completely in pan on cooling rack, about 1 hour.

4 Remove bars from pan by lifting foil; peel foil away. Spread frosting over top. Cut into 27 triangles as follows: Using sharp knife, cut into 3 horizontal rows. Cut each row into 9 triangles so each triangle has about a 2-inch-wide base, cleaning knife with paper towel after each cut to keep frosting clean of crumbs. (See diagram below.) Set aside end pieces for snacking.

5 For each reindeer, press 2 halved pretzels on top corners of cookie triangle for antlers, 2 candy eyeballs in center for eyes, 1 brown candy on tip of triangle for nose (use photo as guide). Repeat with remaining cookie triangles.

kitchen secret:
To easily line bottom of pan, tip upside down, and form foil around bottom and sides. Flip pan over, and place foil insert inside pan for a perfect fit!

how to store:
Store these bars in a tightly covered container in a single layer.

1 Cookie Bar: Calories 170; Total Fat 8g (Saturated Fat 4g, Trans Fat 0g); Cholesterol 20mg; Sodium 140mg; Total Carbohydrate 24g (Dietary Fiber 0g, Sugars 16g); Protein 1g
Exchanges: ½ Starch, 1 Other Carbohydrate, 1½ Fat
Carbohydrate Choices: 1½

Chocolate-Cherry Thumbprint Trees

PREP TIME: 40 Minutes • START TO FINISH: 2 Hours 45 Minutes • 12 cookie trees

COOKIES

1½	cups granulated sugar
1	cup butter, softened
1	teaspoon vanilla
2	eggs
2½	cups all-purpose flour
½	cup unsweetened baking cocoa
¼	teaspoon baking soda
¼	teaspoon salt

FILLING AND DECORATIONS

12	white- and chocolate-striped candy drops or pieces, unwrapped or cherry cordial creme-filled milk chocolate drops or pieces, unwrapped
½	cup cherry fruit spread or preserves
⅓	cup white vanilla baking chips
½	teaspoon vegetable oil
	Assorted sprinkles, if desired
	Powdered sugar, if desired

1 In large bowl, beat granulated sugar, butter, vanilla and eggs with electric mixer on low speed or mix with spoon until well blended. Beat in flour, cocoa, baking soda and salt until well blended. Divide dough in half; wrap and refrigerate 30 minutes.

3 Heat oven to 350°F. Roll dough on lightly floured surface ⅜ inch thick. Cut 12 stars with floured 3½-inch cookie cutter; 12 stars with floured 2½-inch cookie cutter and 12 stars with floured 1½-inch cookie cutter. On ungreased cookie sheet, place cutouts 2 inches apart.

4 Bake 10 to 12 minutes or just until set. With bottom of rounded teaspoon, press shallow indentation into the 3½- and 2½-inch cookies. Cool 2 minutes; remove from cookie sheets to cooling racks. Cool completely, about 30 minutes.

5 Stir fruit spread, breaking up large pieces. Fill each 2½- and 3½-inch cookie with about 1 teaspoon fruit spread.

6 In small microwavable bowl, microwave baking chips and oil uncovered on High 30 to 45 seconds, stirring once, until chips are softened and can be stirred smooth. Place melted chocolate in small resealable food-storage plastic bag; cut small corner of bag. Squeeze bag to drizzle chocolate over the 1½-inch and 3½-inch cookies; sprinkle with sprinkles. Immediately press candy drop into center of each of the 1½-inch cookies. Sprinkle 2½-inch cookies with powdered sugar. Let stand 30 minutes or until glaze is set.

7 To assemble trees, place 2½-inch cookies on 3½-inch cookies. Top each stack with a candy-filled cookie.

why it works:

Our testing shows that placing decorating icings, like the melted baking chips, in a resealable, food-safe plastic bag is the best way to achieve a finely controlled drizzle without needing to use a pastry bag and decorating tip.

why it works:

Thumbprint cookies come in many variations and are so named because the baker would shape a hole in the center of a cookie just after baking. When the cookies cooled, jam or another sweet filling would be spooned into the indentations. For these cookies, use the back of a rounded measuring teaspoon or the handle of a wooden spoon instead of your thumb, so you don't burn yourself!

how to store:

Store these trees in a single layer in a tightly covered container at room temperature.

BAKING
SPIRITS
BRIGHT

1 Cookie Tree: Calories 450; Total Fat 20g (Saturated Fat 12g, Trans Fat 0.5g); Cholesterol 75mg; Sodium 230mg; Total Carbohydrate 62g (Dietary Fiber 2g); Protein 5g
Exchanges: 1½ Starch, 2½ Fruit, 4 Fat
Carbohydrate Choices: 4

Sugar Cookie Candy Bars

PREP TIME: 10 Minutes • **START TO FINISH: 1 Hour 35 Minutes** • **24 bars**

1 pouch (17.5 oz) Betty Crocker sugar cookie mix
½ cup butter, softened
1 egg

1 cup candy-coated milk chocolate candies
1 cup white vanilla baking chips

1 Heat oven to 350°F. Spray bottom only of 13x9-inch pan with cooking spray.

2 In large bowl, mix cookie mix, butter and egg with spoon until soft dough forms. Stir in ½ cup of the candies and the white vanilla baking chips. Press dough in bottom of pan. Sprinkle remaining candies over top.

3 Bake 22 to 24 minutes or until golden brown. Cool completely in pan on cooling rack, about 1 hour. For bars, cut into 6 rows by 4 rows.

ingredient info:
White vanilla baking chips or chocolate chips can also be melted and drizzled on bars for an upscale topping.

how to store: Store these bars in a tightly covered container.

1 Bar: Calories 200; Total Fat 9g (Saturated Fat 6g, Trans Fat 0g); Cholesterol 20mg; Sodium 115mg; Total Carbohydrate 27g (Dietary Fiber 0g); Protein 2g
Exchanges: 1 Starch, 1 Other Carbohydrate, 1 ½ Fat
Carbohydrate Choices: 2

Grinch Pistachio Cookie Bars

PREP TIME: 20 Minutes • START TO FINISH: **1 Hour 45 Minutes** • **24 bars**

BARS

1	cup butter, softened
½	cup granulated sugar
2	boxes (3.4 oz each) instant pistachio pudding mix (not sugar-free)
2	eggs
1	teaspoon vanilla
2	cups all-purpose flour
1	teaspoon baking powder

FROSTING

4	cups powdered sugar
1	cup butter, softened
1	teaspoon vanilla
½	teaspoon almond extract
3	to 4 teaspoons milk
12	drops neon green gel food color
24	red candy heart decors

1 Heat oven to 350°F. Spray 13x9-inch baking pan with cooking spray.

2 In large bowl, mix 1 cup butter, the granulated sugar and pistachio pudding mix with spoon until blended. Add eggs and 1 teaspoon vanilla; mix until smooth. Stir in flour and baking powder. Press dough in bottom of pan.

3 Bake 25 to 27 minutes or until edges are lightly brown. Cool completely in pan on cooling rack, about 1 hour.

4 In large bowl, beat powdered sugar and 1 cup butter with electric mixer until smooth. Add 1 teaspoon vanilla and the almond extract. Add milk, 1 teaspoon at a time, until desired spreading consistency. Spread over bars. Place drops of food color evenly over frosting. Using a small metal spatula, swirl food color to create marbled appearance. Decorate with candy heart decors. For bars, cut into 6 rows by 4 rows.

ingredient info:

Candy heart decors can be found by the cake and cookie decorating supplies in craft stores, grocery stores and discount stores, or purchase them online.

kitchen secret:

For the fun "special effects" in the frosting, use the neon green gel food color. As the gel color is swirled through the frosting, several shades of green color will appear.

how to store:

Store these bars tightly covered at room temperature.

1 Bar: Calories 320; Total Fat 16g (Saturated Fat 10g, Trans Fat 0.5g); Cholesterol 55mg; Sodium 260mg; Total Carbohydrate 41g (Dietary Fiber 0g); Protein 1g
Exchanges: 1 Starch, 1½ Other Carbohydrate, 3 Fat
Carbohydrate Choices: 3

Peanut Butter Blossom Bars

PREP TIME: 10 Minutes • START TO FINISH: 1 Hour 30 Minutes • 16 bars

1 pouch Betty Crocker peanut butter cookie mix
3 tablespoons vegetable oil
2 teaspoons water
1 egg

½ cup miniature milk chocolate candy drops or pieces
3 teaspoons white sparkling sugar
16 milk chocolate candy drops or pieces, unwrapped

1 Heat oven to 350°F. Spray bottom only of 9-inch square pan with cooking spray.

2 In large bowl, mix cookie mix, oil, water and egg with spoon until stiff dough forms. Stir in miniature chocolate candy drops. Press dough in bottom of pan. Sprinkle 2 teaspoons of the sparkling sugar on top.

3 Bake 18 to 20 minutes or until golden. Immediately top with unwrapped candy drops in 4 rows by 4 rows. Sprinkle with remaining 1 teaspoon sparkling sugar. Cool completely in pan on cooling rack, about 1 hour. For bars, cut into 4 rows by 4 rows with one candy in center of each bar.

ingredient info:

If you can't find miniature candy drops, use semisweet chocolate chips instead. For more traditional holiday coloring, swap the white sparkling sugar for red and green colored sugars.

how to store:

Store these bars in a tightly covered container.

1 Bar: Calories 220; Total Fat 10g (Saturated Fat 3.5g, Trans Fat 0g); Cholesterol 15mg; Sodium 180mg; Total Carbohydrate 31g (Dietary Fiber 1g); Protein 3g
Exchanges: 1 Starch, 1 Other Carbohydrate, 2 Fat
Carbohydrate Choices: 2

Santa Heart-Shaped Cookies

PREP TIME: **1 Hour** • START TO FINISH: **2 Hours 50 Minutes** • **About 1 dozen cookies**

COOKIES

- 1 pouch (17.5 oz) Betty Crocker sugar cookie mix
- ½ cup butter, melted
- 3 tablespoons all-purpose flour
- 1 egg

FROSTING AND DECORATIONS

Red gel food color
- 1 container vanilla creamy ready-to-spread frosting
Decorations, as desired
Candy eyeballs, miniature candy-coated milk chocolate candies, semisweet chocolate chips, miniature marshmallows, flaked coconut, white candy sprinkles

1 Heat oven to 375°F. In large bowl, stir cookie mix, butter, flour and egg until soft dough forms.

2 On floured surface, roll dough ¼ inch thick. Cut with floured 3-inch heart-shaped cookie cutter. On ungreased cookie sheets, place cutouts 2 inches apart.

3 Bake 7 to 9 minutes or until edges are light golden brown. Cool 2 minutes; remove from cookie sheets to cooling racks. Cool completely, about 20 minutes.

4 In small bowl, stir food color into ½ cup of frosting to create desired color. Place ⅓ cup untinted frosting into small resealable food-storage plastic bag; partially seal bag. Cut off tiny bottom corner of bag; set aside.

5 Turn cookies so pointed ends are up. Working with one cookie at a time, spread 2 teaspoons of remaining untinted frosting on lower third of cookie for beard. Spread generous teaspoon red frosting on upper third of cookie for hat. Squeeze bag of frosting to pipe dots to attach eyes and nose. Pipe to finish hat, pom pom; decorate with additional decorations as desired (use photo as guide).

6 Decorate each cookie before starting another so frosting does not set. Let stand until frosting is set, about 1 hour.

why it works:
The frosting tends to set quickly once spread, so for best results, completely decorate one cookie before starting another.

why it works:
Use completely cooled cookie sheets so the cookies don't spread too much on a hot, or warm, cookie sheet.

how to store:
Store these cookies at room temperature in a tightly covered container with waxed paper between layers.

95

BAKING
SPIRITS
BRIGHT

1 Cookie: Calories 380; Total Fat 13g (Saturated Fat 7g, Trans Fat 0g); Cholesterol 30mg; Sodium 220mg; Total Carbohydrate 64g (Dietary Fiber 0g, Sugars 43g); Protein 2g
Exchanges: 1 Starch, 3 Other Carbohydrate, 2½ Fat
Carbohydrate Choices: 4

Marbled Sugar Cookie Cutouts

PREP TIME: 25 Minutes • **START TO FINISH: 1 Hour 10 Minutes** • **About 2 dozen cookies**

1   pouch (17.5 oz) Betty
    Crocker sugar cookie mix
½   cup butter, melted

3   tablespoons all-
    purpose flour
1   egg
    Green and red gel
    food colors

why it works:
The cookies become marbled by rolling the red- and green-colored dough together. The more cookies are rolled, the more marbled the cookies become!

how to store:
Store these cookies in a covered container.

1 Cookie: Calories 110; Total Fat 4g (Saturated Fat 2g, Trans Fat 0g); Cholesterol 15mg; Sodium 85mg; Total Carbohydrate 16g (Dietary Fiber 0g, Sugars 9g); Protein 1g
Exchanges: 1 Other Carbohydrate, 1 Fat
Carbohydrate Choices: 1

1   Heat oven to 375°F. In large bowl, mix cookie mix, butter, flour and egg with spoon until soft dough forms. Divide dough into 3 pieces. Place 2 pieces of dough into 2 small bowls. Tint 1 bowl green, 1 bowl red by stirring in food colors.

2   On floured surface, drop scant tablespoons of each dough in random pattern to make large rectangle. Dough pieces should be just touching together.

3   Push dough toward center on all sides to make 6x5-inch rectangle. Roll dough ¼ inch thick to create marbled pattern. Cut with 3-inch cookie cutters. Lightly press back of cookie spatula in flour, and slide under cookie dough. On ungreased cookie sheets, place cutouts 2 inches apart. Press together any leftover scraps, and reroll on floured surface to make more cookies.

4   Bake 6 to 8 minutes or until edges are light golden brown. Cool 2 minutes; remove from cookie sheets to cooling racks. Cool completely, about 15 minutes.

Classic Spritz Cookies

PREP TIME: 1 Hour 5 Minutes • **START TO FINISH: 1 Hour 15 Minutes** • **About 6 dozen cookies**

1	cup butter, softened
½	cup granulated sugar
2¼	cups all-purpose flour
¼	teaspoon salt
¼	teaspoon almond extract or vanilla

1	egg
	Food color, if desired
	Colored sugar, candies or sprinkles or finely chopped nuts, if desired
	Light corn syrup, if desired

how to store:

Store these delicate cookies in a tightly covered container.

1 Cookie: Calories 45; Total Fat 2g (Saturated Fat 2g, Trans Fat 0g); Cholesterol 10mg; Sodium 30mg; Total Carbohydrate 4g (Dietary Fiber 0g, Sugars 1g); Protein 0g
Exchanges: ½ Other Carbohydrate, ½ Fat
Carbohydrate Choices: ½

1 Heat oven to 400°F. In large bowl, beat butter and granulated sugar with electric mixer on medium speed or mix with spoon. Stir in flour, salt, almond extract, egg and a few drops of food color.

2 Place dough in cookie press. On ungreased cookie sheets, form desired shapes. Decorate with colored sugar.

3 Bake 5 to 8 minutes or until set but not brown. Immediately remove from cookie sheets to cooling racks. To decorate cookies after baking, use a drop of corn syrup to attach decorations to cookies.

Chocolate Spritz

Stir 2 oz unsweetened baking chocolate, melted and cooled, into the butter-sugar mixture.

99

BAKING
SPIRITS
BRIGHT

Holiday Cookie Ornaments

PREP TIME: 30 Minutes • **START TO FINISH:** 30 Minutes • **About 1½ dozen cookies**

1 box (5 oz) strawberry
chewy fruit snack rolls
About 18 (3-inch) pieces
string licorice

About 18 vanilla
wafer cookies
Coarse sugar, if desired

1 Line cookie sheet with waxed paper or cooking parchment paper. Unroll and remove paper from fruit snack rolls. Cut each in fourths.

2 Make a loop for ornament using string licorice, and attach to back side of cookie, securing under fruit snack as you wrap fruit snack roll around cookie. Decorate with sugar, or cut pieces from remaining fruit snack to decorate. Place on cookie sheet.

ingredient info:
Try using mini vanilla wafer cookies or other mini cookies to make miniature ornaments.

how to store:
Store these cookies in a tightly covered container at room temperature.

1 Cookie: Calories 60; Total Fat 1g (Saturated Fat 0g, Trans Fat 0g); Cholesterol 0mg; Sodium 50mg; Total Carbohydrate 11g (Dietary Fiber 0g); Protein 0g
Exchanges: 1 Other Carbohydrate
Carbohydrate Choices: 1

Pictured clockwise from top left are Almond Butter Puppy Cookies, page 149; Pumpkin Bread Breakfast Cookies, page 109; and Thumbprint Cookies, page 137.

Lunch Box
&
Cookie Jar
Favorites

Iced Limoncello Cookies

PREP TIME: 55 Minutes • **START TO FINISH: 1 Hour 30 Minutes** • **About 5 dozen cookies**

COOKIES

- 1¼ cups granulated sugar
- 1 cup butter, softened
- ½ cup sour cream (from 8-oz container)
- 3 tablespoons limoncello
- 2 teaspoons grated lemon zest
- 2 eggs
- 3½ cups all-purpose flour
- 1 teaspoon baking powder
- ½ teaspoon baking soda
- ½ teaspoon salt

ICING

- 4 cups powdered sugar
- ½ cup limoncello
- 1 to 2 teaspoons water
- 1 to 2 drops yellow liquid food color, if desired
- Additional grated lemon zest, if desired

1 In large bowl, beat granulated sugar and butter with electric mixer on medium-high speed until light and fluffy. Add sour cream, 3 tablespoons limoncello, 2 teaspoons lemon zest and eggs; beat on low speed until well mixed. Add remaining Cookie ingredients; beat 1 to 2 minutes or until well blended. Cover with plastic wrap; refrigerate 1 hour.

2 Heat oven to 350°F. Line large cookie sheets with cooking parchment paper.

3 Shape dough by level tablespoonfuls into 1-inch balls (dough will be slightly sticky). On cookie sheets, place balls 2 inches apart.

4 Bake 11 to 14 minutes or until edges are set. Cool 2 minutes; remove from cookie sheets to cooling racks. Cool completely, about 30 minutes.

5 In medium bowl, mix powdered sugar and ½ cup limoncello until smooth. Add water, 1 teaspoon at a time, until desired dipping consistency. Stir in food color. Dip tops of cookies in icing; shake off excess icing. Sprinkle with additional lemon zest.

ingredient info:

Limoncello is an Italian liqueur made from the zest of lemons, sugar, water and grappa or vodka. You can find limoncello in your favorite liquor store or make your own. Its bright, pungent lemon flavor adds a pucker-sweet kick to these cookies.

kitchen secret:

These delicious, tender, cakey cookies don't brown while baking but become puffy and are slightly firm when edges are touched.

how to store:

Store these cookies in a tightly covered container at room temperature.

1 Cookie: Calories 110; Total Fat 3.5g (Saturated Fat 2g, Trans Fat 0g); Cholesterol 15mg; Sodium 65mg; Total Carbohydrate 19g (Dietary Fiber 0g); Protein **Carbohydrate Choices: 1**

105

LUNCH
BOX
&
COOKIE
JAR
FAVORITES

White Chocolate Chunk–Macadamia Cookies

PREP TIME: 35 Minutes • **START TO FINISH: 50 Minutes** • **About 2½ dozen cookies**

1   cup packed brown sugar
½   cup granulated sugar
½   cup butter, softened
½   cup shortening
1   teaspoon vanilla
1   egg
2¼   cups all-purpose flour

1   teaspoon baking soda
¼   teaspoon salt
1   package (6 oz) white chocolate baking bars, cut into ¼- to ½-inch chunks
1   jar (3½ oz) macadamia nuts, coarsely chopped

ingredient info:

You can use 6 oz (about 1 cup) white baking chips in place of the white baking bar if you'd prefer.

how to store:

Store these cookies in a tightly covered container.

1 Cookie: Calories 190; Total Fat 11g (Saturated Fat 4g, Trans Fat 0g); Cholesterol 15mg; Sodium 105mg; Total Carbohydrate 22g (Dietary Fiber 0g, Sugars 14g); Protein 2g
Exchanges: 1 Starch, ½ Other Carbohydrate, 2 Fat
Carbohydrate Choices: 1½

1 Heat oven to 350°F. In large bowl, beat brown sugar, granulated sugar, butter, shortening, vanilla and egg with electric mixer on medium speed until light and fluffy or mix with spoon. Stir in flour, baking soda and salt (dough will be stiff). Stir in white baking bar chunks and nuts.

2 Onto ungreased cookie sheets, drop dough by rounded tablespoonfuls about 2 inches apart.

3 Bake 10 to 12 minutes or until light brown. Cool 1 to 2 minutes; remove from cookie sheets to cooling racks. Cool completely.

106

LUNCH
BOX
&
COOKIE
JAR
FAVORITES

Pumpkin Bread Breakfast Cookies

PREP TIME: 30 Minutes • **START TO FINISH: 55 Minutes** • **About 1½ dozen cookies**

¾ cup chopped walnuts
1 cup granulated sugar
½ cup packed brown sugar
1 cup butter, softened
1 cup canned pumpkin (not pumpkin pie mix)
¼ cup real or imitation maple syrup
1⅔ cups all-purpose flour

2 teaspoons pumpkin pie spice
1½ teaspoons ground cinnamon
1 teaspoon baking soda
½ teaspoon salt
2 cups old-fashioned or quick-cooking oats
1 cup sweetened dried cranberries
½ cup raw unsalted hulled pumpkin seeds (pepitas)

1 Heat oven to 350°F. Spray cookie sheets with cooking spray. Finely chop ½ cup of the walnuts. Set aside both the ¼ cup chopped walnuts and the ½ cup finely chopped walnuts.

2 In large bowl, beat granulated sugar, brown sugar and butter with electric mixer on medium speed until blended. Add pumpkin and maple syrup; mix well. Beat in flour, pumpkin pie spice, ground cinnamon, baking soda and salt until well blended. Stir in the oats, cranberries, pumpkin seeds and reserved ½ cup finely chopped walnuts; mix well.

3 On cookie sheets, drop batter by ¼ cupfuls 2 inches apart. Spread each cookie with metal spatula into a 3-inch round. Sprinkle each cookie with about 1½ teaspoons of the remaining ¼ cup chopped walnuts.

4 Bake 15 to 17 minutes or until edges are set. Cool 5 minutes; remove from cookie sheets to cooling racks. Cool completely, about 30 minutes.

ingredient info:

Pepitas are actually pumpkin seeds without the hull, found only in specific types of pumpkins. They are available raw, roasted, salted and unsalted. Each type has a slightly different flavor, but all can be used for snacking, salads, soups and main dishes, as well as in cookies, breads and other baked goods.

why it works:

Pumpkin pie spice is a blend of cinnamon, nutmeg, ginger, cloves and sometimes allspice. Using it eliminates the need to buy several spices to get the yummy flavor we associate with pumpkin.

how to store:

Store these cookies in a tightly covered container in the refrigerator or loosely covered at room temperature. For breakfast on the run or snacking, individually wrap each cookie in plastic wrap and freeze. Let frozen cookies thaw about 15 minutes before serving.

109

LUNCH
BOX
&
COOKIE
JAR
FAVORITES

1 Cookie: Calories 340; Total Fat 16g (Saturated Fat 7g, Trans Fat 0g); Cholesterol 25mg; Sodium 220mg; Total Carbohydrate 45g (Dietary Fiber 3g); Protein 4g
Exchanges: 1½ Starch, 1½ Other Carbohydrate, 3 Fat
Carbohydrate Choices: 3

Spicy Apricot Bacon Breakfast Cookies

PREP TIME: 25 Minutes • **START TO FINISH: 2 Hours 20 Minutes** • **About 2 dozen cookies**

110

LUNCH
BOX
&
COOKIE
JAR
FAVORITES

1½   cups plus 3 tablespoons packed brown sugar
¾   teaspoon ground red pepper (cayenne)
10   slices bacon
1   cup almond butter
½   cup butter, softened
2   teaspoons vanilla
2   eggs
2   cups all-purpose flour

2   cups old-fashioned oats
1   teaspoon baking soda
½   teaspoon baking powder
½   teaspoon salt
1   cup chopped dried apricots (from 6-oz package)
½   cup chopped pistachio nuts
½   cup slivered almonds, toasted

1 Heat oven to 350°F. Line 18x13-inch half-sheet pan with cooking parchment paper.

2 In small bowl, combine 3 tablespoons of the brown sugar and ½ teaspoon of the red pepper until well blended. Place bacon in single layer in baking pan; sprinkle with brown sugar mixture.

3 Bake bacon 15 to 20 minutes or until sugar is hot and bubbly and bacon is slightly crisp. Let cool 10 to 15 minutes or until cool enough to handle. Coarsely chop.

4 Meanwhile, in large bowl, beat the remaining 1½ cups of the brown sugar, almond butter, butter, vanilla and eggs with electric mixer on medium speed until well blended. Add flour, oats, baking soda, baking powder, salt and remaining ¼ teaspoon red pepper; beat on low speed until soft dough forms.

5 Stir in bacon, apricots, pistachios and almonds until well mixed (dough will be slightly crumbly). Onto ungreased large cookie sheets, drop ¼ cupfuls 2 inches apart; flatten each cookie to ¾ inch thick.

6 Bake 15 to 18 minutes or until edges are golden brown. Cool 5 minutes; remove from cookie sheets to cooling racks. Cool completely, about 30 minutes.

ingredient info:

You can find pistachios in shells, unshelled, salted and roasted, and raw. We used the unshelled, salted, roasted pistachio nuts in our recipe for a slightly sweet-and-salty cookie.

ingredient info:

The ground red pepper (cayenne) adds a hint of spice to this breakfast cookie. Customize this spice level by increasing or decreasing the cayenne pepper.

how to store:

Store these cookies in a tightly covered container in the refrigerator.

1 Cookie: Calories 290; Total Fat 14g (Saturated Fat 3.5g, Trans Fat 0g); Cholesterol 30mg; Sodium 230mg; Total Carbohydrate 34g (Dietary Fiber 3g); Protein 7g **Exchanges:** 2 Starch, ½ Other Carbohydrate, 2½ Fat **Carbohydrate Choices:** 2

Brownie Cookies

PREP TIME: 30 Minutes • **START TO FINISH: 1 Hour** • **About 2½ dozen cookies**

2 cups chopped pecans, toasted, if desired
3 cups semisweet chocolate chips (18 oz)
½ cup butter, cut into pieces
4 oz unsweetened baking chocolate, chopped

1½ cups all-purpose flour
½ teaspoon baking powder
½ teaspoon salt
4 eggs
1½ cups sugar
2 teaspoons vanilla

how to store:
Store these cookies in a covered container.

1 Cookie: Calories 280; Total Fat 8g (Saturated Fat 4g, Trans Fat 0g); Cholesterol 0mg; Sodium 85mg; Total Carbohydrate 31g (Dietary Fiber 3g, Sugars 0g); Protein 4g
Exchanges: ½ Starch, 1½ Other Carbohydrate, 3½ Fat
Carbohydrate Choices: 2

1 Heat oven to 350°F. Spread pecans in ungreased shallow pan. Bake uncovered 6 to 10 minutes, stirring occasionally, until light brown. Set aside.

2 In 3-quart heavy saucepan, heat 1½ cups of the chocolate chips, the butter and baking chocolate over low heat, stirring constantly, until butter and chocolate are melted. Remove from heat; cool.

3 In medium bowl, mix flour, baking powder and salt; set aside. In large bowl, beat eggs, sugar and vanilla with electric mixer on medium speed until well blended. On low speed, gradually beat in flour mixture. Add chocolate mixture; beat well. Stir in toasted pecans and remaining 1½ cups chocolate chips.

4 Line cookie sheets with cooking parchment paper. Onto cookie sheets, drop dough by 2 tablespoonfuls about 1 inch apart.

5 Bake 10 minutes. Cool 2 minutes; remove from cookie sheets to cooling racks.

113

LUNCH
BOX
&
COOKIE
JAR
FAVORITES

Toasted Sesame-Chocolate Chip-Cashew Cookies

PREP TIME: 30 Minutes • **START TO FINISH: 1 Hour** • **About 2½ dozen cookies**

1 cup packed brown sugar	1 teaspoon baking soda
½ cup granulated sugar	½ teaspoon salt
¼ cup butter, softened	1 cup milk chocolate chips
2 eggs	1 cup white vanilla baking chips
½ cup cashew butter	½ cup roasted salted cashew pieces
¼ cup toasted sesame oil	¼ cup sesame seed
2 cups all-purpose flour	

1 Heat oven to 375°F. In large bowl, beat brown sugar, granulated sugar, butter and eggs on low speed of electric mixer or mix with spoon until blended. Beat in cashew butter and sesame oil. Beat in flour, baking soda and salt. Stir in milk chocolate chips, white baking chips and cashew pieces.

2 Shape rounded tablespoonfuls of dough into 1¼-inch balls; dip top of balls into sesame seed. On ungreased cookie sheets, place cookies, seed side up, about 2 inches apart.

3 Bake 10 to 12 minutes or until edges are set. Cool 2 minutes; remove from cookie sheets to cooling racks.

1 Cookie: Calories 110; Total Fat 5g (Saturated Fat 2g, Trans Fat 0g); Cholesterol 10mg; Sodium 75mg; Total Carbohydrate 13g (Dietary Fiber 0g); Protein 1g
Exchanges: ½ Starch, ½ Other Carbohydrate, 1 Fat
Carbohydrate Choices: 1

ingredient info:

Toasted sesame oil develops a deep, nutty flavor during production because the sesame seed is roasted before extracting the oil. Used in these cookies, it provides a complex and delicious flavor that complements the chocolate chips and cashew butter. You can also use toasted sesame oil as a finishing oil in Asian stir-fry, seasoning for steamed vegetables or splashed into salad dressing.

ingredient info:

Cashew butter comes in a variety of forms: raw, roasted, salted and unsalted. Any variety will work in these cookies. If the oil and solids have separated, stir together before measuring.

how to store:

Store these cookies in a tightly covered container at room temperature.

114

LUNCH
BOX
&
COOKIE
JAR
FAVORITES

Turtle Chocolate Chip Cookies

PREP TIME: 25 Minutes • **START TO FINISH: 3 Hours 20 Minutes** • **About 4 dozen cookies**

COOKIES

- 1 pouch Betty Crocker chocolate chip cookie mix
- ½ cup butter, softened
- 2 tablespoons all-purpose flour
- 1 egg

TOPPINGS

- About 48 round chewy caramels in milk chocolate, unwrapped
- About 48 pecan halves
- 15 caramels, unwrapped (from 11-oz package)
- 1 tablespoon heavy whipping cream
- ½ teaspoon coarse sea salt

1 Heat oven to 375°F. In large bowl, mix cookie mix, butter, flour and egg with spoon until soft dough forms. Onto ungreased cookie sheets, drop dough by rounded teaspoonfuls 2 inches apart.

2 Bake 5 to 7 minutes or until light golden brown. Remove from oven; press chocolate in center of each cookie. Return to oven 1 minute. Remove from oven; immediately place 1 pecan half on top of chocolate. Press down slightly. Remove from cookie sheets to cooling racks. Cool 30 minutes.

3 In small microwavable bowl, heat caramels and whipping cream uncovered on High 30 to 60 seconds, stirring once, until caramels are melted. Drizzle over cookies. Sprinkle with sea salt. Let stand about 2 hours or until set.

why it works:

When baking batches of cookies, use completely cooled cookie sheets. Cookies will spread too much if put on a hot or warm cookie sheet.

how to store:

Store these cookies in a tightly covered container.

1 Cookie: Calories 120; Total Fat 6g (Saturated Fat 3g, Trans Fat 0g); Cholesterol 10mg; Sodium 100mg; Total Carbohydrate 15g (Dietary Fiber 0g, Sugars 11g); Protein 1g
Exchanges: ½ Starch, ½ Other Carbohydrate, 1 Fat
Carbohydrate Choices: 1

117

LUNCH
BOX
&
COOKIE
JAR
FAVORITES

Salted Butterscotch Pudding Pretzel Cookies

PREP TIME: 25 Minutes • **START TO FINISH: 1 Hour 30 Minutes** • **About 4 dozen cookies**

2½ cups all-purpose flour
1½ teaspoons baking soda
½ teaspoon salt
1 cup butter, softened
¾ cup granulated sugar
¾ cup packed brown sugar
1 box (4-serving size) butterscotch instant pudding and pie filling mix

2 eggs
1 teaspoon vanilla
2 cups mini pretzel twists, coarsely crushed
1 cup semisweet chocolate chips
½ cup milk chocolate toffee bits
1 teaspoon coarse sea salt

ingredient info:
The pudding mix in this recipe is not prepared but added dry to the butter-sugar mixture.

how to store:
Store these cookies covered in a tightly covered container at room temperature.

1 Cookie: Calories 130; Total Fat 6g (Saturated Fat 4g, Trans Fat 0g); Cholesterol 15mg; Sodium 180mg; Total Carbohydrate 18g (Dietary Fiber 0g, Sugars 10g); Protein 1g
Exchanges: ½ Starch, ½ Other Carbohydrate, 1 Fat
Carbohydrate Choices: 1

1 Heat oven to 350°F. In medium bowl, mix flour, baking soda and ½ teaspoon salt; set aside.

2 In large bowl, beat butter, granulated sugar and brown sugar with electric mixer on medium speed about 1 minute or until fluffy; scrape side of bowl. Beat in dry pudding mix. Beat in eggs, one at a time, just until smooth. Stir in vanilla. On low speed, beat flour mixture into sugar mixture until well blended. Stir in crushed pretzels, chocolate chips and toffee bits until blended.

3 Onto ungreased cookie sheets, drop dough by rounded tablespoonfuls about 2 inches apart. Sprinkle each cookie lightly with coarse salt.

4 Bake 9 to 11 minutes or until light brown. Cool 2 minutes; remove from cookie sheets to cooling racks. Cool completely, about 15 minutes.

Cinnamon-Maple Sugar Crinkles

PREP TIME: 45 Minutes • **START TO FINISH: 2 Hours 5 Minutes** • **About 4½ dozen cookies**

1½ cups packed brown sugar
1 cup butter, softened
1 teaspoon maple extract
2 eggs
3¼ cups all-purpose flour
2 teaspoons baking powder

1 teaspoon baking soda
1½ teaspoons ground cinnamon
½ teaspoon salt
⅔ cup white sparkling decorating sugar
½ teaspoon nutmeg

1 Heat oven to 350°F. In large bowl, beat brown sugar, butter and maple extract with electric mixer on medium speed until fluffy, scraping sides of bowl. Beat in eggs, one at a time, just until smooth. On low speed, beat in flour, baking powder, baking soda, ½ teaspoon of the cinnamon and the salt until well mixed.

2 In small bowl, mix remaining 1 teaspoon cinnamon, the decorating sugar and nutmeg. Shape dough into 1½-inch balls. For each cookie, place a ball into the sugar mixture, spooning over the balls and rolling to coat. On ungreased cookie sheets, place balls about 2 inches apart.

3 Bake 8 to 10 minutes or until cookies are light brown around the edges. Cool 2 minutes; remove from cookie sheets to cooling racks. Cool completely.

ingredient info: We like the light-catching texture of the sparkling decorating sugar in this recipe. Sparkling decorating sugar can be purchased in the baking aisle of most grocery stores or in craft stores carrying baking supplies. To use granulated sugar instead, adjust your amount to ⅓ cup.

why it works: Spices tend to settle near the bottom of the rolling sugar mixture. By spooning the mixture over the cookie balls, you guarantee an even coating of spices and sugar.

how to store: Store these cookies in a tightly covered container at room temperature.

1 Cookie: Calories 100; Total Fat 3.5g (Saturated Fat 2g, Trans Fat 0g); Cholesterol 15mg; Sodium 95mg; Total Carbohydrate 14g (Dietary Fiber 0g); Protein 1g **Exchanges:** ½ Starch, ½ Other Carbohydrate, ½ Fat **Carbohydrate Choices:** 1

The Cookie Goes Round

FROM *BETTY CROCKER COOKY BOOK*: MOLASSES CRINKLES—FROM THE EARLY 1930s

"COOKIES BANISH DEPRESSION BLUES—After the stock market crash, money was scarce and families enjoyed simple pleasures like reading aloud, taking nature hikes, and visiting friends—all occasions for chewy, hearty cookies like these." Molasses crinkles were so named for their appealing characteristic cracks on the sugary-crusted tops of the cookies that formed while baking.

TODAY: CINNAMON-MAPLE SUGAR CRINKLES

We still love crinkles, so we combined the fall-like flavors of cinnamon and maple for a new flavor twist. They also form cracks while baking, which makes them as much fun to make as they are to eat!

Vanilla Bean Sugar Cookie Crinkles

PREP TIME: 25 Minutes • **START TO FINISH: 2 Hours 5 Minutes** • **About 5 dozen cookies**

3 cups all-purpose flour
2 teaspoons baking powder
½ teaspoon baking soda
½ teaspoon salt
1½ cups granulated sugar
1 cup butter, softened

2 vanilla beans, cut in half lengthwise, scraped
2 eggs
1 cup powdered sugar
Additional powdered sugar for sprinkling, if desired

1 Heat oven to 325°F. In medium bowl, mix flour, baking powder, baking soda and salt; set aside.

2 In large bowl, beat granulated sugar, butter and seeds from vanilla beans with electric mixer on medium speed about 1 minute or until fluffy; scrape side of bowl. Beat in eggs, one at a time, just until smooth. On low speed, beat flour mixture into sugar mixture until well blended. Cover and let dough stand at room temperature 10 minutes.

3 Shape dough into 1¼-inch balls. In small bowl, place 1 cup powdered sugar. Roll each cookie in powdered sugar; shake off excess. On ungreased cookie sheets, place balls 2 inches apart.

4 Bake 12 to 14 minutes or until edges are light brown. Cool 2 minutes; remove from cookie sheets to cooling racks. Cool completely, at least 15 minutes. Sprinkle with additional powdered sugar.

ingredient info:

To remove seeds from a vanilla bean, cut the bean in half lengthwise. Run the blade of a knife across the inside of the bean, gathering seeds on the edge of the knife.

ingredient info:

No vanilla beans? No problem! Substitute 2 teaspoons vanilla extract for the 2 beans.

how to store:

Store these cookies in a tightly covered container at room temperature.

1 Cookie: Calories 80; Total Fat 4g (Saturated Fat 2g, Trans Fat 0g); Cholesterol 15mg; Sodium 75mg; Total Carbohydrate 12g (Dietary Fiber 0g, Sugars 7g); Protein 1g
Exchanges: 1 Other Carbohydrate, ½ Fat
Carbohydrate Choices: 1

Brown Sugar Crackle Cookies

PREP TIME: 25 Minutes • START TO FINISH: **1 Hour 45 Minutes** • **About 5½ dozen cookies**

3 cups all-purpose flour
½ teaspoon baking soda
½ teaspoon salt
2 cups packed brown sugar

1 cup butter, softened
2 eggs
1 tablespoon vanilla
¾ cup coarse white sparkling sugar

1 Heat oven to 350°F. In medium bowl, mix flour, baking soda and salt; set aside.

2 In large bowl, beat brown sugar and butter with electric mixer on medium speed about 1 minute or until fluffy; scrape side of bowl. Beat in eggs, one at a time, just until smooth. Beat in vanilla. On low speed, gradually beat flour mixture into butter mixture until well blended.

3 Shape dough into 1½-inch balls; roll in sparkling sugar. On ungreased cookie sheets, place balls 2 inches apart.

4 Bake 10 to 13 minutes or until edges are light golden brown. Cool on cookie sheets 2 minutes; remove from cookie sheets to cooling racks. Cool completely, about 15 minutes.

ingredient info:

Coarse sparkling sugar adds extra sparkle to cookies and can be found in the cake decorating section at most grocery stores.

why it works:

For even baking, make sure cookies are the same shape and size.

how to store:

Store these cookies in a tightly covered container at room temperature.

1 Cookie: Calories 100; Total Fat 4g (Saturated Fat 2g, Trans Fat 0g); Cholesterol 15mg; Sodium 65mg; Total Carbohydrate 16g (Dietary Fiber 0g, Sugars 10g); Protein 1g
Exchanges: ½ Starch, ½ Other Carbohydrate, ½ Fat
Carbohydrate Choices: 1

125

LUNCH
BOX
&
COOKIE
JAR
FAVORITES

Chocolate-Stuffed Snickerdoodles

PREP TIME: 25 Minutes • **START TO FINISH: 1 Hour 20 Minutes** • **About 2 dozen cookies**

⅓ cup sugar
1½ teaspoons ground cinnamon
1 pouch (17.5 oz) Betty Crocker sugar cookie mix

½ cup butter, softened
2 tablespoons all-purpose flour
1 egg
About 18 milk chocolate nuggets, unwrapped

1 Heat oven to 375°F. In small bowl, mix sugar and cinnamon. Remove 2 tablespoons of mixture to second small bowl; reserve.

2 In large bowl, stir cookie mix, butter, flour and egg with spoon until soft dough forms. Shape dough into 1½-inch balls; flatten each ball to 2½-inch circle. Press 1 chocolate into center of each cookie, making sure to form dough around chocolate to enclose; reshape into balls. Roll in remaining sugar-cinnamon mixture. On ungreased large cookie sheets, place balls 2 inches apart. Discard sugar-cinnamon mixture after rolling balls.

3 Bake 8 to 10 minutes or until edges are set and light golden brown. Cool 2 minutes; remove from cookie sheets to cooling racks. Sprinkle reserved 2 tablespoons sugar-cinnamon mixture on tops of warm cookies. Cool completely, about 30 minutes.

why it works:

Take the time to seal all cracks when forming the dough around the chocolate so that none of it leaks out during baking.

how to store:

Store these surprise Snickerdoodles in a tightly covered container.

1 Cookie: Calories 190; Total Fat 8g (Saturated Fat 4.5g, Trans Fat 0g); Cholesterol 20mg; Sodium 105mg; Total Carbohydrate 26g (Dietary Fiber 0g, Sugars 17g); Protein 2g
Exchanges: 1 Starch, 1 Other Carbohydrate, 1½ Fat
Carbohydrate Choices: 2

126

LUNCH
BOX
&
COOKIE
JAR
FAVORITES

Chai Ginger Cookies

PREP TIME: 30 Minutes • **START TO FINISH: 50 Minutes** • **About 4 dozen cookies**

3   tea bags chai black tea
¾   cup packed brown sugar
1   cup butter, softened
2   cups all-purpose flour
1   teaspoon vanilla

¼   cup finely chopped crystallized ginger (from 3-oz package)
2   tablespoons granulated sugar

1 Heat oven to 375°F. Cut open tea bags; set aside.

2 In large bowl, beat brown sugar and butter with electric mixer on medium speed until well mixed. Stir in contents of 2 of the tea bags, the flour and vanilla until mixed. Stir in ginger.

3 In small bowl, mix granulated sugar and contents of remaining tea bag. Shape dough by scant tablespoonfuls into 1-inch balls; roll balls in sugar mixture. On ungreased cookie sheets, place balls about 2 inches apart. Press bottom of drinking glass on each ball until about ¼-inch thick.

4 Bake 7 to 8 minutes or until light golden brown. Cool 2 minutes; remove from cookie sheets to cooling racks. Cool completely, about 20 minutes.

1 Cookie: Calories 70; Total Fat 4g (Saturated Fat 2.5g, Trans Fat 0g); Cholesterol 10mg; Sodium 30mg; Total Carbohydrate 9g (Dietary Fiber 0g, Sugars 4g); Protein 0g
Exchanges: ½ Other Carbohydrate, 1 Fat **Carbohydrate Choices:** ½

ingredient info:

The word "chai" is the Hindi word for "tea," but we often think of chai tea as a black tea infused with spices like cinnamon, cardamom, cloves and ginger. Its subtle flavor blends well with the crystallized ginger in the cookie.

ingredient info:

Crystallized ginger may vary from brand to brand. Some are chopped into small pieces and tend to be harder. Others are in flat pieces and are more pliable. You can use either form, but be sure to finely chop the ginger so it is incorporated throughout the cookie dough.

how to store:

Store these cookies at room temperature in resealable food-storage plastic bags or tightly covered containers.

129

LUNCH
BOX
&
COOKIE
JAR
FAVORITES

Baking Fun with Kids

Baking with your kids can be so rewarding if you know the secrets to keeping it low-key and stress-free! It's a great experience to share that not only fosters conversation but memories in the making. Your youngsters get to see that baking is more than just getting food on the table— it's an expression of love and creativity. And learning some kitchen and math skills along the way is a bonus!

Use these tips when baking with your pint-size protégés, for a super-fun experience together:

1. **PICK YOUR TEAM** Consider whether you wish to bake with multiple kids (depending on the occasion and time you have) or if you want to bake with just one at a time. It can be a special treat to get that one-on-one time with you. Make it a tradition by baking the same cookie recipe together year after year if you like!

2. **SET THE STAGE** Pick out some fun, upbeat music to work to. It can be songs to sing along with, holiday favorites or something new that you can talk about. Allow more time than you'd think it would take to make the cookies, so that you won't be rushed. Focus more on the time together than a perfect batch of cookies.

3. **GEAR UP** Start with freshly washed hands. Wear aprons to stay clean and to mark this time together as special. Chef hats are optional! Look for kid-size aprons and hats online. If your kids are too short to reach the counter, find a stepping stool or chair that won't tip over to get them into the action safely.

4. **READ IT THROUGH** Reading through the recipe together before you get started will be a great way to teach your kids one step in how to be successful when baking. If they are old enough, have them read it to you!

5. **PREP FIRST** Chop ingredients such as nuts and dried fruits before you get started so that little hands don't get their fingers near the sharp knives. For older kids, have them chop with supervision while you gather the other ingredients.

   Measuring can be hard for wee ones (those under 5 years old) . . . and messy. Premeasure ingredients before you start, if your kids are very young. (They'd rather get to the fun of mixing and decorating anyway.) Older kids (5 years and older) can break an egg at a time into a small custard cup and then transfer it to the mixing bowl. Even older kids can learn how to measure ingredients successfully, following the guidelines on page 10. Be sure to allow extra time for first-timers!

6. **PREPARE FOR NIBBLING** It's hard for little tummies to wait to eat the finished cookies, so have small bowls of some of the ingredients that are designated specifically for nibbling. Chocolate chips, raisins and coconut are just a few of the ingredients that are fun to look at, touch, taste and smell. It's a great sensory experience!

7. **AVOID ACCIDENTS** Use a stand mixer, if possible, that has a bowl locked in place and can't tip over rather than using a hand mixer and a loose bowl. Allow kids to pour milk or other liquids from small, lightweight containers rather than from the large, heavy jugs we purchase. To keep the mess contained, use baking pans with sides when frosting or decorating cookies.

8. **KEEP IT SIMPLE** Choose the simplest recipes for very young children, or consider a recipe such as sugar cookies, where you make and chill the dough ahead of time. Then the kids can jump into the process when it's time to roll and cut out the dough shapes and decorate the finished cookies. If choosing a cutout cookie recipe, select larger, simple-shaped cookie cutters without much detail so the cookies are easier to cut out and decorate. For older kids, consider working your way up to more complex recipes with each baking experience to keep their interest piqued and to expand their skills.

9. **DIG IN** Allow your kids to be inquisitive. Let them squish the dough, roll it in their hands and shape it so they feel connected to what they are making. It's like getting to play in a muddy puddle, but with much better-tasting results!

10. **EMBRACE THE MESS** Inevitably there will be flour on the counter and crumbs on the floor. If you are prepared for this to happen, it won't be as hard to deal with. Depending on their age, let your kids help clean up. Whether it's putting away ingredients or sweeping the floor, it's good for them to see the entire process and realize all that goes into it.

Brownie Monster Cookies

PREP TIME: 15 Minutes • **START TO FINISH: 45 Minutes** • **About 1½ dozen cookies**

1 box (1 lb 2.3 oz) Betty Crocker fudge brownie mix
½ cup quick-cooking oats
½ cup butter, melted
1 tablespoon water

1 egg
¾ cup candy-coated chocolate candies
½ cup peanut butter chips
½ cup semisweet chocolate chips

how to store:
Store these cookies in a tightly covered container.

1 Cookie: Calories 270; Total Fat 11g (Saturated Fat 6g, Trans Fat 0g); Cholesterol 30mg; Sodium 160mg; Total Carbohydrate 40g (Dietary Fiber 1g, Sugars 29g); Protein 2g
Exchanges: 1 Starch, 1½ Other Carbohydrate, 2 Fat
Carbohydrate Choices: 2½

1 Heat oven to 350°F. Line cookie sheets with cooking parchment paper.

2 In large bowl, stir together brownie mix and oats. Add melted butter, water and egg; stir until well blended. Stir in candies and chips.

3 Shape dough into 2-inch balls. On cookie sheets, place balls 3 inches apart; press slightly to flatten each ball.

4 Bake 12 to 14 minutes or until tops of cookies are no longer wet looking. Cool 5 minutes; remove from cookie sheets to cooling racks.

132

LUNCH
BOX
&
COOKIE
JAR
FAVORITES

Texas Sheet Cake Chocolate-Pecan Cookies

PREP TIME: **30 Minutes** • START TO FINISH: **1 Hour 30 Minutes** • **About 2½ dozen cookies**

COOKIES
- ¾ cup packed brown sugar
- ½ cup butter, softened
- ¼ cup buttermilk
- 1 teaspoon vanilla
- 1 egg
- 1¾ cups all-purpose flour
- ¼ cup unsweetened baking cocoa
- ½ teaspoon baking soda
- ½ teaspoon salt
- ½ cup chopped pecans

CHOCOLATE ICING
- ¼ cup butter
- 2 cups powdered sugar
- ¼ cup chopped pecans
- 3 tablespoons unsweetened baking cocoa
- 3 tablespoons milk

1 Heat oven to 400°F. In large bowl, beat brown sugar, ½ cup butter, the buttermilk, vanilla and egg with an electric mixer on medium speed until well blended. Beat in flour, ¼ cup cocoa, baking soda and salt until well mixed. Stir in ½ cup pecans.

2 Onto ungreased cookie sheets, drop dough by rounded tablespoonfuls about 2 inches apart.

3 Bake 7 to 9 minutes or until edges are set and almost no indentation remains when touched in center. Immediately remove from cookie sheets to cooling racks. Cool completely, about 15 minutes.

4 In 2-quart saucepan, melt ¼ cup butter over low heat; remove from heat. Stir in remaining ingredients until icing is of spreading consistency. If icing is too thick, add milk 1 teaspoon at a time until spreading consistency. Spread each cookie with about 2 teaspoons of the icing. Let stand until glaze hardens, about 15 minutes.

ingredient info:
If you don't have buttermilk on hand, stir together ¼ cup milk and 1 teaspoon vinegar and let stand 5 minutes.

why it works:
Texas Sheet Cake is a popular dessert in the south. It's typically baked in a sheet pan and iced with a glossy icing. We've captured the texture and flavor of this cake in a cookie form, so no fork is needed!

how to store:
Store these moist cookies tightly covered at room temperature.

1 Cookie: Calories 150; Total Fat 7g (Saturated Fat 3.5g, Trans Fat 0g); Cholesterol 20mg; Sodium 105mg; Total Carbohydrate 20g (Dietary Fiber 1g); Protein 1g
Exchanges: ½ Starch, 1 Other Carbohydrate, 1½ Fat
Carbohydrate Choices: 1

135

LUNCH
BOX
&
COOKIE
JAR
FAVORITES

Browned Butter Shortbread Cookies

PREP TIME: 35 Minutes • **START TO FINISH: 1 Hour 20 Minutes** • **About 2½ dozen cookies**

1   cup butter
½   cup packed brown sugar
¼   cup powdered sugar
1   teaspoon vanilla

2   cups all-purpose flour
1   tablespoon granulated sugar or 2 tablespoons coarse white sparkling sugar

1 Heat oven to 350°F. In 2-quart saucepan, heat butter over medium heat, stirring constantly, 16 to 20 minutes, or until light golden brown. Remove from heat. Cool 15 minutes.

2 In medium bowl, mix browned butter, brown sugar, powdered sugar and vanilla with a spoon. Add flour; mix well.

3 Shape dough by rounded tablespoonfuls into 1¼-inch balls. On ungreased cookie sheets, place balls 2 inches apart. Press bottom of drinking glass on each ball until about ½ inch thick. Sprinkle with granulated sugar.

4 Bake 8 to 10 minutes or until set and bottoms are light golden brown. Cool 2 minutes; remove from cookie sheets to cooling racks. Cool completely, about 20 minutes.

1 Cookie: Calories 110; Total Fat 6g (Saturated Fat 4g, Trans Fat 0g); Cholesterol 15mg; Sodium 50mg; Total Carbohydrate 11g (Dietary Fiber 0g); Protein 1g
Exchanges: ½; Other Carbohydrate, 1½ Fat
Carbohydrate Choices: 1

138

LUNCH
BOX
&
COOKIE
JAR
FAVORITES

why it works:

Brown butter is butter that is heated until it starts to turn brown. As you cook it, the water in it evaporates, browning the milk solids and giving it a beautiful color and a delicate nutty flavor.

Use a light-colored pan so you can clearly see the color of the butter as it changes.

Stir constantly to ensure the butter is cooking evenly.

Butter will become foamy as the water evaporates. Carefully watch the butter at this point as can change color very quickly.

Remove from heat as soon as the butter is light golden brown. It will continue to darken slightly.

kitchen secret:

You can make a subtle design on the cookies, if you like, by pressing the balls with a glass that has a design on the bottom or a cookie stamp with deep ridges.

how to store:

Store these cookies in a tightly covered container at room temperature.

Tie-Dye Swirl Cookies

PREP TIME: 30 Minutes • **START TO FINISH:** 3 Hours 10 Minutes • **About 4 dozen cookies**

1½	cups powdered sugar
1	cup butter, softened
1	teaspoon vanilla
1	egg
2¾	cups all-purpose flour

1	teaspoon baking soda
1	teaspoon cream of tartar
	Blue, red, yellow, green and orange gel food colors
¼	cup rainbow nonpareils

1 In large bowl, beat powdered sugar, butter, vanilla and egg with electric mixer on medium speed until well blended. Stir in flour, baking soda and cream of tartar. Divide dough in half; set one half aside. Divide one half into 5 portions in separate small bowls. Using the various gel food colors, tint each portion, just until dough is partially colored with streaks of color.

2 Place plain dough onto lightly floured 17x12-inch sheet of cooking parchment paper. Roll into 12x9-inch rectangle. Drop tablespoonfuls of colored dough in random pattern on top of plain dough. Press lightly to bottom layer, and use rolling pin to flatten. Using parchment to guide dough, starting with the long side, tightly roll dough into log about 12 inches long and 2½ inches wide.

3 Place nonpareils in 15x10x1-inch pan. Transfer roll to pan. Press and roll dough in nonpareils to evenly coat roll. Wrap roll tightly in parchment and refrigerate 2 hours or until firm.

4 Heat oven to 375°F. Unwrap dough; trim ends of dough if necessary and discard. Cut dough into ¼-inch slices. On ungreased cookie sheets, place slices 2 inches apart.

5 Bake 7 to 9 minutes or until edges are light brown. Cool 2 minutes; remove from cookie sheets to cooling racks.

why it works:

For nicely shaped round cookies, turn the dough log a couple of times during the refrigeration step before it has a chance to settle and lose its round shape.

why it works:

For the best tie-dye effect, do not fully mix the color into the dough. Dough should have a streaked, swirled appearance. For fun, try combining two different colors in one dough.

how to store:

Store these cookies in a tightly covered container at room temperature.

1 Cookie: Calories 80; Total Fat 4g (Saturated Fat 2.5g, Trans Fat 0g); Cholesterol 15mg; Sodium 60mg; Total Carbohydrate 10g (Dietary Fiber 0g); Protein 1g
Exchanges: ½ Other Carbohydrate, 1 Fat
Carbohydrate Choices: ½

141

LUNCH BOX & COOKIE JAR FAVORITES

Refrigerator Cookies Three Ways

PREP TIME: 20 Minutes • START TO FINISH: 3 Hours • About 4½ dozen cookies

1 cup butter, softened
1 cup granulated sugar
½ cup packed brown sugar
1 teaspoon vanilla

1 egg
2½ cups all-purpose flour
1½ teaspoons baking powder
½ teaspoon salt

1 In large bowl, beat butter, granulated sugar, brown sugar, vanilla and egg with electric mixer on medium speed until well blended. Stir in remaining ingredients (as well as specific ingredients called for from chosen recipe below).

2 Shape dough into 2 (8-inch-long) round, rectangular or triangular logs. Wrap logs tightly in plastic wrap, and refrigerate until firm.

3 Heat oven to 375ºF. Unwrap dough; trim ends of dough and discard. With sharp knife, cut into ¼-inch slices. On ungreased cookie sheets, place slices about 2 inches apart.

4 Bake 8 to 10 minutes or until edges are light golden brown. Cool 2 minutes; remove from cookie sheets to cooling racks. Cool completely. Continue as directed in chosen recipe.

Toffee-Pecan Cookies

Add ½ cup finely chopped toasted pecans and ½ cup toffee bits with the dry ingredients. In small microwavable bowl, microwave 2 cups semisweet chocolate chips and 2 teaspoons shortening uncovered on High 1 to 2 minutes, stirring once, or until mixture can be stirred smooth. Dip half of each cooled cookie into melted chocolate, shaking off excess. Place on waxed paper and sprinkle with ½ cup finely chopped toasted pecans; allow to set.

Ginger-Orange Cookies

Stir in 3 tablespoons chopped crystallized ginger and 1 tablespoon orange zest with the dry ingredients. In small microwavable bowl, microwave ⅓ cup dark chocolate chips uncovered on High 30 seconds to 1 minute, stirring once, or until chips can be stirred smooth. Spoon melted chocolate into small resealable food-storage plastic bag; seal bag. Cut off tiny corner of bag; squeeze bag to drizzle onto cookies; allow to set about 15 minutes.

Piña Colada Cookies

Stir in ½ cup shredded toasted coconut, ⅓ cup finely chopped sweetened dried mango and ⅓ cup finely chopped sweetened dried pineapple with the dry ingredients.

why it works:

For nicely shaped cookies, rotate the logs in the refrigerator every 30 minutes during refrigeration so the dough doesn't have a chance to settle and alter the shape of the log.

how to store:

Since these are refrigerator or "icebox" cookies, dough may be stored tightly wrapped in the refrigerator and sliced and baked as you'd like them. Keep dough for no longer than 1 week in the refrigerator. Store leftover baked cookies in a tightly covered container at room temperature for up to 5 days.

1 Cookie: Calories 80; Total Fat 3.5g (Saturated Fat 2g, Trans Fat 0g); Cholesterol 10mg; Sodium 65mg; Total Carbohydrate 10g (Dietary Fiber 0g); Protein 0g
Exchanges: ½ Starch, ½ Fat
Carbohydrate Choices: ½

Clockwise from top left: Piña Colada Cookies, Ginger-Orange Cookies, Toffee-Pecan Cookies

Rosemary Shortbread Cookies

PREP TIME: 35 Minutes • **START TO FINISH: 35 Minutes** • **About 1½ dozen cookies**

1½ cups all-purpose flour
½ cup cold butter, cut into pieces
¼ cup powdered sugar

2 tablespoons finely chopped fresh rosemary leaves
2 tablespoons granulated sugar or coarse white sparkling sugar

1 Heat oven to 325°F. Spray cookie sheet with cooking spray.

2 In food processor bowl with metal blade, place flour, butter, powdered sugar and rosemary. Cover; process until dough forms a ball.

3 Roll dough on lightly floured surface to ¼ inch thickness. Cut with floured scalloped 2-inch cookie cutter. On cookie sheet, place cutouts about 2 inches apart.

4 Bake 18 to 20 minutes or until edges are lightly browned. Sprinkle with granulated sugar. Remove from cookie sheet to cooling rack.

ingredient info:

Fresh rosemary adds a fragrant quality to these delicate cookies. And because the herb traditionally represents remembrance, a batch of these treats is ideal as a thank-you or birthday gift.

how to store:

Store these cookies in a tightly covered container at room temperature.

1 Cookie: Calories 100; Total Fat 5g (Saturated Fat 4g, Trans Fat 0g); Cholesterol 0mg; Sodium 45mg; Total Carbohydrate 11g (Dietary Fiber 0g, Sugars 0g); Protein 1g
Exchanges: ½ Starch, 1 Fat
Carbohydrate Choices: 1

Zebra Cookies

PREP TIME: 45 Minutes • **START TO FINISH: 2 Hours 30 Minutes** • **About 3 dozen cookies**

1 cup butter, softened
1 cup sugar
1 egg
1½ teaspoons baking powder
1 teaspoon vanilla
½ teaspoon salt

2¼ cups all-purpose flour
¼ cup unsweetened baking cocoa
¼ cup chocolate, pink or multicolored sprinkles or nonpareils

1 In large bowl, beat butter and sugar with electric mixer on medium speed until smooth and creamy. Add egg, baking powder, vanilla and salt; beat on medium speed until smooth. In medium bowl, place half of mixture (about 1 cup); add 1¼ cups of the flour. Beat on low speed until well mixed. To remaining mixture in other bowl, add the remaining 1 cup flour and the cocoa. Beat on low speed until well mixed.

2 Divide dough from each bowl in half. Form each dough portion into a 3¼x1-inch log. Wrap in plastic wrap and refrigerate 30 minutes.

3 Cut each roll crosswise into 6 equal pieces. On lightly floured surface, pat pieces into 4½x2-inch rectangles. Alternately stack 3 chocolate and 3 white dough strips, brushing lightly with water between each layer to form a striped stack. Place 2 tablespoons of the candy sprinkles on a piece of plastic wrap or waxed paper. Coat each side of stack in sprinkles, pressing to adhere to roll. Wrap log in plastic wrap or waxed paper. Repeat with remaining dough strips and sprinkles to form an additional stack. Refrigerate logs at least 1 hour.

4 Heat oven to 375°F. Unwrap dough; trim ends of dough and discard. Cut into ¼-inch slices. On ungreased cookie sheets, place slices 2 inches apart.

5 Bake 10 to 12 minutes or until edges are light golden brown. Cool 1 minute; remove from cookie sheets to cooling racks.

ingredient info:

We've just offered a few suggestions for colored sprinkles for these striped cookies, but feel free to use whatever color sprinkles you like to match your occasion. You can also add a few drops of food color or gel to the white dough for a zebra cookie of a different color!

why it works:

Patting the dough to a thinner size and then stacking and brushing the layers with a little water helps make the dough firm enough for cutting into nice slices without the layers separating.

how to store:

Store these cookies in a tightly covered container at room temperature.

1 Cookie: Calories 110; Total Fat 6g (Saturated Fat 3.5g, Trans Fat 0g); Cholesterol 20mg; Sodium 95mg; Total Carbohydrate 13g (Dietary Fiber 0g); Protein 1g
Exchanges: ½ Starch, ½ Other Carbohydrate, 1 Fat
Carbohydrate Choices: 1

LUNCH BOX & COOKIE JAR FAVORITES

Almond Butter Puppy Cookies

PREP TIME: 2 Hours 25 Minutes • **START TO FINISH:** 4 Hours 45 Minutes • **About 3½ dozen cookies**

1 cup almond butter
½ cup butter, softened
¾ cup granulated sugar
¾ cup packed brown sugar
2 eggs
2 cups all-purpose flour
½ cup almonds, ground
1 teaspoon baking soda

1 teaspoon cream of tartar
About 88 semisweet chocolate chips
About 44 small (1-inch) chewy chocolate candies, unwrapped
Decorating frosting and assorted candies, as desired

1 In large bowl, beat almond butter, butter, granulated sugar, brown sugar and eggs with electric mixer on medium speed until well mixed. Add flour, ground almonds, baking soda and cream of tartar; beat until well mixed. Divide dough in half. Wrap each with plastic wrap, and refrigerate at least 2 hours.

2 Heat oven to 375°F. Spray 2 large cookie sheets with cooking spray.

3 Roll each dough half on lightly floured surface until ¼ inch thick. Cut with floured 2- to 2½-inch heart-shaped cookie cutters. On cookie sheets, place cutouts about 1 inch apart.

4 Bake 6 to 8 minutes or until edges are just set. Using the photo as a guide, immediately press two chocolate chips in each cookie for the eyes. Remove cookies from cookie sheets to cooling racks. Cool completely, about 15 minutes.

5 Cut each chocolate candy diagonally in half; flatten halves to look like dog ears by pressing narrow ends to form longer points. Squeeze a small amount of decorating frosting on back of ears, and, using the photo as a guide, attach to cookies. Use decorating frosting and candies as desired to make nose and mouth.

ingredient info:

To make ground almonds, process ½ cup slivered almonds in mini food processor until ground. You can also toast the almonds before processing if you like, for an additional layer of flavor.

kitchen secret:

This recipe makes enough cookies to share with a large group, but if you don't need all the cookies at one time, freeze the baked, cooled cookies in an tightly covered container. When you are ready to decorate a few, or all of them, let stand at room temperature 15 to 20 minutes before decorating.

how to store:

Store these cookies in tightly covered container at room temperature.

1 Cookie: Calories 140; Total Fat 7g (Saturated Fat 2g, Trans Fat 0g); Cholesterol 15mg; Sodium 65mg; Total Carbohydrate 16g (Dietary Fiber 1g); Protein 2g
Exchanges: ½ Starch, ½ Other Carbohydrate, 1½ Fat
Carbohydrate Choices: 1

149

LUNCH
BOX
&
COOKIE
JAR
FAVORITES

Butterscotch Blondies

PREP TIME: 15 Minutes • **START TO FINISH: 1 Hour 55 Minutes** • **48 bars**

½ cup plus 2 tablespoons unsalted butter
2½ cups packed light brown sugar

2 cups all-purpose flour
2 teaspoons baking powder
½ teaspoon salt
3 eggs

how to store:
Store these bars in a tightly covered container.

1 Bar: Calories 90; Total Fat 3g (Saturated Fat 1.5g, Trans Fat 0g); Cholesterol 20mg; Sodium 50mg; Total Carbohydrate 15g (Dietary Fiber 0g); Protein 1g
Exchanges: 1 Other Carbohydrate, ½ Fat
Carbohydrate Choices: 1

1 Heat oven to 350°F. Spray bottom and sides of 13x9-inch pan with cooking spray.

2 In 1-quart saucepan, heat butter over medium heat 6 minutes, stirring occasionally, until lightly browned. Pour into small bowl; cool 10 minutes.

3 Meanwhile, in large bowl, mix brown sugar, flour, baking powder and salt. Add eggs to browned butter; stir with whisk. Pour butter mixture over flour mixture; stir just until moistened. Spoon batter into pan; smooth top with spatula.

4 Bake 30 minutes or until toothpick inserted in center comes out clean. Cool completely in pan on cooling rack, about 1 hour. For bars, cut into 8 rows by 6 rows.

Stuffed S'more Cookies

PREP TIME: 40 Minutes • **START TO FINISH:** 1 Hour 50 Minutes • **2 dozen cookies**

FILLING
- 1 cup marshmallow creme (from 7-oz jar)
- 1 tablespoon all-purpose flour
- 4 oz (half of 8-oz package) cream cheese, softened

COOKIES
- ¾ cup packed brown sugar
- ½ cup granulated sugar
- 1 cup butter, melted and cooled slightly
- 1 teaspoon vanilla
- 1 egg
- 2¼ cups all-purpose flour
- 1½ cups coarsely crushed honey graham cereal squares
- 1 teaspoon baking powder
- ½ teaspoon baking soda
- ½ teaspoon salt
- ½ cup miniature semi-sweet chocolate chips
- ½ cup marshmallow bits (from 3-oz container)

1 Line 15x10x1-inch baking pan with cooking parchment paper.

2 In medium bowl, beat Filling ingredients with electric mixer on medium speed until well mixed. Drop cream cheese mixture into 24 mounds onto baking pan (about 1½ teaspoons each). Freeze 1 hour or until set.

3 Heat oven to 350°F. In large bowl, beat brown sugar, granulated sugar, butter, vanilla and egg with electric mixer on medium speed until well mixed. Add flour, graham cereal, baking powder, baking soda and salt; beat until dough forms. Stir in miniature chocolate chips and marshmallow bits until well mixed.

4 Divide dough into 24 portions (about 2 tablespoonfuls dough each). Flatten each mound of dough into a 2½-inch round. Using metal spatula or knife, place 1 dollop frozen marshmallow mixture in center of round. Wrap dough around frozen marshmallow mixture, forming a ball, making sure marshmallow is completely covered. On ungreased cookie sheets, place 2 inches apart.

5 Bake 13 to 15 minutes or until light golden brown. Cool 3 minutes; remove from cookie sheets to cooling racks. Cool completely, about 30 minutes.

ingredient info:
Easily crush the graham cereal by placing it in a 1-gallon resealable food-storage plastic bag and rolling over it with a rolling pin or pounding it with a meat mallet. Two cups cereal will make 1½ cups coarsely crushed crumbs. Coarsely crushed cereal adds texture to this recipe that finely crushed cereal doesn't provide.

ingredient info:
Marshmallow bits are tiny vanilla-flavored pieces that have the flavor of marshmallows but retain their shape when baked. You can find them at your favorite discount store in the baking aisle.

how to store:
Store these cookies in a tightly covered container at room temperature.

1 Cookie: Calories 220; Total Fat 11g (Saturated Fat 7g, Trans Fat 0g); Cholesterol 35mg; Sodium 200mg; Total Carbohydrate 26g (Dietary Fiber 0g); Protein 2g
Exchanges: 1 Starch, 1 Other Carbohydrate, 2 Fat
Carbohydrate Choices: 2

Cookie Biscotti Sticks

PREP TIME: 15 Minutes • **START TO FINISH: 3 Hours** • **About 2 dozen biscotti sticks**

1 cup packed brown sugar
⅔ cup butter
¼ cup light corn syrup
¾ cup creamy peanut butter
1 teaspoon vanilla
3½ cups old-fashioned oats

1 bag (12 oz) semisweet chocolate chips (2 cups)
1 cup butterscotch chips
2 tablespoons shortening
½ cup coarsely chopped peanuts

how to store:
Store these cookies tightly covered at room temperature.

1 Biscotti Stick: Calories 653; Total Fat 38g (Saturated Fat 19g, Trans Fat 0g); Cholesterol 0mg; Sodium 222mg; Total Carbohydrate 74g (Dietary Fiber 5g, Sugars 0g); Protein 11g
Exchanges: 1 Starch, 4 Other Carbohydrate, 1 High-Fat Meat, 6 Fat
Carbohydrate Choices: 5

1 Heat oven to 375°F. Line 13x9-inch pan with foil, leaving foil overhanging at 2 opposite sides of pan.

2 In 3-quart saucepan, stir together brown sugar, butter and corn syrup; cook over medium heat until sugar is dissolved and butter is melted. Remove from heat. Stir in ¼ cup of the peanut butter and the vanilla. Gently stir in oats. Press in bottom of pan.

3 Bake 20 to 22 minutes or until brown.

4 In 2-quart saucepan, heat chocolate chips, butterscotch chips and shortening over medium heat, stirring constantly, until melted and smooth. Remove from heat. Stir in remaining ½ cup peanut butter. Spread mixture over baked cookie crust; sprinkle with peanuts. Cool in pan on cooling rack 20 minutes.

5 Cover; refrigerate 2 to 3 hours or until firm. Use foil to lift out of pan. Using large chef's knife, cut bars lengthwise in half and then crosswise into approximately 1-inch-wide sticks.

Pictured clockwise from top left are Festive White Velvet Star Stacks, page 187; Birthday Cake Cookies, page 213; and Brownies on a Stick, page 212.

Sparkling Orange Ricotta Sandwich Cookies

PREP TIME: 45 Minutes • **START TO FINISH:** 3 Hours 45 Minutes • **About 4 dozen sandwich cookies**

COOKIES

- 1 cup granulated sugar
- ⅓ cup butter, softened
- 1 egg
- ¼ cup whole milk ricotta cheese (from 8-oz container)
- 1 teaspoon grated orange zest
- 4½ teaspoons fresh orange juice
- 1½ cups all-purpose flour
- ½ teaspoon baking powder
- ¼ teaspoon baking soda
- ¼ teaspoon salt
- ⅛ teaspoon orange gel food color
- 1 tablespoon water

FILLING

- ¾ cup powdered sugar
- ⅓ cup butter, softened
- ½ cup whole milk ricotta cheese (from 8-oz container)
- 2 teaspoons grated orange zest

GARNISH

Candied orange slices, cut into small triangles, if desired

Small mint leaves, cut in half, if desired

1 In large bowl, beat ¾ cup of the granulated sugar and ⅓ cup butter with electric mixer on medium speed until light and fluffy. Add egg and beat well. Beat in ¼ cup ricotta cheese, 1 teaspoon orange zest, and the orange juice until well mixed. Add flour, baking powder, baking soda and salt; beat until well blended. Cover and refrigerate 1 hour.

2 Heat oven to 350°F. Line large cookie sheets with cooking parchment paper.

3 Onto cookie sheets, drop dough by rounded teaspoonfuls 2 inches apart (dough will be sticky).

4 Bake for 9 to 11 minutes or until edges are set. Cool 2 minutes; remove from cookie sheets to cooling racks. Cool completely, about 20 minutes.

5 In small resealable bag, add remaining ¼ cup granulated sugar and the food color; seal bag and shake to color sugar. Transfer colored sugar to small bowl. Lightly brush tops of cookie with pastry brush dipped in water; dip tops in colored sugar; return sugar side up to cooling rack for sugar to dry.

6 In medium bowl, mix powdered sugar and ⅓ cup butter until no lumps remain. Stir in ½ cup ricotta and 2 teaspoons orange zest until mixed well.

7 To assemble cookies, pipe or spread about 2 teaspoons filling on the flat side of one cookie; press flat side of another cookie to filling at one spot to look like an open clam. Press a piece of candied orange slice and mint leaf into filling for garnish and place on tray. Loosely cover and refrigerate about 30 minutes or until filling is firm.

ingredient info:

Candied orange slices can be found packaged in the specialty area of some grocery stores. Coat in additional granulated sugar to make them extra special.

why it works:

Making your own sparkling colored sugar is easy using a resealable food-storage plastic bag and food gel color. Just shake bag, pressing color into sugar to get the best color. The gel works best for this, as traditional liquid food coloring may cause your sugar to clump.

1 Sandwich Cookie: Calories 70;
Total Fat 3g (Saturated Fat 2g, Trans
Fat 0g); Cholesterol 15mg; Sodium 50mg;
Total Carbohydrate 9g (Dietary Fiber 0g);
Protein 1g
Exchanges: ½ Starch, ½ Fat
Carbohydrate Choices: ½

why it works:

Piping your filling works great using a resealable food-storage plastic bag. Just transfer your filling to bag, seal and cut about ¼-inch opening from one corner. Gently squeeze filling onto bottom cookies, top with another cookie. Make sure filling is not refrigerated before piping, as it may be too firm to squeeze through the bag.

how to store:

Store the assembled cookies in single layer in a tightly covered container in the refrigerator for up to 3 days.

Lemon Meltaways

PREP TIME: 35 Minutes • **START TO FINISH:** 2 Hours 30 Minutes • **About 3 dozen cookies**

COOKIES
1 cup butter, softened
2 cups powdered sugar
3 tablespoons finely grated lemon zest

2 cups all-purpose flour

ICING
1 cup powdered sugar
1 to 2 tablespoons lemon juice

1 Heat oven to 400°F. In large bowl, beat butter, ½ cup of the powdered sugar and the lemon zest with electric mixer on medium speed until fluffy. Stir in flour until soft dough forms.

2 Shape dough into 1¼-inch balls. On ungreased cookie sheets, place balls 1½ inches apart; flatten each ball to 1½-inch circle.

3 Bake 6 to 8 minutes or until edges are set but not brown. Cool 2 minutes; remove from cookie sheets to cooling racks. In small bowl, place 1½ cups powdered sugar. Roll each warm cookie in powdered sugar and place on cooling rack. Cool completely, about 30 minutes. Roll cookies again in powdered sugar to coat.

4 In small bowl, beat 1 cup powdered sugar and 1 tablespoon of the lemon juice until smooth. If too stiff to drizzle, add more lemon juice, 1 teaspoon at a time. Spoon into resealable food-storage plastic bag; partially seal bag. Cut small tip from corner of bag; pipe over tops of cookies. Let stand about 1 hour or until icing is set.

ingredient info:
1 medium lemon yields about 3 tablespoons juice and 2 to 3 teaspoons grated lemon zest.

how to store:
Store these lemon gems covered in a tightly covered container.

1 Cookie: Calories 110; Total Fat 5g (Saturated Fat 4g, Trans Fat 0g); Cholesterol 15mg; Sodium 40mg; Total Carbohydrate 15g (Dietary Fiber 0g, Sugars 10g); Protein 0g
Exchanges: 1 Other Carbohydrate, 1 Fat
Carbohydrate Choices: 1

161

MAKE
IT
SPECIAL

Cookie-Stuffed Chocolate Chip Cookie Bombs

PREP TIME: 50 Minutes • **START TO FINISH:** 5 Hours 45 Minutes • **About 3 dozen cookie bombs**

1 pouch Betty Crocker chocolate chip cookie mix
½ cup butter, softened
2 tablespoons all-purpose flour
1 egg

About 36 miniature creme-filled chocolate sandwich cookies (from 8-oz bag)
1 container chocolate creamy ready-to-spread frosting
⅓ cup white vanilla baking chips
1 teaspoon shortening

kitchen secret:
Have only one mini muffin pan? Refrigerate the rest of the dough while baking the first batch. Cool the pan about 10 minutes, then bake the rest of the dough, adding 1 to 2 minutes to the bake time.

how to store:
Store these cookie bombs covered in a tightly covered container at room temperature.

1 Heat oven to 375°F. In large bowl, stir cookie mix, butter, flour and egg until soft dough forms. Shape into 36 (1¼-inch) balls; place in 36 ungreased mini muffin cups. Press miniature sandwich cookie in center of each cookie.

2 Bake 10 to 12 minutes or until edges are golden brown. Cool in pan 10 minutes. Carefully run small knife around outside edge of cookie to loosen; remove to cooling rack. Cool completely, about 30 minutes. Place cooling rack of cookies over cookie sheet or waxed paper. Turn cookies over so bottom side is up and miniature sandwich cookie side is down.

3 In small microwavable bowl, microwave frosting uncovered on High 30 to 60 seconds or until thin enough to pour. Pour slightly less than 1 tablespoon warmed frosting over each cookie to completely cover, using spoon to help spread if needed. Rewarm frosting in microwave to maintain pouring consistency, if needed.

4 In another small microwavable bowl, microwave white vanilla baking chips and shortening uncovered on High 30 to 60 seconds or until mixture can be stirred smooth. Drizzle melted chips over cookies. Let stand about 4 hours or until frosting glaze is set.

162

MAKE
IT
SPECIAL

1 Cookie Bomb: Calories 160; Total Fat 7g (Saturated Fat 4g, Trans Fat 0g); Cholesterol 10mg; Sodium 125mg; Total Carbohydrate 21g (Dietary Fiber 0g, Sugars 15g); Protein 1g
Exchanges: 1½ Other Carbohydrate, 1½ Fat
Carbohydrate Choices: 1½

Cinnamon Dolce Latte Sandwich Cookies

PREP TIME: **55 Minutes** • START TO FINISH: **1 Hour** • **About 3 dozen sandwich cookies**

COOKIES

4	teaspoons espresso powder
3	teaspoons water
1	cup plus 3 tablespoons granulated sugar
1	cup butter, softened
1	teaspoon vanilla
1	egg
2¼	cups all-purpose flour
½	teaspoon baking soda
¼	teaspoon salt
1	teaspoon ground cinnamon

FILLING

½	cup butter, softened
2¼	cups powdered sugar
3	tablespoons cinnamon-flavored coffee syrup

1 Heat oven to 375°F. In small bowl, dissolve espresso powder in water; set aside.

2 In large bowl, mix 1 cup of the granulated sugar and the butter with spoon until well blended. Stir in espresso mixture, vanilla and egg. Stir in flour, baking soda and salt; mix well.

3 In small bowl, mix remaining 3 tablespoons granulated sugar and cinnamon. For each cookie, shape 1½ teaspoons of the dough into ball; roll in cinnamon-sugar mixture. On ungreased cookie sheets, place balls about 2 inches apart. Press bottom of drinking glass on each ball until about ¼ inch thick.

4 Bake 7 to 9 minutes or until edges are set. Cool 3 minutes; remove from cookie sheets to cooling racks. Cool completely, about 15 minutes.

5 Meanwhile, in medium bowl, mix together Frosting ingredients until smooth and creamy. For each sandwich cookie, spread or pipe about 2 teaspoons frosting on flat side of 1 cookie; top with second cookie, flat side down.

ingredient info:

Coffee syrups are often used to make the flavorful specialty coffee beverages we enjoy. This syrup can be found in the grocery store where the coffee and tea products are sold or at specialty food stores. If you prefer, substitute 1 tablespoon milk and ¼ teaspoon ground cinnamon for the cinnamon-flavored coffee syrup.

why it works:

When balls of cookie dough are rolled in a sugar mixture before baking, you may have a little extra of the sugar mixture left over. Since there is variation in how much sugar mixture sticks to the balls, we always want to make sure you have enough to successfully make a recipe.

how to store:

Store these cookies in tightly covered container at room temperature.

1 Sandwich Cookie: Calories 160; Total Fat 8g (Saturated Fat 5g, Trans Fat 0g); Cholesterol 25mg; Sodium 95mg; Total Carbohydrate 21g (Dietary Fiber 0g); Protein 1g **Exchanges:** ½ Starch, 1 Other Carbohydrate, 1½ Fat **Carbohydrate Choices:** 1½

Sweetheart Cookies

PREP TIME: 15 Minutes • **START TO FINISH: 1 Hour** • **About 3 dozen cookies**

1   pouch (17.5 oz) Betty Crocker sugar cookie mix
½   cup butter, softened
2   tablespoons all-purpose flour
1   egg
3   tablespoons white sparkling sugar or granulated sugar

3   tablespoons coarse pink sparkling sugar or pink decorator sugar
1   tablespoon instant coffee powder or granules
    About 36 chocolate-striped candy drops or pieces, unwrapped
    About 36 milk chocolate candy drops or pieces, unwrapped

1 Heat oven to 375°F. In medium bowl, stir cookie mix, butter, flour and egg until soft dough forms.

2 Roll dough into 1-inch balls. In small bowl, combine white sugar, pink sugar and coffee powder. Roll balls in sugar-coffee mixture. On ungreased cookie sheets, place balls about 2 inches apart.

3 Bake 7 to 9 minutes or until set. Immediately press 1 chocolate-striped candy into center of each cookie. Allow to stand about 5 minutes until soft; press lightly. Top melted candy with chocolate candy. Remove cookies to cooling racks. Cool completely.

why it works:

For even baking, make sure cookies are the same shape and size. You can make it look like you made two different types of cookies with only one batch by swapping the placement of the candies. In step 3, press chocolate striped candies into half of the cookies as directed and then press a chocolate candy into each of the other half of the cookies. Top softened striped candies with a chocolate candy for half of the cookies as directed in step 3 and top the remaining cookies with the softened chocolate candies with a striped candy.

how to store:

Store these cookies covered at room temperature.

1 Cookie: Calories 140; Total Fat 7g (Saturated Fat 4g, Trans Fat 0g); Cholesterol 15mg; Sodium 70mg; Total Carbohydrate 19g (Dietary Fiber 0g, Sugars 13g); Protein 1g
Exchanges: ½ Starch, 1 Other Carbohydrate, 1 Fat
Carbohydrate Choices: 1

Glazed Toffee Bonbons

PREP TIME: 1 Hour 10 Minutes • **START TO FINISH: 1 Hour 30 Minutes** • **About 4 dozen cookies**

COOKIES
- ½ cup butter, softened
- ½ cup packed brown sugar
- ½ teaspoon vanilla
- 1 egg
- 1¾ cups all-purpose flour
- ¼ teaspoon baking soda
- ¼ teaspoon salt
- 3 bars (1.4 oz each) chocolate-covered English toffee candy, finely chopped

GLAZE
- ½ cup packed brown sugar
- ¼ cup butter
- 3 tablespoons milk
- 1⅓ cups powdered sugar
- ⅓ cup semisweet chocolate chips
- ⅓ cup white vanilla baking chips

kitchen secret:

You don't need to wait to drizzle the second melted chip mixture over the first melted chip mixture—just be sure to not touch the soft melted chocolate.

how to store:

Store these cookies covered, in a single layer, at room temperature.

1 Cookie: Calories 100; Total Fat 4g (Saturated Fat 3g, Trans Fat 0g); Cholesterol 15mg; Sodium 55mg; Total Carbohydrate 15g (Dietary Fiber 0g, Sugars 11g); Protein 1g
Exchanges: 1 Other Carbohydrate, 1 Fat
Carbohydrate Choices: 1

169

MAKE IT SPECIAL

1 Heat oven to 325°F. In large bowl, beat ½ cup butter, ½ cup brown sugar, the vanilla and egg with electric mixer on medium speed until light and fluffy. On low speed, beat in flour, baking soda and salt.

2 Reserve one-third of the chopped candy for garnish. Stir remaining chopped candy into dough. Shape dough into 1-inch balls. On ungreased cookie sheets, place balls 1 inch apart.

3 Bake 11 to 14 minutes or until edges start to brown and tops of cookies feel set when tapped. Place cooling racks on waxed paper. Immediately remove cookies from cookie sheets to cooling racks.

4 Meanwhile, in 1-quart saucepan, heat ½ cup brown sugar, ¼ cup butter and milk over medium-low heat, stirring frequently, until mixture just comes to a boil and sugar is dissolved. Stir in powdered sugar; beat with whisk if necessary to remove lumps. Immediately dip tops of cookies into glaze or spread glaze on tops of cookies. (Cookies don't need to be completely cooled, just firm and set.) Place on cooling racks; let stand about 10 minutes or until glaze is set. If glaze starts to set in saucepan, reheat over medium-low heat and beat with whisk until softened.

5 Place chocolate chips and vanilla chips in separate small microwavable bowls. Microwave each on High 1½ to 2 minutes, stirring every 30 seconds, until melted and smooth. Using tip of spoon, generously drizzle each flavor over cookies. Sprinkle with remaining candy. Refrigerate about 20 minutes or until set.

Springtime Baby Chick Cookies

PREP TIME: 1 Hour 30 Minutes • **START TO FINISH: 3 Hours 30 Minutes** • **15 cookie chicks**

COOKIES

1	cup granulated sugar
½	cup butter, softened
1	teaspoon vanilla
1	egg
2	cups all-purpose flour
1	teaspoon baking powder
¼	teaspoon salt
15	pretzel sticks, broken in half
½	cup shredded coconut
	Yellow food coloring
16	candied orange slices or large orange gumdrops

GLAZE

2	cups powdered sugar
2	tablespoons milk
¼	teaspoon almond extract or vanilla
30	miniature chocolate chips

1 In large bowl, beat granulated sugar, butter, 1 teaspoon vanilla and egg with electric mixer on medium speed or mix with spoon until fluffy. Beat in flour, baking powder and salt until well blended.

2 Heat oven to 375°F. Shape dough into 15 (1¼-inch) balls, using rounded tablespoon of dough per ball; and shape 15 (¾-inch) balls, using scant tablespoon of dough per ball. On ungreased cookie sheets, place 1 small ball and 1 large ball next to each other, 2 inches apart and pressing gently to touch to form chick.

3 Bake 9 to 11 minutes or until edges are set. Cool 2 minutes; remove from cookie sheet to cooling rack. Cool 5 minutes or just until cool enough to handle. Using photo as a guide, carefully push pretzel sticks into body of chicks to form legs. Cool completely, about 30 minutes longer.

4 In jar, place coconut and 2 to 3 drops food coloring. Cover and shake until coconut is evenly yellow. Cut 1 orange slice into 15 small triangles to use as beaks. Line the same cookie sheets with waxed paper.

5 In medium bowl, mix all Glaze ingredients except chocolate chips until smooth. Dip tops of each chick into glaze; shake off excess. Place on cookie sheets. Attach 2 mini chocolate chips for eyes, a small orange triangle for beak and sprinkle body with coconut for feathers. Repeat with remaining chicks. Let stand 30 minutes or until glaze hardens.

6 Flatten each of the remaining orange slices with rolling pin to ¼ inch thickness. Cut in half crosswise to form 2 flat triangles. With kitchen shears, cut chicken feet, using photo as a guide. Carefully push feet into pretzels.

kitchen secret:

If orange slices are sticky to roll and cut, coat rolling pin, work surface and kitchen shears with granulated sugar.

kitchen secret:

Have fun with these little chicks by arranging legs, feet and feathers to give each one its own personality. If attaching legs to the bottom of the chicks, use a little of the glaze as "glue."

how to store:

Store these chicks in a single layer in a tightly covered container at room temperature.

1 Cookie Chick: Calories 290; Total Fat 8g (Saturated Fat 5g, Trans Fat 0g); Cholesterol 30mg; Sodium 140mg; Total Carbohydrate 53g (Dietary Fiber 0g); Protein 2g **Exchanges:** 1 Starch, 2½ Other Carbohydrate, 1½ Fat **Carbohydrate Choices:** 3½

MAKE IT SPECIAL

Easter Nest Cookies

PREP TIME: 1 Hour • **START TO FINISH: 1 Hour** • **About 2 dozen cookies**

1 pouch (17.5 oz) Betty Crocker sugar cookie mix
⅓ cup butter, softened
1 tablespoon all-purpose flour
1 egg

1 container fluffy white whipped ready-to-spread frosting
1 cup flaked coconut
Food color
Jelly beans

1 Heat oven to 375°F. In medium bowl, stir cookie mix, butter, flour and egg until dough forms.

2 Shape dough into 2-inch balls. On ungreased cookie sheets, place cookies 1 inch apart.

3 Bake 7 to 9 minutes or until edges are light golden brown. Cool 1 minute; remove from cookie sheets to cooling racks. Cool completely, about 15 minutes.

4 Frost cookies. Add coconut to a 1-quart resealable food-storage plastic bag. Add 2 to 3 drops food color, shaking bag to blend color. It may be necessary to add 1 to 2 teaspoons water to help disperse the color evenly or additional food color until desired color is reached.

5 Sprinkle about 1 teaspoon coconut onto each cookie. Top with jelly beans.

why it works:
Going lightly on the coconut in the center of the cookies will leave some frosting exposed for the jelly beans to stick to.

how to store:
Store these showy nests in a tightly covered container.

1 Frosted Cookie (undecorated):
Calories 190; Total Fat 8g (Saturated Fat 4g, Trans Fat 1g); Cholesterol 15mg; Sodium 105mg; Total Carbohydrate 27g (Dietary Fiber 0g, Sugars 19g); Protein 1g
Exchanges: ½ Starch, 1½ Other Carbohydrate, 1½ Fat
Carbohydrate Choices: 2

MAKE
IT
SPECIAL

Mini Burger Cookies

PREP TIME: 40 Minutes • **START TO FINISH:** 1 Hour 40 Minutess • **16 sandwich cookies**

1 pouch (17.5 oz) Betty Crocker sugar cookie mix

⅓ cup butter, softened

3 tablespoons all-purpose flour

1 egg

½ cup vanilla creamy ready-to-spread frosting (from 16-oz container)

16 chocolate-covered peppermint patties (1.5 oz), unwrapped

2 tablespoons green tinted flaked coconut (see ingredient info)

1 can (6.4-oz) each red and yellow decorating icing

1 teaspoon honey

1 teaspoon water

2 teaspoons sesame seed

kitchen secret:
To tint coconut, shake coconut and a few drops green food color in tightly covered jar or resealable food-storage plastic bag.

how to store:
Store these "burgers" in a covered container at room temperature.

1 Heat oven to 375ºF. In medium bowl, combine cookie mix, butter, flour and egg until soft dough forms. Shape dough into 32 (1-inch) balls. On ungreased cookie sheets, place balls 1 inch apart.

2 Bake for 10 to 12 minutes or until set and edges are light golden brown. Cool 1 minute; remove from cookie sheets to cooling racks. Cool completely.

3 Spread about ½ teaspoon vanilla frosting on bottom of each cookie. Top 1 cookie, frosted side up, with 1 peppermint patty. Pipe red and yellow icing on peppermint patties for mustard and ketchup; top each with ½ teaspoon green coconut and a remaining cookie, frosting side down. Repeat with remaining cookies.

4 In small bowl, combine honey and water. Brush on top of each cookie; sprinkle with sesame seeds.

174

MAKE
IT
SPECIAL

1 Sandwich Cookie: Calories 410; Total Fat 14g (Saturated Fat 6g, Trans Fat 2g); Cholesterol 25mg; Sodium 160mg; Total Carbohydrate 69g (Dietary Fiber 1g, Sugars 53g); Protein 2g
Exchanges: 1 Starch, 3½ Other Carbohydrate, 2½ Fat
Carbohydrate Choices: 4½

Pumpkin Cream-Filled Gingerbread Thumbprint Cookies

PREP TIME: 45 Minutes • **START TO FINISH:** 1 Hour 45 Minutes • About 4 dozen cookies

COOKIES

- ½ cup packed brown sugar
- ½ cup butter, softened
- ½ cup dark molasses
- 1 teaspoon vanilla
- 2 eggs
- 3 cups all-purpose flour
- 1 teaspoon ground cinnamon
- ½ teaspoon baking powder
- ½ teaspoon ground ginger
- ¼ teaspoon baking soda
- ¼ teaspoon salt
- ¼ cup chopped crystallized ginger (from 3-oz package)
- 3 tablespoons granulated sugar

PUMPKIN FILLING

- 4 oz (half of 8-oz package) cream cheese, softened
- ¼ cup butter, softened
- ¼ cup canned pumpkin (not pumpkin pie mix)
- 4 cups powdered sugar
- ¼ teaspoon ground cinnamon

1 Heat oven to 350°F. Line large cookie sheets with cooking parchment paper.

2 In large bowl, beat brown sugar, ½ cup butter, molasses, vanilla and eggs with electric mixer on medium speed until well blended. Add remaining Cookie ingredients except crystalized ginger and granulated sugar; beat until dough forms. Stir in 2 tablespoons of the crystallized ginger until well mixed.

3 Shape rounded tablespoonfuls dough into 1¼-inch balls. Roll each ball in granulated sugar. On cookie sheets, place balls 2 inches apart. Press thumb into center of each cookie to make indentation, but do not press all the way through the bottom of dough.

4 Bake 8 to 10 minutes or until edges are set. With back of round measuring teaspoon or end of a wooden spoon, remake indentation in center of each cookie. Cool 2 minutes; remove from cookie sheets to cooling racks. Cool completely, about 15 minutes.

5 In medium bowl, beat cream cheese, ¼ cup butter and pumpkin with electric mixer on high speed until well blended. On medium speed, gradually add powdered sugar and ¼ teaspoon cinnamon. Beat filling until smooth and creamy. Spoon heaping 2 teaspoonfuls of the pumpkin mixture into indentation in each cookie. Sprinkle with remaining 2 tablespoons crystallized ginger.

ingredient info:

Dark molasses is darker in color and has a more robust flavor than light molasses. Either can be used in this recipe, but we prefer the less sweet darker molasses for both color and flavor.

kitchen secret:

For a festive, sparkly cookie, roll balls in coarse white sparkling sugar and omit the 3 tablespoons granulated sugar in this recipe. Sparkling sugar can be found in most grocery stores or craft stores with baking supplies.

how to store:

Store these filled cookies in a tightly covered container in the refrigerator.

1 Cookie: Calories 130; Total Fat 4g (Saturated Fat 2.5g, Trans Fat 0g); Cholesterol 20mg; Sodium 60mg; Total Carbohydrate 23g (Dietary Fiber 0g); Protein 1g
Exchanges: 1½ Other Carbohydrate, 1 Fat
Carbohydrate Choices: 1½

177

MAKE IT SPECIAL

Pop Art Cookie Pops

PREP TIME: 25 Minutes • **START TO FINISH: 1 Hour 5 Minutes** • **About 1 dozen cookie pops**

COOKIES

1   pouch (17.5 oz) Betty
     Crocker sugar cookie
     mix
⅓   cup butter, softened
2   tablespoons all-
     purpose flour
1   egg

FROSTING AND DECORATIONS

12   wooden sticks with
     rounded ends
1   container creamy ready-
     to-spread frosting (any
     white variety)
     Gel food colors (in
     desired colors)
     Assorted candy
     decorations, if desired

ingredient info:

You can tint the frosting with
either liquid, gel or paste food
colors. You may like to try the
newer neon liquid food colors.
Gel and paste food colors will
give you a very vibrant color.

how to store:

Store these cookies in a tightly
covered container.

1 Heat oven to 375°F. In medium bowl, stir cookie mix, butter, flour
and egg until dough forms.

2 Roll dough on floured surface until about ¼ inch thick. Cut with
3-inch round cookie cutter. On ungreased cookie sheet, place cutouts
2 inches apart. Carefully insert a wooden stick into side of each cookie.

3 Bake 9 to 11 minutes or until edges are light golden brown.
Cool 1 minute; remove from cookie sheet to cooling rack. Cool
completely, about 30 minutes.

4 Divide frosting among 4 small bowls. Tint frosting in 3 of the bowls
with different color of food color. Reserve some of the tinted frostings
for piping on designs. Frost cookies with remaining white and tinted
frostings. For piping, place each tinted frosting in small resealable
food-storage plastic bag; snip off tiny corner of bag. Pipe frostings on
cookies in desired designs. Decorate with candy decorations.

1 Cookie Pop: Calories 380; Total Fat 14g
(Saturated Fat 5g, Trans Fat 2g);
Cholesterol 30mg; Sodium 250mg;
Total Carbohydrate 62g (Dietary Fiber 0g,
Sugars 43g); Protein 2g
Exchanges: 1 Starch, 3 Other Carbohydrate,
2½ Fat
Carbohydrate Choices: 4

Raspberry Cream–Filled Buttons

PREP TIME: 1 Hour • **START TO FINISH: 2 Hours** • **About 4 dozen sandwich cookies**

BUTTONS

1	cup butter, softened
¾	cup powdered sugar
½	teaspoon vanilla
2	cups all-purpose flour
4	teaspoons coarse white sparkling sugar

RASPBERRY BUTTERCREAM

2	cups powdered sugar
3	tablespoons butter, softened
¼	cup red raspberry syrup
2	to 3 teaspoons milk

1 In large bowl, beat 1 cup butter, ¾ cup powdered sugar and the vanilla with electric mixer on medium speed or mix with spoon until well blended. Beat in flour on low speed just until mixed. Divide dough in half. Wrap in plastic wrap. Refrigerate 30 minutes.

2 Heat oven to 325°F. Roll dough on lightly floured surface until ⅛-inch thick. Cut with floured 1½-inch round cutter. On ungreased cookie sheets, place cutouts 1 inch apart. Press 1- or 1¼-inch round cutter lightly into each round. With toothpick or small round pastry tip, cut 4 holes in center of each round to resemble a button. Sprinkle with sparkling sugar.

3 Bake 10 to 13 minutes until light golden brown. Remove from cookie sheets to cooling racks. Cool completely, about 15 minutes.

4 In medium bowl, beat 2 cups powdered sugar, 3 tablespoons butter and the raspberry syrup on low speed until combined. Beat in milk, 1 teaspoon at a time, until frosting is spreadable. Spread about 1 teaspoon each on flat side of half the cookies. Place remaining cookies over buttercream flat sides down, pressing lightly to form sandwiches. Repeat with remaining cookies and buttercream.

ingredient info:

Raspberry syrup, found with the pancake syrup, makes a flavorful and colorful addition to the buttercream. Try other flavors, too, such as blueberry or strawberry.

why it works:

Place 2 clean wooden rulers on either side of dough to use as a guide for rolling the dough to ⅛-inch thickness.

how to store:

Store these buttons tightly covered at room temperature.

181

MAKE
IT
SPECIAL

1 Sandwich Cookie: Calories 90; Total Fat 4.5g (Saturated Fat 3g, Trans Fat 0g); Cholesterol 10mg; Sodium 35mg; Total Carbohydrate 12g (Dietary Fiber 0g); Protein 0g
Exchanges: 1 Other Carbohydrate, 1 Fat
Carbohydrate Choices: 1

Clever Uses for Cookie Cutters

Cookie cutters can be used for so much more than cutting cookie dough. Give yours some love with these clever ways to get them out of your cupboard more often!

FOOD IDEAS

APPETIZER ORGANIZER Use cookie cutters on a flat platter to organize small foods, such as olives, crackers, nuts or candies for serving.

BREAKFAST MOLD Use a metal cookie cutter as a mold to make shaped pancakes or eggs. Spray inside of cookie cutter with cooking spray, and place on griddle or in pan before pouring the batter or scrambled eggs (hold down cutter for a few seconds until batter is set on bottom).

COOKIE PLACE CARDS Cut out cookie dough using a large cookie cutter, and bake to use as place cards at your table. Decorate each cookie with the name of a guest. Place a cookie on the plate at each setting.

EDIBLE CENTERPIECE Cut out and bake cookies with cookie cutters. Arrange cookies around a candle on a serving platter to use as a wreath.

FUN-SHAPES FRUIT SALAD Cut slices of fruit with small cookie cutters before making salad.

PRETTY PIE DECORATIONS Cut out shapes from pastry scraps with small cookie cutters to decorate the edge or top of pie before baking.

SHAPED BAKED GOODS Cut shapes with cookie cutters from your baked one-layer cake, brownies or bars for a fun shape when served.

SHAPED ROASTED POTATOES Cut potatoes with small, simple-shaped cookie cutters before roasting in the oven.

SURPRISING SANDWICHES Cut peanut butter and jelly or grilled cheese sandwiches with large cookie cutters for an unexpected lunch treat.

DECORATING IDEAS

GIFT WRAPPING Attach a cookie cutter to the bow of a present with a piece of ribbon for an extra-special gift wrapping.

DECORATIVE JACK O' LANTERNS Pound metal cookie cutters into the side of the pumpkin; pull out cutters and pumpkin inside the cookie cutters.

HOLIDAY ORNAMENTS Trace a photo or heavy decorative paper with the cookie cutter; cut out shape. Thread a ribbon through the cookie cutter and make a loop for a hanger; glue the cut shape to the back of the cutter. Use to hang on holiday tree or as gifts.

WIND CHIMES Hang metal cookie cutters from a wire wreath frame (found at craft stores) with ribbons or raffia at varying heights to make a wind chime.

182

CLEVER
USES
FOR
COOKIE
CUTTERS

Betty Crocker Cookies

Valentine Cream Wafers

PREP TIME: 1 Hour 10 Minutes • **START TO FINISH:** 2 Hours 10 Minutes • **About 3½ dozen sandwich cookies**

WAFERS

- 2 cups all-purpose flour
- 1 cup butter, softened
- ⅓ cup heavy whipping cream
- Granulated sugar or colored sugar

CREAMY FILLING

- 1½ cups powdered sugar
- ½ cup butter, softened
- 1 teaspoon vanilla
- Red liquid food color

1 In medium bowl, mix flour, 1 cup butter and the whipping cream with spoon. Cover and refrigerate about 1 hour or until firm.

2 Heat oven to 375°F. Roll one-third of dough at a time ⅛ inch thick on lightly floured surface. (Keep remaining dough refrigerated until ready to roll.) Cut with 2¼-inch heart-shaped cookie cutter. Generously cover large piece of waxed paper with granulated sugar. Using pancake turner, transfer cutouts to waxed paper. Turn each cutout to coat both sides. On ungreased cookie sheets, place cutout cookies. Prick each cutout with fork about four times.

3 Bake 7 to 9 minutes or just until set but not brown. Cool 1 minute; remove from cookie sheets to cooling racks. Cool completely, about 15 minutes.

4 Meanwhile, in medium bowl, beat powdered sugar and ½ cup butter until smooth. Add vanilla. Beat until fluffy. Divide frosting among 6 small bowls. Add the following different amounts of red liquid food color to one of each of the bowls starting with a toothpick, 1 drop, 3 drops, 7 drops, 12 drops and 25 drops to make different shades of pink.

5 For each sandwich cookie, spread about 1 teaspoon frosting on flat side of 1 cooled cookie. Top with second cookie, flat side down; gently press cookies together.

kitchen secret:

To make rolled cookies, start with properly chilled dough. To bake the most tender cookies, avoid rerolling the dough more than twice.

how to store:

Store these cookies in a tightly covered container.

1 Sandwich Cookie: Calories 100; Total Fat 7g (Saturated Fat 4g, Trans Fat 0g); Cholesterol 20mg; Sodium 55mg; Total Carbohydrate 10g (Dietary Fiber 0g, Sugars 5g); Protein 0g
Exchanges: ½ Other Carbohydrate, 1½ Fat
Carbohydrate Choices: ½

Festive White Velvet Star Stacks

PREP TIME: 1 Hour 30 Minutes • **START TO FINISH: 4 Hours** • **About 18 star stacks**

COOKIES

1	cup butter, softened
1	cup granulated sugar
1	teaspoon vanilla
1	egg yolk
4	oz (half of 8-oz package) cream cheese, softened
2¼	cups all-purpose flour
¼	teaspoon salt

GLAZE AND DECORATIONS

5	cups powdered sugar
5	tablespoons milk
½	teaspoon almond extract or vanilla
	Blue and red gel food color
	About 18 small red or white gumdrops, cut horizontally in half

1 In large bowl, beat butter, granulated sugar, vanilla, egg yolk and cream cheese with electric mixer on medium speed until well mixed. Beat in flour and salt on low speed. Divide dough in half; wrap in plastic wrap. Refrigerate 1 hour.

2 Heat oven to 350°F. Line large cookie sheets with cooking parchment paper. Roll dough ¼ inch thick on lightly floured surface. Cut with various-size star cookie cutters. On cookie sheets, place cutouts 1 inch apart.

3 Bake 8 to 10 minutes or until edges are set. Remove from cookie sheets to cooling racks. Cool completely, about 30 minutes.

4 In medium bowl, mix powdered sugar, 4 tablespoons of the milk and the almond extract until smooth. Stir in additional milk, 1 teaspoon at a time, until spreading consistency. Divide glaze among 3 bowls. Tint one bowl with blue food coloring and one bowl with red food coloring. Place about ¼ cup of each colored glaze into each of 3 small resealable food-storage plastic bags. Cut a very small corner of each bag.

5 Using photo as a guide and working with a few cookies at a time, spread glaze over cookies. With bags of alternating color glaze, pipe glaze into firework, stars and stripes designs. Run toothpick through design, if desired. Let stand 30 minutes or until glaze hardens. (Cover bowls with remaining glaze until ready to stack cookies.)

6 To assemble each cookie stack, dip top and bottom of gumdrop piece in glaze. Place in center of large cookie. Top with a medium-sized cookie. Repeat with another gumdrop piece and smaller cookie.

why it works:

Baking on parchment promotes even browning and easy removal of baked cookies from cookie sheet. If you don't have cooking parchment paper, remove cookies immediately to prevent excess browning.

why it works:

The thin glaze is the secret behind making these cookies beautiful. Dropping a dot of glaze onto the cookie and pulling a toothpick through the dot can create stars, shooting stars or an abstract design.

ingredient info:

Love the look? Try the same recipe and technique for other holidays and special occasions by varying the shape of the cookies, the colors of the glazes and the designs.

how to store:

Store these stacks in a single layer or between sheets of waxed paper in a tightly covered container at room temperature.

MAKE IT SPECIAL

1 Star Stack: Calories 360; Total Fat 13g (Saturated Fat 8g, Trans Fat 0g); Cholesterol 45mg; Sodium 140mg; Total Carbohydrate 60g (Dietary Fiber 0g, Sugars 46g); Protein 2g
Exchanges: 1 Starch, 3 Other Carbohydrate, 2½ Fat
Carbohydrate Choices: 4

Ginger Frankenstein Cookies

PREP TIME: **1 Hour** • START TO FINISH: **2 Hours 20 Minutes** • **3 dozen cookies**

1½ cups sugar
1 cup butter, softened
3 tablespoons mild-flavor (light) molasses
2 tablespoons milk
1 egg
3¼ cups all-purpose flour
2 teaspoons baking soda
2 teaspoons ground cinnamon
1½ teaspoons ground ginger
½ teaspoon ground cloves
½ teaspoon ground cardamom
1 container vanilla creamy ready-to-spread frosting
5 drops green food color
⅓ cup candy-coated milk chocolate candies (72 candies)
¾ cup candy corn (72 candies)
1 cup semisweet chocolate chips

ingredient info:

Molasses is available in both light and dark varieties. We prefer the light variety for these cookies.

how to store:

Store these cookies in a single layer in a covered container at room temperature.

1 Cookie: Calories 230; Total Fat 9g (Saturated Fat 5g, Trans Fat 0.5g); Cholesterol 20mg; Sodium 150mg; Total Carbohydrate 36g (Dietary Fiber 0g); Protein 1g
Exchanges: 2½ Other Carbohydrate, 2 Fat
Carbohydrate Choices: 2½

1 In large bowl, beat sugar, butter and molasses with electric mixer on medium speed until well blended. Beat in milk and egg. Stir in flour, baking soda, cinnamon, ginger, cloves and cardamom until dough forms. Divide dough in half; flatten each ball to make 4-inch disk. Wrap each in plastic wrap and refrigerate about 1 hour or until firm.

2 Heat oven to 350°F. Roll each half on floured surface into 12x9-inch rectangle. Cut each 12x9-inch rectangle into 3 rows by 6 rows to make 18 smaller rectangles (36 total). On ungreased large cookie sheets, place cookies 1 inch apart.

3 Bake 6 to 8 minutes or until set. Immediately remove from cookie sheet to cooling rack. Cool completely, about 15 minutes.

4 In small bowl, stir frosting and food color until well blended. Frost each cookie with slightly less than 1 tablespoon frosting. Add 2 candy-coated candies for eyes and 2 candy corn pieces for neck "bolts."

5 In small microwavable bowl, microwave chocolate chips uncovered on High 60 seconds, stirring once, until chips are softened and can be stirred smooth. Spoon melted chocolate into small resealable food-storage plastic bag; seal bag. Cut off tiny corner of bag; squeeze bag to drizzle melted chips on cookies for hair and mouth.

Chocolate Mocha Mummy Cookies

PREP TIME: 1 Hour 30 Minutes • **START TO FINISH: 1 Hour 40 Minutes** • **20 cookies**

1 cup butter, softened
1 cup powdered sugar
1 teaspoon vanilla
1¾ cups all-purpose flour
⅓ cup unsweetened baking cocoa

1 teaspoon instant coffee granules or crystals
1¼ cups white vanilla baking chips (from 11-oz bag)
¼ cup miniature candy-coated semisweet chocolate baking bits (40 bits)

1 Heat oven to 350°F. In large bowl, beat butter, powdered sugar and vanilla with electric mixer on medium speed until creamy. On low speed, beat in flour, cocoa and coffee granules until well mixed. Divide dough in half; press each to form disk. Wrap each disk in plastic wrap; freeze 10 minutes.

2 Roll each half on lightly floured surface until ⅛ inch thick. Cut with floured 5-inch gingerbread boy cookie cutter. On ungreased cookie sheets, place cutouts 1 inch apart.

3 Bake 9 to 10 minutes or until set. Cool 1 minute; remove from cookie sheets to cooling racks. Cool completely, 15 to 20 minutes.

4 In small microwavable bowl, microwave baking chips uncovered on High 60 seconds, stirring once, until chips are softened and can be stirred smooth. Spoon melted chips into small resealable food-storage plastic bag; seal bag. Cut off tiny corner of bag. Squeeze bag to drizzle melted chips over cookies for mummy wrapping. Add 2 baking bits to each cookie for eyes.

ingredient info:
You can use prepared frosting instead of white vanilla baking chips in a small resealable food-storage plastic bag. There's no need to melt frosting, just pipe it on cookies.

ingredient info:
Instead of mini baking bits, you can use raisins for the mummy eyes.

how to store:
Store these cookies in a tightly covered container.

191

MAKE
IT
SPECIAL

1 Cookie: Calories 220; Total Fat 13g (Saturated Fat 8g, Trans Fat 0g); Cholesterol 25mg; Sodium 75mg; Total Carbohydrate 23g (Dietary Fiber 1g, Sugars 14g); Protein 2g
Exchanges: ½ Starch, 1 Other Carbohydrate, 2½ Fat
Carbohydrate Choices: 1½

Lavender-Lemon Cookies

PREP TIME: 45 Minutes • **START TO FINISH: 2 Hours 30 Minutes** • **About 4 dozen cookies**

COOKIES

1½	cups powdered sugar
1	cup butter, softened
2	tablespoons chopped fresh or 1 tablespoon dried lavender flowers, crushed
1	teaspoon grated lemon zest
1	egg
2½	cups all-purpose flour

WHITE CHOCOLATE FROSTING

3	oz white chocolate baking bars, chopped (from 6-oz package)
3	tablespoons heavy whipping cream
2	cups powdered sugar
½	cup butter, softened
	Additional dried lavender flowers, if desired

1 In large bowl, beat 1½ cups powdered sugar and 1 cup butter on low speed of electric mixer until fluffy. Beat in lavender, lemon zest and egg. Stir in flour. Divide dough in half. Wrap in plastic wrap; cover and refrigerate 1 hour.

2 Heat oven to 375°F. Roll each half on lightly floured surface until 3/16 inch thick. Cut with floured 2½-inch flower cookie cutter. On ungreased cookie sheets, place cutouts 1 inch apart.

3 Bake 8 to 10 minutes or until edges begin to brown. Remove from cookie sheets to cooling racks. Cool completely, about 10 minutes.

4 In small microwavable bowl, microwave white chocolate and whipping cream uncovered on High 30 to 45 seconds, stirring once, or until chocolate is softened and can be stirred smooth.

5 In medium bowl, beat powdered sugar and ½ cup butter with electric mixer on medium speed until blended. Add white chocolate mixture; blend well.

6 Frost cookies; sprinkle with additional lavender.

ingredient info:

Look for fresh lavender at the farmers' market or in the produce section of the grocery store. Dried lavender may be found at health food stores. If lavender is not available, 1 tablespoon chopped fresh thyme can be substituted for an equally unique cookie with a different flavor.

why it works:

When 1/8 inch is too thin and 1/4 inch is too thick for rolling cookies, try 3/16 inch! We love rolling cookies between 2 sticks of wood or dowels cut exactly at the right height.

how to store:

Store these cookies in a single layer in a tightly covered container at room temperature.

1 Cookie: Calories 110; Total Fat 6g (Saturated Fat 4g, Trans Fat 0g); Cholesterol 20mg; Sodium 45mg; Total Carbohydrate 14g (Dietary Fiber 0g, Sugars 8g); Protein 1g
Exchanges: ½ Starch, ½ Other Carbohydrate, 1 Fat
Carbohydrate Choices: 1

MAKE IT SPECIAL

Easy Cinnamon Roll Cookies

PREP TIME: 25 Minutes • **START TO FINISH: 1 Hour 10 Minutes** • **About 1½ dozen cookies**

1   pouch (17.5 oz) Betty Crocker sugar cookie mix
½   cup butter, softened
¼   cup all-purpose flour
1   egg
1   tablespoon butter, melted

¼   cup granulated sugar
1   tablespoon ground cinnamon
¾   cup powdered sugar
1   tablespoon milk

how to store:
Store these cookies covered at room temperature.

1 Cookie: Calories 190; Total Fat 8g (Saturated Fat 4g, Trans Fat 0g); Cholesterol 0mg; Sodium 107mg; Total Carbohydrate 28g (Dietary Fiber 0g, Sugars 0g); Protein 1g
Exchanges: 2 Other Carbohydrate, ½ Fat
Carbohydrate Choices: 2

1   In medium bowl, stir cookie mix, butter, flour and egg until dough forms. Roll dough on lightly floured surface until ¼ inch thickness. Brush with melted butter.

2   In small bowl, mix granulated sugar and cinnamon; sprinkle evenly over dough. Roll up dough jelly-roll fashion, starting at long side. Wrap roll in plastic wrap, and refrigerate 2 hours or until firm.

3   Heat oven to 375°F. Cut dough into ¾-inch slices. On ungreased cookie sheets, place slices 2 inches apart.

4   Bake 11 to 12 minutes or until edges are light golden brown. Cool 2 minutes; remove from cookie sheets to cooling racks. Cool completely, about 15 minutes.

5   In small bowl, mix powdered sugar and milk until smooth. Drizzle over cooled cookies.

MAKE IT SPECIAL

Mocha Biscotti

PREP TIME: 30 Minutes • **START TO FINISH: 2 Hours 30 Minutes** • **About 3½ dozen cookies**

BISCOTTI

- 2 tablespoons instant espresso or coffee crystals
- 2 teaspoons hot water
- 1 cup sugar
- ½ cup butter, softened
- 1 teaspoon vanilla
- 2 eggs
- 3½ cups all-purpose flour
- 1½ oz semisweet baking chocolate, grated (about ½ cup)
- ¼ cup chopped slivered almonds, toasted
- 1 teaspoon baking powder
- ½ teaspoon salt

CHOCOLATE DRIZZLE

- 3 oz semisweet baking chocolate
- ½ teaspoon shortening

1 Heat oven to 350°F. Dissolve coffee crystals in hot water. In large bowl, beat sugar, butter, vanilla, eggs and coffee with electric mixer on medium speed or mix with spoon. Stir in all remaining Biscotti ingredients.

2 On ungreased cookie sheets, shape half of dough at a time into rectangle, 10x3 inches. Bake about 30 minutes or until center is firm to the touch. Cool on cookie sheet 15 minutes.

3 Cut crosswise into ½-inch slices. Place slices, cut sides down, on cookie sheets. Bake about 15 minutes, turning once, until crisp and edges are light brown. Immediately remove from cookie sheets to cooling racks. Cool completely.

4 If desired, in 1-quart saucepan, heat Chocolate Drizzle ingredients over low heat, stirring occasionally, until melted and smooth. Drizzle chocolate over one side of each biscotti. Let stand until chocolate is set.

kitchen secret:

To toast nuts, heat oven to 350°F. Spread nuts in ungreased shallow pan. Bake uncovered 6 to 10 minutes, stirring occasionally, until light brown.

how to store:

Cover and store these biscotti at room temperature.

1 Cookie: Calories 90; Total Fat 3g (Saturated Fat 2g, Trans Fat 0g); Cholesterol 15mg; Sodium 60mg; Total Carbohydrate 14g (Dietary Fiber 0g, Sugars 5g); Protein 1g
Exchanges: ½ Starch, ½ Other Carbohydrate, ½ Fat
Carbohydrate Choices: 1

195

MAKE
IT
SPECIAL

Frosted Turkey Cookies

PREP TIME: 1 Hour 15 Minutes • START TO FINISH: **1 Hour 15 Minutes** • **About 2 dozen cookies**

1   pouch (17.5 oz) Betty Crocker sugar cookie mix
½   cup butter, softened
1   egg
1   container chocolate whipped ready-to-spread frosting
    Candy corn

1   tube (4.25 oz) yellow decorating icing
    Miniature candy-coated semisweet chocolate baking bits
1   tube (0.68 oz) black decorating gel
    Fall-colored sprinkles, if desired

how to store:

Store these "turkeys" at room temperature in a covered container.

1 Frosted Cookie (Undecorated):
Calories 180; Total Fat 9g (Saturated Fat 4g, Trans Fat 2g); Cholesterol 20mg; Sodium 120mg; Total Carbohydrate 24g (Dietary Fiber 0g, Sugars 16g); Protein 1g
Exchanges: ½ Starch, 1 Other Carbohydrate, 2 Fat
Carbohydrate Choices: 1½

1 Heat oven to 375°F. In medium bowl, stir cookie mix, butter and egg until soft dough forms.

2 On ungreased cookie sheets, drop dough by rounded tablespoonfuls 2 inches apart.

3 Bake 11 to 14 minutes or until edges are light golden brown. Cool 1 minute; remove from cookie sheets to cooling racks. Cool completely, about 15 minutes.

4 Frost and decorate 1 cookie at a time. After spreading frosting on cookie, add candy corn for feathers. Pipe yellow icing for beak and feet. Add baking bits for eyes; pipe black gel for center of each eye. Sprinkle tops of cookies with sprinkles.

Unicorn Cookies

PREP TIME: 40 Minutes • **START TO FINISH: 1 Hour 55 Minutes** • **About 2½ dozen cookies**

COOKIES

1	cup butter, softened
1	cup powdered sugar
½	cup granulated sugar
1	teaspoon vanilla
½	teaspoon almond extract
1	egg
2	cups all-purpose flour
½	teaspoon baking soda
½	teaspoon cream of tartar
¼	teaspoon salt

Pink, blue, purple and yellow gel food color (about ¼ teaspoon each)

FROSTING

1½	cups powdered sugar
½	cup butter, softened
2	to 4 teaspoons milk
½	teaspoon vanilla
	Gold candy sprinkles
	Pastel-colored star decors and nonpareils

1 Heat oven to 375°F. Line two 8-inch round cake pans with foil, leaving about 2 inches to overhang sides. Spray foil with cooking spray.

2 In large bowl, beat 1 cup butter, 1 cup powdered sugar and the granulated sugar with electric mixer on medium speed until well blended. Add 1 teaspoon vanilla, almond extract and egg; mix well. Add flour, baking soda, cream of tartar and salt; beat until well blended.

3 Divide dough into 4 equal portions. Color each portion with enough gel food color to make 4 different deep-colored doughs. Drop spoonfuls of each colored dough randomly and equally into each pan. Press dough evenly in pans with floured fingers.

4 Bake 20 to 22 minutes or until edges are golden brown. Cool 15 minutes. Lift foil to remove cookie rounds from pans. Place cookie rounds with foil on cooling racks, peeling foil away from edge of rounds. Cool completely, about 45 minutes.

5 Place cookie rounds on cutting board. Using sharp knife, cut each round into 16 wedges. Carefully loosen wedges from foil.

6 In large bowl, beat 1½ cups powdered sugar, ½ cup butter and 2 teaspoons milk until well mixed. Stir in additional milk, 1 teaspoon at a time, until desired piping consistency.

7 Using decorator bag fitted with small star decorating tip or quart-size resealable food-storage plastic bag, fill bag with frosting. (Cut tiny corner from bag if using a resealable bag.) Pipe frosting on cookies in elongated spirals to look like unicorn horns. Sprinkle gold sprinkles on the frosting. Sprinkle the edge with star decors and nonpareils.

ingredient info:

Pastel-colored nonpareils, candy sprinkles and colored star decors and even premixed unicorn sprinkle mixes can be found at craft stores and grocery stores. Check out online options as well. Or, make your own mix by combining a variety of pastel-colored candy sprinkles.

how to store:

Store these cookies in a tightly covered container at room temperature.

1 Cookie: Calories 170; Total Fat 9g (Saturated Fat 6g, Trans Fat 0g); Cholesterol 30mg; Sodium 115mg; Total Carbohydrate 20g (Dietary Fiber 0g); Protein 1g
Exchanges: 1½ Other Carbohydrate, 2 Fat
Carbohydrate Choices: 1

199

MAKE
IT
SPECIAL

Cookie Pizza

PREP TIME: **10 Minutes** • START TO FINISH: **40 Minutes** • **8 wedges**

1 pouch Betty Crocker
   chocolate chip cookie mix
½ cup butter, softened

1 egg
1 pint vanilla ice cream
   Hot fudge topping,
   if desired

1 Heat oven to 350°F. Spray 10-inch ovenproof skillet with cooking spray.

2 In medium bowl, stir cookie mix, butter and egg until soft dough forms. Spread dough evenly in skillet, pressing to flatten and cover bottom.

3 Bake about 25 minutes or until edges are light golden brown. Do not overbake; cookie will continue to cook once out of oven.
Cool skillet on cooling rack 5 minutes. Cut into 8 wedges; serve warm with scoops of ice cream and drizzled with hot fudge topping.

why it works:
The cookie can also easily be baked in a nonstick ovenproof skillet. No cooking spray is needed.

how to store:
If you have leftover "pizza," store in a tightly covered container at room temperature.

1 Wedge: Calories 450; Total Fat 23g (Saturated Fat 13g, Trans Fat 0g); Cholesterol 70mg; Sodium 370mg; Total Carbohydrate 57g (Dietary Fiber 0g, Sugars 39g); Protein 4g
Exchanges: 1 Starch, 3 Other Carbohydrate, 4½ Fat
Carbohydrate Choices: 4

Strawberry-Rhubarb Pavlova Cookies

PREP TIME: **25 Minutes** • START TO FINISH: **3 Hours** • **About 2 dozen cookies**

COOKIES

3	egg whites, room temperature (see tip at right)
¼	teaspoon cream of tartar
¼	teaspoon almond extract
½	cup granulated sugar

TOPPING

1	cup chopped fresh or frozen (thawed) rhubarb
¼	cup granulated sugar
¼	cup water
1½	teaspoons cornstarch
⅓	cup chopped strawberries

GARNISH

6	small strawberries, quartered
	Powdered sugar, if desired

1 Heat oven to 225°F. Line 2 cookie sheets with cooking parchment paper.

2 In medium bowl, beat egg whites, cream of tartar and almond extract on high speed until foamy. Beat in ½ cup sugar, 1 tablespoon at a time; continue beating 5 to 6 minutes, or until stiff, glossy peaks form.

3 On cookie sheets, drop meringue by heaping tablespoonfuls. Shape into 2½-inch rounds, building up sides and making a small indentation in center of each with back of spoon, pressing only to ½-inch from bottom of meringues.

4 Bake 1 hour, rotating cookie sheets halfway. Turn off oven; leave cookies in oven with door closed for 1 hour. Place cookie sheets on cooling racks. Cool completely, about 15 minutes.

5 Meanwhile, in 1-quart saucepan, combine Topping ingredients except strawberries. Heat mixture to boiling over medium heat, stirring occasionally. Reduce heat to low and simmer uncovered 4 to 6 minutes, stirring occasionally, until rhubarb is tender. Stir in chopped strawberries; heat just to boiling. Remove from heat; cool 15 minutes. Cover and refrigerate 30 minutes or until chilled.

6 To serve, remove meringues from parchment paper. Top each with about 1½ teaspoons strawberry-rhubarb filling. Place one strawberry quarter in filling of each cookie and sprinkle with powdered sugar.

why it works:

Room temperature egg whites whip better than cold egg whites, but for food safety reasons, do not leave eggs out of the refrigerator for more than 30 minutes. To quickly bring the whites to room temperature, soak whole eggs in a bowl of hot water for about 10 minutes before cracking and separating.

why it works:

Spreading meringues to an equal thickness and size will ensure even baking and doneness. Keeping ½-inch thickness of meringue below the indentations helps ensure the integrity of the cookies when filled with meringue, so that they can be picked up without breaking.

how to store:

Meringues should be assembled and served the same day they are prepared.

1 Cookie: Calories 30; Total Fat 0g (Saturated Fat 0g, Trans Fat 0g); Cholesterol 0mg; Sodium 5mg; Total Carbohydrate 7g (Dietary Fiber 0g); Protein 0g
Exchanges: ½ Other Carbohydrate
Carbohydrate Choices: ½

Strawberry Cream French Macarons

PREP TIME: 30 Minutes • START TO FINISH: 2 Hours 10 Minutes • 16 sandwich cookies

COOKIES

1	cup almond flour
1½	cups powdered sugar
3	eggs whites, at room temperature (see tip at right)
¼	teaspoon salt
⅛	teaspoon cream of tartar
3	tablespoons granulated sugar
½	teaspoon vanilla
⅛	to ¼ teaspoon pink gel food color

FILLING

½	cup chopped strawberries
1¼	cups powdered sugar
¼	cup butter, softened

1 Trace thirty-two 2-inch circles, 1½ inches apart, onto 2 sheets of cooking parchment paper for cookie templates. Place pencil side down on 2 large cookie sheets.

2 In food processor bowl with metal blade, place almond flour and powdered sugar. Cover; process 15 to 30 seconds or until well mixed and very finely ground.

3 In large bowl of stand mixer, beat egg whites, salt and cream of tartar with whisk attachment on high speed just until foamy. Gradually add granulated sugar, 1 tablespoon at a time, beating on high speed 1 to 2 minutes or just until stiff peaks form. Beat in vanilla and food color on low speed just until evenly colored. Using a rubber spatula, fold half of the almond mixture into egg white mixture. Fold in remaining almond mixture until completely incorporated.

4 Spoon batter into large decorating bag fitted with ½-inch round tip. Pipe dollops of batter onto template within ¼ inch of template line. If tops have a peak, wet fingertips lightly on damp paper towel and press down to flatten. Tap bottom of cookie sheets on counter a few times to flatten cookies. Let stand uncovered at room temperature 30 minutes to allow a light crust to form on tops.

5 Heat oven to 300°F.

6 Bake 17 to 18 minutes or until tops look set. Cool 10 minutes; remove to cooling racks. Cool completely, about 15 minutes.

7 Meanwhile, in food processor with a metal blade, place strawberries. Cover; process 1 minute, scraping bowl once or twice, or until pureed. Strain mixture through wire strainer; discard solids. In medium bowl of electric mixer on medium speed, beat powdered sugar, butter and 1 tablespoon plus 1 teaspoon pureed strawberries.

8 For each sandwich cookie, spread about 2 teaspoons filling on flat of 1 macaron. Top with second macaron, flat side down; gently press together.

why it works:

For the prettiest macarons, prepare them when the humidity is below 50%, so that they will stay light and fluffy when baked.

how to store:

Store these macarons loosely covered in the refrigerator for up to 3 days. Macarons will absorb moisture from the filling during storage. Serve cold or remove from refrigerator 15 minutes before serving.

1 Sandwich Cookie: Calories 160; Total Fat 6g (Saturated Fat 2g, Trans Fat 0g); Cholesterol 10mg; Sodium 70mg; Total Carbohydrate 24g (Dietary Fiber 0g, Sugars 23g); Protein 2g **Exchanges:** ½ Starch, 1 Other Carbohydrate, 1 Fat **Carbohydrate Choices:** 11½

Hot Cocoa Meringues

PREP TIME: 25 Minutes • **START TO FINISH:** 5 Hours 25 Minutes • **About 3 dozen cookies**

4 egg whites, room temperature
½ teaspoon vanilla
¼ teaspoon cream of tartar
1 cup sugar

2 tablespoons unsweetened dark baking cocoa
½ cup dark chocolate chips
3 tablespoons vanilla marshmallow bits

1 Heat oven to 275°F. Place oven racks in upper and lower third of oven. Line 2 large cookie sheets with cooking parchment paper.

2 In large bowl, beat egg whites, vanilla and cream of tartar with electric mixer on high speed until foamy. Beat in sugar, 1 tablespoon at a time; continue beating until stiff, glossy peaks form and sugar is almost dissolved, 5 to 6 minutes, scraping side of bowl occasionally. Do not underbeat.

3 In small bowl, place 2 cups of the meringue. Sprinkle cocoa through fine mesh strainer over top; fold cocoa into mixture. Place large piping bag fitted with large star piping tip on its side. Using large icing spatula, spoon half of white meringue so it covers half of the length of inside of piping bag. Carefully spoon half of the cocoa meringue on top of the white in bag. On cookie sheets, pipe meringue into 2-inch circles. Repeat filling piping bag and piping with remaining meringues.

4 Place both cookie sheets in oven. Bake 30 minutes. Turn off oven; leave meringues in oven with door closed 1 hour. Remove cookie sheets to cooling racks; cool about 2 hours. Remove from parchment paper; place meringues on cooling racks.

5 Place waxed paper or cooking parchment paper under cooling racks. In small microwavable bowl, microwave chocolate chips uncovered on High 30 to 60 seconds, stirring halfway through, until chips can be stirred smooth. Spoon into resealable food-storage plastic bag; partially seal bag. Cut small tip from corner of bag; drizzle chocolate over tops of cookies. Sprinkle marshmallow bits on tops of cookies. Let stand 1 hour 30 minutes or until chocolate is set.

ingredient info:

We tested with unsweetened dark cocoa, but unsweetened natural baking cocoa will also work.

why it works:

Egg whites whip best at room temperature; for food safety reasons, limit to 30 minutes at room temperature.

why it works:

Make sure egg whites are yolk-free, or your meringue may deflate. To prevent mixing yolk into the whites, crack eggs, one at a time, and place each white into a custard cup to ensure it is free of yolk before transferring it to the mixing bowl. A clean glass, metal or copper bowl is best for whipping meringue.

how to store:

Store these meringues in a tightly covered container at room temperature.

207

MAKE
IT
SPECIAL

1 Cookie: Calories 40; Total Fat 1g (Saturated Fat 0g, Trans Fat 0g); Cholesterol 0mg; Sodium 5mg; Total Carbohydrate 7g (Dietary Fiber 0g, Sugars 7g); Protein 0g
Exchanges: ½ Other Carbohydrate
Carbohydrate Choices: ½

Chocolate Marshmallow Hearts

PREP TIME: 30 Minutes • START TO FINISH: **1 Hour 45 Minutes** • **About 1½ dozen cookies**

CRUST

1	cup all-purpose flour
1	cup chocolate O-shaped toasted whole-grain cereal, crushed
⅔	cup packed brown sugar
½	cup butter, softened
1	teaspoon vanilla
½	teaspoon baking powder
3	cups miniature marshmallows

TOPPING

⅔	cup light corn syrup
¼	cup butter
1	teaspoon vanilla
1	bag (11.5 oz) milk chocolate chips
4	cups chocolate O-shaped toasted whole-grain cereal
	Candy sprinkles, if desired

why it works:

Use your favorite shape cookie cutter for these cookies. Depending on the size of the cookie cutter, you may get more or less cookies. For a quicker treat, cut into bars.

how to store:

Store these cookies loosely covered.

1 Cookie: Calories 230; Total Fat 10g (Saturated Fat 6g, Trans Fat 0g); Cholesterol 15mg; Sodium 105mg; Total Carbohydrate 33g (Dietary Fiber 1g, Sugars 21g); Protein 2g **Exchanges:** ½ Starch, 1½ Other Carbohydrate, 2 Fat **Carbohydrate Choices:** 2

1   Heat oven to 350°F. Line bottom and sides of 13x9-inch pan with foil. In large bowl, mix all Crust ingredients except marshmallows with electric mixer on low speed until crumbly. Press firmly into bottom of pan.

2   Bake 12 to 15 minutes or until light golden brown. Immediately sprinkle with marshmallows. Return to oven; bake an additional 1 to 2 minutes or until marshmallows just begin to puff. Cool in pan on cooling rack while preparing topping.

3   In large saucepan, place all Topping ingredients except cereal and sprinkles. Heat over medium-low heat just until chips are melted and mixture is smooth, stirring constantly. Remove from heat; stir in 4 cups cereal. Immediately spoon warm topping over marshmallows; spread to cover. Sprinkle with candy sprinkles. Cool completely, at least 1 hour.

4   Using foil to lift, remove mixture from pan; remove foil. With deep 2½-inch heart-shaped cookie cutter, cut out 18 hearts.

Baklava Tassies

PREP TIME: 30 Minutes • **START TO FINISH: 1 Hour** • **2 dozen cookies**

FILLING

- ⅓ cup roasted pistachio nuts
- ⅓ cup sliced almonds
- ⅓ cup chopped walnuts
- 2 tablespoons honey
- 1 tablespoon butter
- 1 tablespoon brown sugar
- ¼ teaspoon grated lemon zest
- 1 teaspoon fresh lemon juice
- ⅛ teaspoon ground cinnamon

PHYLLO CUPS

- 2 teaspoons granulated sugar
- ⅛ teaspoon ground cinnamon
- 4 sheets frozen phyllo (filo) pastry (14x9-inch), thawed
- 4 teaspoons butter, melted

CREAMY TOPPING

- 2 oz cream cheese, softened
- 1 teaspoon honey
  Dash of ground cinnamon
  Additional ground cinnamon, if desired

1 Heat oven to 350°F. Spray 24 mini muffin cups with cooking spray.

2 In food processor bowl with metal blade, combine all Filling ingredients. Cover; process with on-and-off pulses until finely chopped; set aside.

3 In small bowl, stir together granulated sugar and ⅛ teaspoon cinnamon; set aside. Trim phyllo sheets to measure 12x8 inches; discard scraps. Place 1 phyllo sheet on large cutting board, and lightly brush with butter. Sprinkle with ½ teaspoon of the cinnamon-sugar blend. Top with another phyllo sheet, and lightly brush with butter. Again sprinkle with ½ teaspoon of the cinnamon-sugar blend. Continue building layers by repeating with remaining 2 phyllo sheets, the butter and remaining cinnamon-sugar mixture.

4 Cut phyllo stack into 6 rows by 4 rows for 24 two-inch squares. For each phyllo cup, gently lift top 2 phyllo sheets off stack; turn sheets an eighth turn and restack layers to create 8 corners. Press stack lightly into cup. Repeat with remaining phyllo stacks. Spoon about 1½ teaspoons filling into each cup.

5 Bake 11 to 13 minutes or until filling and phyllo begin to brown. Gently remove cookies from muffin cups. Cool on cooling rack, about 15 minutes.

6 In small bowl, stir together cream cheese, 1 teaspoon honey and dash of cinnamon. Place in small resealable food-storage plastic bag. Cut off tiny corner of bag. Squeeze bag to dollop about 1½ teaspoons filling on each cookie. Sprinkle with additional cinnamon.

ingredient info:

Many nations, in the Middle East, Mediterranean, Balkans and Caucasia, consider baklava their national dessert. Each region has its own variation of this flaky pastry that contains nuts, sweeteners, citrus and sometimes other fruit. These little cookies are a twist on the original.

why it works:

Look for phyllo dough in the freezer section. For best results, thaw overnight in the refrigerator. When working with the layers, place on a clean, dry surface. To keep the sheets from drying out, cover with plastic wrap and then a damp towel while working with them. Unused phyllo sheets can be rolled up, wrapped in plastic wrap and stored in the refrigerator for up to 2 weeks.

how to store:

Store these cookies in a single layer in a loosely-covered container in the refrigerator. Let stand at room temperature 15 minutes before serving.

211

MAKE
IT
SPECIAL

1 Cookie: Calories 70; Total Fat 4.5g (Saturated Fat 1.5g, Trans Fat 0g); Cholesterol 5mg; Sodium 35mg; Total Carbohydrate 6g (Dietary Fiber 0g); Protein 1g
Exchanges: ½ Starch, 1 Fat
Carbohydrate Choices: ½

Brownies on a Stick

PREP TIME: **30 Minutes** • START TO FINISH: **3 Hours 45 Minutes** • **15 brownie pops**

1   box (1 lb 6.25 oz) Betty Crocker Supreme brownie mix
½   cup vegetable oil
¼   cup water
2   eggs

15   craft sticks (flat wooden sticks with round ends)
⅔   cup semisweet chocolate chips
1½   teaspoons shortening
    Assorted decorating candy sprinkles, if desired

1   Heat oven to 350°F. Line 9-inch square pan with foil so foil extends about 2 inches over sides of pan. Spray foil with cooking spray. Make brownies as directed on box for 9-inch pan using oil, water and eggs. Cool completely in pan on cooling rack, about 1½ hours.

2   Place in freezer 30 minutes. Remove from pan by lifting foil; peel foil away. Cut into 15 rectangular brownies, 5 rows by 3 rows. Gently insert craft stick into end of each. Place on cookie sheet; freeze 30 minutes.

3   In small microwavable bowl, microwave chocolate chips and shortening uncovered on High about 1 minute or until chips are softened and can be stirred smooth. (If necessary, microwave additional 5 seconds at a time.) Dip top one-third to one-half of each brownie into chocolate; sprinkle with candy sprinkles. Lay flat on waxed paper or foil to dry.

MAKE
IT
SPECIAL

ingredient info:

You can use white vanilla baking chips for the chocolate chips if you like. Visit a craft store or cake-decorating supply store, or shop online to find an array of candy sprinkles.

how to store:

Store these brownie pops in a tightly covered container at room temperature.

1 Brownie Pop: Calories 290; Total Fat 12g (Saturated Fat 4g, Trans Fat 0g); Cholesterol 25mg; Sodium 160mg; Total Carbohydrate 42g (Dietary Fiber 1g, Sugars 29g); Protein 2g **Exchanges:** ½ Starch, 2½ Other Carbohydrate, 2½ Fat **Carbohydrate Choices:** 3

Photo appears in the chapter opener on page 155.

Birthday Cake Cookies

PREP TIME: 45 Minutes • **START TO FINISH: 1 Hour** • **10 sandwich cookies**

1   box yellow cake mix
    with pudding
¼   cup rainbow mix
    candy sprinkles
½   cup butter, melted
1   tablespoon milk

1   egg
1   container vanilla creamy
    ready-to-spread frosting
¼   cup multicolored
    candy sprinkles

1   Heat oven to 350°F. In large bowl, stir cake mix, ¼ cup of the candy sprinkles, the butter, milk and egg with spoon until soft dough forms. Onto ungreased cookie sheets, drop dough by tablespoonfuls to make 20 cookies.

2   Bake 8 to 10 minutes or until set. Immediately remove from cookie sheets to cooling racks. Cool completely, about 15 minutes.

3   To make each sandwich cookie, spread frosting on flat of 1 cookie. Top with second cookie, flat side down; gently press together. Roll edges of cookies in candy sprinkles. If desired, top each cookie with a birthday candle.

ingredient info:

Adding rainbow candy sprinkles to the batter gives a bright, party-like feel. If you don't have sprinkles in your pantry, feel free to omit them. The cookies will still bake up perfectly and taste totally delicious. You can also use any favorite cake mix and frosting for these cookies.

how to store:

Store these cookies in a tightly covered container.

1 Sandwich Cookie: Calories 480; Total Fat 20g (Saturated Fat 11g, Trans Fat 3g); Cholesterol 45mg; Sodium 490mg; Total Carbohydrate 72g (Dietary Fiber 0g, Sugars 5g); Protein 2g
Exchanges: ½ Starch, 4½ Other Carbohydrate, 4 Fat
Carbohydrate Choices: 5

213

MAKE
IT
SPECIAL

Photo appears in the chapter opener on page 155.

Samoas Bars

PREP TIME: **20 Minutes** • START TO FINISH: **1 Hour 35 Minutes** • **25 bars**

CRUST
- ½ cup butter, softened
- ¼ cup packed brown sugar
- 1 cup all-purpose flour
- 1½ cups shredded coconut, toasted

CARAMEL FILLING AND TOPPING
- 3 tablespoons heavy whipping cream
- 2 tablespoons butter
- 25 caramels (from 11- or 14-oz bag), unwrapped
- ¼ cup hot fudge topping

1 Heat oven to 350°F. In medium bowl, mix ½ cup butter and the brown sugar until creamy. Add the flour and ½ cup of the coconut; mix well. Press into ungreased 9-inch square pan.

2 Bake 15 minutes or until the edges are light brown.

3 Meanwhile, in 1½-quart saucepan, heat whipping cream, 2 tablespoons butter and the caramels over medium-low heat, stirring frequently, until caramels are melted and mixture is smooth. Remove from heat.

4 Sprinkle ¾ cup of the remaining coconut over hot crust. Pour hot caramel filling over coconut, carefully spreading to sides of the pan. Sprinkle with remaining ¼ cup coconut.

5 In small microwavable bowl, microwave hot fudge topping uncovered on Medium (50%) for 30 to 60 seconds or until topping is thin enough to drizzle. Drizzle topping over bars. Let cool completely, about 30 minutes. For bars, cut into 5 rows by 5 rows.

why it works:
Be sure to use hot fudge topping, not chocolate sauce, for these rich, gooey bars. Chocolate sauce is too thin to drizzle nicely.

kitchen secret:
For a little more ease in cutting these bars, try spraying the knife with cooking spray before cutting. If too much topping and caramel adhere to the knife, clean and reapply cooking spray.

how to store:
Store these bars in a single layer in a tightly covered container at room temperature.

1 Bar: Calories 150; Total Fat 8g (Saturated Fat 5g, Trans Fat 0g); Cholesterol 15mg; Sodium 90mg; Total Carbohydrate 18g (Dietary Fiber 0g); Protein 1g
Exchanges: ½ Starch, ½ Other Carbohydrate, 1½ Fat
Carbohydrate Choices: 1

MAKE IT SPECIAL

Mint Brookies

PREP TIME: 10 Minutes • START TO FINISH: 3 Hours 55 Minutes • 16 bars

1   box (1 lb 2.3 oz) Betty
    Crocker fudge brownie
    mix
½   cup vegetable oil
3   tablespoons water
3   eggs

1   pouch (17.5 oz) Betty
    Crocker sugar cookie mix
½   cup butter, softened
1¼ cups green candy-coated
    milk chocolate candies
12 chocolate mint creme
    sandwich cookie thins, cut
    into fourths (about 1 cup)

ingredient info:
Regular creme-filled mint
sandwich cookies also work
in this recipe. Cut 7 cookies
into quarters.

how to store:
Store these combination
brownie-cookies in a tightly
covered container.

1 Bar: Calories 480; Total Fat 21g
(Saturated Fat 9g, Trans Fat 0g);
Cholesterol 50mg; Sodium 280mg;
Total Carbohydrate 68g (Dietary Fiber 1g,
Sugars 46g); Protein 4g
Exchanges: 1½ Starch, 3 Other
Carbohydrate, 4 Fat
Carbohydrate Choices: 4½

1 Heat oven to 350°F. Line 9-inch square pan with foil, allowing foil
to hang over sides of pan. Spray with cooking spray.

2 Make brownie batter as directed on box using oil, water and 2 of
the eggs. Spread in pan.

3 Bake 32 to 35 minutes or until brownies are set around sides and
toothpick inserted in center of brownies comes out almost clean. Cool
in pan on cooling rack for 10 minutes.

4 Meanwhile, in medium bowl, make cookie dough as directed on
pouch for drop cookies using butter and 1 egg. Stir in 1 cup of the
candies. Drop half of the cookie dough mixture in chunks on top
of baked brownie layer; add half of the cookie pieces. Repeat with
remaining cookie dough and cookie pieces. With back of spoon or
offset metal spatula, gently press cookie dough together to form
even layer. Top with remaining ¼ cup candies, pressing gently into
cookie dough.

5 Bake 23 to 28 minutes or until cookie layer is set, covering with foil
last 10 minutes if necessary to prevent overbrowning. Cool in pan on
cooling rack at least 2½ hours. Remove bars from pan; cut into 4 rows
by 4 rows.

217

MAKE
IT
SPECIAL

Chocolate Caramel Pretzel Bars

PREP TIME: 30 Minutes • START TO FINISH: 2 Hours 15 Minutes • 48 bars

BARS

- ½ cup granulated sugar
- ½ cup packed brown sugar
- ½ cup extra chunky peanut butter
- ½ cup butter, softened
- 1 egg
- 1¼ cups all-purpose flour
- ¾ teaspoon baking soda
- ½ teaspoon baking powder
- ¼ teaspoon salt
- 1 cup dark chocolate baking chips

FILLING

- 1 bag (11 oz) caramels, unwrapped
- ⅓ cup heavy whipping cream

GANACHE

- 2 cups dark chocolate baking chips
- ⅓ cup heavy whipping cream
- ½ cup thin pretzel sticks broken into pieces

why it works:

Lining the pan with foil makes cutting the bars easier. Just lift the bars out of the pan using the foil. Foil also makes for easier cleanup.

why it works:

Refrigerated, the bars are a breeze to cut, however, we liked eating them better when they were allowed to sit at room temperature a few minutes. The caramel begins to soften, making it a perfectly gooey delight!

how to store:

Store these bars in a tightly covered container in the refrigerator.

1 Heat oven to 350°F. Line 13x9-inch pan with foil extending 2 inches over short sides of pan.

2 In large bowl, beat granulated sugar, brown sugar, peanut butter, butter and egg with electric mixer on medium speed until well blended. Beat in flour, baking soda, baking powder and salt until well mixed. Stir in 1 cup of the baking chips until well blended. Press dough evenly into bottom of pan.

3 Bake 18 to 22 minutes or until golden brown. Cool completely in pan on cooling rack, about 30 minutes. Refrigerate 1 hour or until cool.

4 In 2-quart saucepan, heat Filling ingredients over medium heat, 5 to 10 minutes, stirring constantly until caramels are melted. Remove from heat; spread evenly over crust.

5 In medium microwavable bowl, microwave 2 cups baking chips and ⅓ cup whipping cream uncovered on High 1 minute, stirring once, until chips are softened and can be stirred smooth. Spread chocolate mixture over caramel. Sprinkle with pretzels; press into chocolate. Refrigerate 1 hour.

6 Lift bars and foil out of pan to cutting board; remove foil. For bars, cut into 6 rows by 4 rows. Cut each bar in half diagonally into triangles. Let stand at room temperature for 15 minutes before serving.

218

MAKE
IT
SPECIAL

1 Bar: Calories 160; Total Fat 8g (Saturated Fat 4.5g, Trans Fat 0g); Cholesterol 15mg; Sodium 90mg; Total Carbohydrate 19g (Dietary Fiber 1g); Protein 2g
Exchanges: ½ Starch, 1 Other Carbohydrate, 1½ Fat
Carbohydrate Choices: 1

Pumpkin Tiramisu Cheesecake Bars

PREP TIME: 35 Minutes • **START TO FINISH: 5 Hours 30 Minutes** • **24 bars**

CRUST
- 1 pouch Betty Crocker oatmeal cookie mix
- ½ cup butter, softened

CHEESECAKE LAYER
- 8 oz mascarpone cheese
- 1 package (8 oz) cream cheese, softened
- ½ cup sugar
- 2 tablespoons all-purpose flour
- 1 egg
- ½ cup canned pumpkin (not pumpkin pie mix)
- ½ teaspoon pumpkin pie spice
- ¼ cup semisweet chocolate chips, melted
- 2 tablespoons cognac
- 1 tablespoon instant espresso powder

CHOCOLATE GANACHE
- ⅓ cup heavy whipping cream
- ⅔ cup semisweet chocolate chips

1 Heat oven to 350°F. Line 13x9-inch pan with foil; spray with cooking spray. In medium bowl, place cookie mix; cut in butter using pastry blender or fork until mixture is crumbly. Press mixture in bottom of pan.

2 Bake 8 to 10 minutes or until set. Meanwhile, in large bowl, beat mascarpone, cream cheese, sugar, flour and egg with electric mixer on medium speed until smooth. Remove ¾ cup of the cheesecake mixture and place in small bowl; set aside. Stir pumpkin and pumpkin pie spice into original bowl of remaining cheesecake mixture. Stir melted chocolate, cognac and espresso powder into reserved ¾ cup cheesecake mixture.

3 Pour pumpkin cheesecake mixture on top of crust. Spoon chocolate cheesecake mixture over pumpkin mixture; use knife to carefully swirl mixtures.

4 Bake 30 to 35 minutes or until edges are set (center will be just slightly jiggly). Cool 30 minutes.

5 In microwavable bowl, microwave whipping cream 1 minute to 1 minute 30 seconds or until hot. Add ⅔ cup chocolate chips; stir until smooth. Spread mixture on top of cheesecake.

6 Refrigerate about 4 hours or until completely cool. For bars, cut into 4 rows by 6 rows.

ingredient info:
Look for mascarpone in the gourmet cheese section of your grocery store. It's usually found near the deli cheeses.

how to store:
Store these bars in a single layer in a tightly covered container in refrigerator.

kitchen secret:
If desired, top each bar with a dollop of whipped cream just before serving.

1 Bar: Calories 260; Total Fat 16g (Saturated Fat 9g, Trans Fat 0g); Cholesterol 45mg; Sodium 150mg; Total Carbohydrate 27g (Dietary Fiber 0g, Sugars 8g); Protein 3g
Exchanges: 1 Starch, 1 Other Carbohydrate, 3 Fat
Carbohydrate Choices: 2

221

MAKE
IT
SPECIAL

Toffee Brown Ale Cheesecake Bars

PREP TIME: 25 Minutes • START TO FINISH: 3 Hours 35 Minutes • 32 bars

1 pouch Betty Crocker oatmeal cookie mix
½ cup cold butter
2 packages (8 oz each) cream cheese, softened
¼ cup granulated sugar
¼ cup packed brown sugar
2 tablespoons all-purpose flour

⅓ cup brown ale beer
1 teaspoon vanilla
1 egg
½ cup chopped pecans
½ cup toffee bits
¼ cup caramel topping
1 tablespoon brown ale beer

why it works:
Cold butter is needed to create the perfect streusel and crust texture.

how to store:
Store these bars in a single layer covered in the refrigerator.

1 Bar: Calories 200; Total Fat 11g (Saturated Fat 6g, Trans Fat 0g); Cholesterol 35mg; Sodium 150mg; Total Carbohydrate 22g (Dietary Fiber 0g, Sugars 15g); Protein 2g
Exchanges: ½ Starch, 1 Other Carbohydrate, 2 Fat
Carbohydrate Choices: 1½

1 Heat oven to 350°F. Spray bottom and sides of 13x9-inch pan with cooking spray. Place cookie mix in bowl; cut in butter using pastry blender or fork until mixture is crumbly. Reserve 1½ cups mixture for topping. Press remaining mixture in bottom of pan.

2 Bake 10 minutes. Meanwhile, in large bowl, beat cream cheese, granulated sugar, brown sugar, flour, ⅓ cup of the beer, the vanilla and egg with electric mixer on medium speed until smooth.

3 Spread cream cheese mixture evenly over partially baked cookie base. Sprinkle with reserved crumb topping, pecans and toffee bits.

4 Bake 35 to 40 minutes or until light golden brown. Cool in pan on cooling rack for 30 minutes. Refrigerate about 2 hours or until chilled. For bars, cut into 8 rows by 4 rows. To serve, stir together caramel topping and 1 tablespoon beer; drizzle over top of each bar.

222

MAKE
IT
SPECIAL

Pictured clockwise from top left are Mango Raspberry Bars, page 268; Tangerine-Cookie Cheesecake Bars, page 242; and Pumpkin-Turmeric Bars with Coconut Cream Frosting, page 250.

Totable Treats

Rhubarb Cheesecake Bars

PREP TIME: 20 Minutes • **START TO FINISH:** 4 Hours 40 Minutes • 60 bars

2½ cups all-purpose flour	¾ cup granulated sugar
2 cups quick-cooking or old-fashioned oats	3 packages (8 oz each) cream cheese, softened
1 cup packed brown sugar	3 eggs
1 cup butter, softened	1 teaspoon vanilla
½ teaspoon salt	2 cups chopped fresh rhubarb
½ teaspoon baking soda	

1 Heat oven to 350°F. Spray bottom and sides of 15x10x1-inch pan with cooking spray.

2 In large bowl, beat flour, oats, brown sugar, butter, salt and baking soda with electric mixer on medium speed until crumbly or mix with spoon. Press about 4 cups of the mixture in pan.

3 In another large bowl, beat remaining ingredients except rhubarb with electric mixer on medium speed until blended. Stir in rhubarb. Spread over crust. Sprinkle with remaining crumb mixture; press lightly.

4 Bake 40 to 50 minutes or until center is set. Cool in pan on cooling rack for 30 minutes. Cover and refrigerate at least 3 hours but no longer than 48 hours. For bars, cut into 10 rows by 6 rows.

ingredient info:

Rhubarb is actually a vegetable that originated in China more than 4,000 years ago. The deeper the red, the more flavorful the rhubarb stalks are likely to be. Medium-size stalks are generally more tender than large ones, which may be stringy.

how to store:

Store these creamy cheesecake bars covered in the refrigerator.

1 Bar: Calories 130; Total Fat 7g (Saturated Fat 4g, Trans Fat 0g); Cholesterol 30mg; Sodium 95mg; Total Carbohydrate 13g (Dietary Fiber 0g, Sugars 7g); Protein 2g
Exchanges: 1 Starch, 1½ Fat
Carbohydrate Choices: 1

227

TOTABLE TREATS

Raspberry Lemonade Cheesecake Bars

PREP TIME: **25 Minutes** • START TO FINISH: **3 Hours 50 Minutes** • **24 bars**

CRUST

- 1 pouch (17.5 oz) Betty Crocker sugar cookie mix
- ½ cup butter, softened
- 1 egg
- 1 teaspoon finely grated lemon zest

FILLING

- 2 packages (8 oz each) cream cheese, softened
- ½ cup sugar
- 1 tablespoon finely grated lemon zest
- 2 eggs
- ⅓ cup fresh lemon juice
- 1 cup fresh raspberries

1 Heat oven to 325°F. Spray bottom only of 13x9-inch pan with cooking spray.

2 In large bowl, mix Crust ingredients with spoon until soft dough forms. Press dough in bottom of pan.

3 Bake 15 minutes. Cool for 10 minutes.

4 In medium bowl, beat cream cheese, sugar and 1 tablespoon lemon zest with electric mixer on medium speed until smooth, scraping down side of bowl frequently. Add eggs, one at a time, beating until just blended. Beat in lemon juice. Reserve ¼ cup filling; set aside. Spread remaining filling evenly over cooled crust.

5 In small bowl, mash raspberries with fork. Push mixture through small strainer with back of spoon to make ¼ cup raspberry puree. Stir puree into reserved filling. Drop tablespoonfuls raspberry mixture on cream cheese layer. With knife, carefully swirl into top of cream cheese layer.

6 Bake 30 to 35 minutes or until filling is set. Cool in pan on cooling rack for 30 minutes. Refrigerate about 2 hours or until cooled completely. For bars, cut in 6 rows by 4 rows.

kitchen secret:

To quickly soften cream cheese, remove from wrapper and place on microwavable plate; microwave uncovered on High about 15 seconds or just until softened.

why it works:

Line your pan with foil or parchment paper (leave it an inch or two longer on two sides to use as handles) before spraying with cooking spray. When the bars are cooled, you can lift them with the foil out of the pan to cut them easily without breaking the edges.

how to store:

Cover and store these bars in the refrigerator.

1 Bar: Calories 210; Total Fat 12g (Saturated Fat 7g, Trans Fat 0g); Cholesterol 55mg; Sodium 170mg; Total Carbohydrate 23g (Dietary Fiber 0g, Sugars 15g); Protein 2g
Exchanges: ½ Starch, 1 Other Carbohydrate, 2½ Fat
Carbohydrate Choices: 1½

Fig Bars

PREP TIME: **20 Minutes** • START TO FINISH: **1 Hour 40 Minutes** • **16 bars**

CRUST
- ½ cup butter, softened
- ¼ cup granulated sugar
- ¼ teaspoon vanilla
- 1 cup all-purpose flour

FILLING
- 1 cup boiling water
- ¼ cup granulated sugar
- 1 bag (9 oz) dried Mission figs, chopped (1 cup)

TOPPING
- ¼ cup all-purpose flour
- ¼ cup packed brown sugar
- 3 tablespoons cold butter (do not use margarine)
- ¼ cup quick-cooking oats
- ¼ cup chopped walnuts

ingredient info:
Mission figs are a delicious deep purple fruit with a creamy interior that are in season for only a short time. This fig bar recipe, though, uses dried figs, which can be found with other dried fruits in the grocery store.

how to store:
Store these fruity bars in a tightly covered container at room temperature.

1 Bar: Calories 210; Total Fat 9g (Saturated Fat 5g, Trans Fat 0g); Cholesterol 20mg; Sodium 60mg; Total Carbohydrate 28g (Dietary Fiber 2g, Sugars 17g); Protein 2g **Exchanges:** 1 Starch, 1 Other Carbohydrate, 1½ Fat
Carbohydrate Choices: 2

1 Heat oven to 350°F. Spray 9-inch square pan with cooking spray. In small bowl, beat all Crust ingredients except flour with electric mixer on medium speed until well blended. On low speed, beat in flour until soft dough forms. Press dough in bottom of pan.

2 Bake 10 to 15 minutes or until center is set.

3 Meanwhile, in 2-quart saucepan, cook Filling ingredients over medium-high heat 5 to 10 minutes, stirring frequently, until figs are tender and most of the liquid is absorbed. Spread over crust.

4 In small bowl, mix ¼ cup flour, the brown sugar and 3 tablespoons butter, using pastry blender or fork, until crumbly. Stir in oats and walnuts. Sprinkle over filling.

5 Bake 15 to 20 minutes longer or until edges are bubbly and topping is light golden brown. Cool completely in pan on cooling rack, about 1 hour. For bars, cut into 4 rows by 4 rows.

Dark Chocolate–Cherry Macadamia Bars

PREP TIME: **20 Minutes** • START TO FINISH: **2 Hours 50 Minutes** • **36 bars**

CRUST AND TOPPING
- 1 cup sugar
- 1 cup butter, softened
- 2½ cups all-purpose flour
- ½ cup finely chopped macadamia nuts

FILLING
- 1 can (12 oz) sweetened condensed milk
- ½ cup chopped macadamia nuts
- ½ cup chopped drained maraschino cherries (from 10-oz jar)
- 1 bar (3 to 3.5 oz) dark chocolate candy bar, chopped

1 Heat oven to 350°F. In large bowl, mix sugar and butter with a spoon until well mixed. Stir in flour and nuts until mixture resembles coarse crumbs. Reserve ¾ cup of mixture; set aside. Press remaining mixture evenly onto bottom of ungreased 13x9-inch pan.

2 Bake 10 minutes or until top is just set.

3 Drizzle ½ cup of the sweetened condensed milk over the crust. Sprinkle with macadamia nuts, cherries and chocolate. Drizzle evenly with the remaining condensed milk; sprinkle with reserved crust mixture.

4 Bake 25 to 30 minutes or until light golden brown. Run a table knife around the edges of the pan to loosen. Cool completely in pan on cooling rack, about 2 hours. For bars, cut into 9 rows by 4 rows.

ingredient info:
We used a 70% cocoa bar for this recipe to get a deep, dark chocolate flavor. There are lots of sizes and types of dark chocolate bars, so choose your favorite. These can be found in the baking aisle or in the candy aisle of your grocery store.

kitchen secret:
Since these bars are very rich, we cut them smaller. To make cutting 9 rows easier, along the long side of the pan, cut the bars into thirds; then cut each section into thirds again for 9 rows.

how to store:
Store these bars loosely covered at room temperature.

1 Bar: Calories 170; Total Fat 9g (Saturated Fat 4.5g, Trans Fat 0g); Cholesterol 15mg; Sodium 55mg; Total Carbohydrate 20g (Dietary Fiber 0g); Protein 2g
Exchanges: 1 Starch, ½ Other Carbohydrate, 1½ Fat
Carbohydrate Choices: 1

233

TOTABLE TREATS

Banana Bars

PREP TIME: 15 Minutes • **START TO FINISH: 1 Hour 45 Minutes** • **24 bars**

BARS

1 cup granulated sugar
1 cup mashed very ripe bananas (2 medium)
⅓ cup vegetable oil
2 eggs
1 cup all-purpose flour
1 teaspoon baking powder
½ teaspoon baking soda
½ teaspoon ground cinnamon
¼ teaspoon salt

CREAM CHEESE FROSTING

3 oz cream cheese, softened
⅓ cup butter, softened
1 teaspoon vanilla
2 cups powdered sugar
Chopped walnuts, if desired

1 Heat oven to 350°F. Spray bottom and sides of 13x9-inch pan with cooking spray. In large bowl, mix granulated sugar, bananas, oil and eggs with spoon. Stir in flour, baking powder, baking soda, cinnamon and salt. Spread in pan.

2 Bake 25 to 30 minutes or until toothpick inserted in center comes out clean. Cool completely in pan on cooling rack, about 1 hour.

3 In medium bowl, mix cream cheese, butter and vanilla with electric mixer on medium speed until blended. Gradually beat in powdered sugar with spoon, scraping bowl occasionally, until smooth and spreadable. Spread frosting on bars. Sprinkle with chopped walnuts. For bars, cut into 6 rows by 4 rows.

1 Bar: Calories 170; Total Fat 7g (Saturated Fat 3g, Trans Fat 0g); Cholesterol 25mg; Sodium 110mg; Total Carbohydrate 25g (Dietary Fiber 0g, Sugars 19g); Protein 1g
Exchanges: ½ Starch, 1 Other Carbohydrate, 1½ Fat
Carbohydrate Choices: 1½

234

TOTABLE
TREATS

ingredient info:

The moist banana bars are terrific, but if you don't have bananas on hand or would prefer, you can substitute 1 cup canned pumpkin (not pumpkin pie mix) for the bananas. Stir in ¼ teaspoon ground ginger and ¼ teaspoon ground cloves with the cinnamon. Sprinkle ¼ cup chopped nuts over frosted bars if desired.

ingredient info:

We've topped these bars with a homemade Cream Cheese Frosting, but if you prefer, you can substitute 1 container cream cheese creamy ready-to-spread frosting.

why it works:

The secret to making these old-fashioned bars moist and flavorful is to use very ripe bananas. As bananas ripen, the starches are converted to sugar, lending a natural sweetness and increased moistness to recipes made from them.

how to store:

Store these bars tightly covered in the refrigerator.

Cinnamon-Fig Bars with Orange Buttercream Frosting

PREP TIME: **30 Minutes** • START TO FINISH: **2 Hours 35 Minutes** • **16 bars**

FILLING

1¼	cups water
¼	cup granulated sugar
1	bag (7 oz) dried Mission figs, stems removed, chopped (about 1 ⅓ cups)

CRUST

¾	cup all-purpose flour
½	cup butter, softened
¼	cup quick-cooking oats

¼	cup packed brown sugar
1	teaspoon ground cinnamon

FROSTING

3	tablespoons butter, softened
1½	cups powdered sugar
3	to 4 teaspoons milk
1	teaspoon grated orange zest

kitchen secret:

You can save a few minutes by substituting 1 cup vanilla creamy ready-to-spread frosting for the homemade frosting. Be sure to stir 1 teaspoon grated orange zest into the frosting.

how to store:

Store these spiced bars in a tightly covered container at room temperature.

1 Bar: Calories 200; Total Fat 8g (Saturated Fat 5g, Trans Fat 0g); Cholesterol 20mg; Sodium 60mg; Total Carbohydrate 31g (Dietary Fiber 1g, Sugars 23g); Protein 1g
Exchanges: ½ Starch, 1½ Other Carbohydrate, 1½ Fat
Carbohydrate Choices: 2

237

TOTABLE TREATS

1 In 1-quart saucepan, heat Filling ingredients to boiling over medium-high heat, stirring frequently, until figs are tender and most of the liquid is absorbed. Remove from heat; cool 5 to 10 minutes. In food processor bowl with metal blade, place filling. Cover; process with on-and-off pulses until figs are pureed; set aside.

2 Heat oven to 350°F. Spray 8-inch square pan with cooking spray. In large bowl, beat Crust ingredients with electric mixer on low speed until crumbly. Press in bottom of pan.

3 Bake 25 to 30 minutes or until center is set. Spread filling over crust. Bake 6 to 10 minutes longer or just until filling sets. Cool completely in pan on cooling rack, about 1 hour 15 minutes.

4 In medium bowl, beat 3 tablespoons butter with electric mixer on medium speed until blended. Beat in powdered sugar. Add milk, 1 teaspoon at a time, beating on low speed until frosting is smooth and desired spreading consistency. Stir in orange zest. Carefully spread frosting over bars. For bars, cut into 4 rows by 4 rows.

Key Lime Bars

PREP TIME: 15 Minutes • **START TO FINISH: 4 Hours 20 Minutes** • **36 bars**

1½ cups coconut cookie crumbs (17 cookies)

3 tablespoons butter, melted

1 package (8 oz) cream cheese, softened

1 can (14 oz) sweetened condensed milk (not evaporated)

1 tablespoon grated lime zest

¼ cup Key lime juice or regular lime juice

Lime zest or strawberries, if desired

1 Heat oven to 350°F. Spray 9-inch square pan with cooking spray.

2 In medium bowl, stir together cookie crumbs and butter thoroughly with fork. Press evenly in bottom of pan. Refrigerate while preparing cream cheese mixture.

3 In small bowl, beat cream cheese with electric mixer on medium speed until light and fluffy. Gradually beat in milk until smooth. Beat in lime zest and lime juice. Spread over layer in pan.

4 Bake about 35 minutes or until center is set. Cool in pan on cooling rack for 30 minutes. Cover loosely and refrigerate at least 3 hours until chilled. For bars, cut into 6 rows by 6 rows. Garnish with lime zest or strawberries.

ingredient info:

Melting butter and softening cream cheese are easy when you microwave. Microwave butter 1 minute on High in a microwavable bowl to melt and unwrapped cream cheese 15 seconds on High to soften.

how to store:

Store these tangy citrus bars covered in the refrigerator.

1 Bar: Calories 90; Total Fat 5g (Saturated Fat 3g, Trans Fat 0g); Cholesterol 15mg; Sodium 45mg; Total Carbohydrate 9g (Dietary Fiber 0g, Sugars 7g); Protein 1g
Exchanges: ½ Starch, 1 Fat
Carbohydrate Choices: ½

Cranberry Crumb Bars

PREP TIME: **20 Minutes** • START TO FINISH: **4 Hours 15 Minutes** • **24 bars**

CRUST AND TOPPING

2½	cups all-purpose flour
1	cup sugar
½	cup ground almonds
1	teaspoon baking powder
¼	teaspoon salt
1	cup cold butter
1	egg
¼	teaspoon ground cinnamon

FILLING

4	cups fresh or frozen cranberries
1	cup sugar
4	teaspoons orange juice
1	tablespoon cornstarch
1	teaspoon vanilla

1 Heat oven to 375°F. Spray bottom and sides of 13x9-inch pan with cooking spray.

2 In large bowl, mix flour, 1 cup sugar, the almonds, baking powder and salt. Cut in butter, using pastry blender or fork, until mixture looks like coarse crumbs. Stir in egg. Press 2½ cups of crumb mixture in bottom of pan. Stir cinnamon into remaining crumb mixture; set aside.

3 In medium bowl, stir Filling ingredients together. Spoon evenly over crust. Spoon reserved crumb mixture over filling.

4 Bake 45 to 55 minutes or until top is light golden brown. Cool completely in pan on cooling rack, about 1 hour. Refrigerate until chilled, about 2 hours. For bars, cut into 6 rows by 4 rows.

ingredient info:

Stock up on cranberries while they're abundant in stores. Store them in the freezer and use as needed; they'll be good for about a year. If you're using frozen cranberries for this recipe, there is no need to thaw them first.

kitchen secret:

A food processor works great for grinding the almonds. You will need about ⅔ cup slivered almonds to measure ½ cup ground almonds.

how to store:

Store these bars tightly covered in the refrigerator.

1 Bar: Calories 210; Total Fat 9g (Saturated Fat 5g, Trans Fat 0g); Cholesterol 30mg; Sodium 105mg; Total Carbohydrate 30g (Dietary Fiber 1g, Sugars 18g); Protein 2g
Exchanges: 1 Starch, ½ Fruit, ½ Other Carbohydrate, 1½ Fat
Carbohydrate Choices: 2

Tangerine-Cookie Cheesecake Bars

PREP TIME: 25 Minutes • **START TO FINISH: 3 Hours 25 Minutes** • **24 bars**

2   packages (8 oz each) mini creme-filled chocolate sandwich cookies
¼   cup butter, melted
3   tablespoons all-purpose flour

2   packages (8 oz each) cream cheese, softened
1   cup sugar
3   teaspoons shredded tangerine zest
¼   cup tangerine juice
2   eggs

1 Heat oven to 325°F. Coarsely chop 1½ cups cookies; set aside.

2 In food processor bowl with metal blade, place remaining cookies. Cover; process until cookies become fine crumbs. In medium bowl, mix cookie crumbs, butter and flour. Press into bottom of ungreased 13x9-inch pan.

3 In medium bowl, beat cream cheese, sugar, 1½ teaspoons of the zest, the juice and eggs with electric mixer on medium speed until smooth. Stir in 1 cup of the reserved cookies. Pour evenly over cookie crust. Sprinkle top with remaining ½ cup cookies and remaining 1½ teaspoons tangerine zest.

4 Bake 33 to 37 minutes or until top is firm to the touch. Cool in pan on cooling rack for 45 minutes. Cover loosely and refrigerate at least 2 hours or until chilled. For bars, cut into 6 rows by 4 rows.

242

TOTABLE TREATS

ingredient info:
Tangerines give a lovely, unique flavor to these bars, but because they aren't available year round, feel free to substitute your favorite variety of orange.

ingredient info:
Mini creme-filled cookies can be found with the snacks and crackers in the grocery store. You can substitute regular creme-filled sandwich cookies if you prefer. Use one 14.3-oz package of creme-filled sandwich cookies. Coarsely chop 12 sandwich cookies. Place 24 sandwich cookies in food processor bowl. Cover and process until cookies become fine crumbs.

how to store:
Store these bars loosely covered in the refrigerator.

1 Bar: Calories 210; Total Fat 12g (Saturated Fat 6g, Trans Fat 0g); Cholesterol 40mg; Sodium 150mg; Total Carbohydrate 23g (Dietary Fiber 0g); Protein 2g
Exchanges: 1 Starch, ½ Other Carbohydrate, 2½ Fat
Carbohydrate Choices: 1½

Cranberry-Almond Triangles

PREP TIME: 35 Minutes • **START TO FINISH: 1 Hour 35 Minutes** • **24 triangles**

¾ cup all-purpose flour
¾ cup quick-cooking oats
½ cup powdered sugar
¾ cup butter, softened
⅓ cup cherry-flavored sweetened dried cranberries

¼ cup packed brown sugar
¼ cup light corn syrup
2 tablespoons whipping cream
¾ cup sliced almonds
½ cup milk chocolate chips

ingredient info:
Dried fruits tend to darken as they are exposed to air. For the brightest color, use a fresh package of sweetened dried cranberries.

how to store:
Store these fruity-and-nut triangles in a tightly covered container at room temperature.

1 Heat oven to 350°F. Line 8-inch square pan with foil; spray foil with cooking spray.

2 In large bowl, beat flour, oats and powdered sugar with electric mixer on low speed until mixed. Add ½ cup of the butter. Beat on low speed until well combined (mixture will be crumbly). Press mixture in pan. Sprinkle with cranberries; lightly push into dough.

3 Bake 15 minutes or until very light golden brown.

4 In 1-quart saucepan, stir brown sugar, corn syrup, remaining ¼ cup butter and the whipping cream. Cook over medium-high heat until smooth and mixture boils, stirring frequently. Boil 4 minutes, stirring frequently. Stir in almonds.

5 Sprinkle chocolate chips over partially baked crust; let stand 2 minutes. Spread melted chips over cranberries. Immediately spoon hot almond mixture over chocolate; spread carefully.

6 Bake 15 to 20 minutes or until bubbly and almonds start to brown. Cool completely in pan on cooling rack, about 30 minutes. Use foil to lift bars from pan; remove foil. For triangles, cut into 4 rows by 3 rows; cut each square diagonally into 2 triangles.

1 Triangle: Calories 150; Total Fat 9g (Saturated Fat 4g, Trans Fat 0g); Cholesterol 20mg; Sodium 45mg; Total Carbohydrate 16g (Dietary Fiber 1g, Sugars 9g); Protein 1g
Exchanges: 1 Other Carbohydrate, 2 Fat
Carbohydrate Choices: 1

Zucchini Bars with Browned Butter Frosting

PREP TIME: **20 Minutes** • START TO FINISH: **2 Hours** • **48 bars**

BARS

1½	cups granulated sugar
1	cup vegetable oil
3	eggs
2	cups all-purpose flour
1½	teaspoons ground cinnamon
1	teaspoon baking powder
½	teaspoon salt
2	cups shredded zucchini (about 2 medium)
1½	cups chopped pecans
48	pecan halves, if desired

BROWNED BUTTER FROSTING

6	tablespoons butter (do not use margarine)
6	cups powdered sugar
1	teaspoon vanilla
8	to 10 tablespoons milk

how to store:
Store these bars covered in the refrigerator.

1 Bar: Calories 190; Total Fat 9g (Saturated Fat 2g, Trans Fat 0g); Cholesterol 15mg; Sodium 50mg; Total Carbohydrate 26g (Dietary Fiber 0g, Sugars 21g); Protein 1g **Exchanges:** 1½ Other Carbohydrate, 2 Fat **Carbohydrate Choices:** 2

1 Heat oven to 350°F. Spray bottom and sides of 15x10x1-inch pan with cooking spray.

2 In large bowl, beat granulated sugar, oil and eggs with electric mixer on medium speed or mix with spoon. Stir in flour, cinnamon, baking powder and salt. Stir in zucchini and chopped pecans. Spread in pan.

3 Bake 30 to 40 minutes or until toothpick inserted in center comes out clean and top is golden brown. Cool completely in pan on cooling rack, about 1 hour.

4 Meanwhile, for Frosting, in 4-quart saucepan, heat butter over medium heat until light golden brown; remove from heat. Stir in powdered sugar, vanilla and milk until smooth and spreadable. Spread frosting on cooled bars. For bars, cut into 8 rows by 6 rows. Top each bar with pecan half.

Pumpkin Cheesecake Squares

PREP TIME: **20 Minutes** • START TO FINISH: **3 Hours 5 Minutes** • **16 bars**

BASE
- 1 cup all-purpose flour
- ¾ cup packed brown sugar
- ½ cup butter or margarine
- 1 cup quick-cooking oats
- ½ cup finely chopped walnuts

FILLING
- 1 package (8 oz) cream cheese, softened
- ¾ cup sugar
- 1 can (15 oz) pumpkin (not pumpkin pie mix)
- 1½ teaspoons ground cinnamon
- 1 teaspoon ground ginger
- 3 eggs

TOPPING
- 2 cups sour cream
- ⅓ cup sugar
- ½ teaspoon vanilla
  Additional finely chopped walnuts, if desired

1 Heat oven to 350°F. Spray 13x9-inch pan with cooking spray. In medium bowl, mix flour and brown sugar. Using pastry blender, cut in butter until mixture looks like coarse crumbs. Stir in oats and ½ cup walnuts. Press in bottom of pan; bake 15 minutes.

2 In large bowl, beat Filling ingredients with electric mixer on medium speed until well blended. Pour over hot base. Bake 20 to 25 minutes or until set and dry in center.

3 Meanwhile, in small bowl, mix Topping ingredients. Drop mixture by spoonfuls over pumpkin layer; spread evenly over hot filling. Bake about 5 minutes or until topping is set. Cool completely, about 2 hours. Sprinkle with additional chopped walnuts. Cut into 4 rows by 4 rows. Store covered in refrigerator.

kitchen secret:

Here's a great alternative to pumpkin pie. They can be made up to a day ahead of time.

how to store:

Store these bars covered in the refrigerator.

1 Bar: Calories 340; Total Fat 19g (Saturated Fat 11g, Trans Fat 0g); Cholesterol 50mg; Sodium 110mg; Total Carbohydrate 37g (Dietary Fiber 2g, Sugars 26g); Protein 4g
Exchanges: 1 Starch, 1½ Other Carbohydrate, 3½ Fat
Carbohydrate Choices: ½

249

TOTABLE TREATS

Pumpkin-Turmeric Bars
with Coconut Cream Frosting

PREP TIME: 25 Minutes • **START TO FINISH: 1 Hour 55 Minutes** • **40 bars**

BARS

- 1 cup granulated sugar
- 1 cup canned pumpkin (not pumpkin pie mix)
- ¾ cup coconut oil
- ½ cup honey
- 3 eggs
- 1½ cups all-purpose flour
- 1¾ teaspoons ground turmeric
- 1½ teaspoons baking powder
- 1 teaspoon baking soda
- 1 teaspoon ground cinnamon
- ½ teaspoon salt

COCONUT CREAM FROSTING

- ⅓ cup plus 2 tablespoons cream of coconut (from 15-oz can)
- 1 teaspoon vanilla or coconut extract
- ⅛ teaspoon salt
- 3 cups powdered sugar
  Additional ground cinnamon and turmeric, if desired

1 Heat oven to 350°F. Spray 13x9-inch baking pan with cooking spray.

2 In large bowl, beat granulated sugar, pumpkin, coconut oil, honey and eggs with electric mixer on low speed until well blended. Beat in flour, turmeric, baking powder, baking soda, cinnamon and salt on low speed until well mixed (batter may be lumpy). Spread in pan.

3 Bake 24 to 28 minutes or until toothpick inserted in center comes out clean. Cool completely in pan on cooling rack, about 1 hour.

4 In medium bowl, beat ⅓ cup cream of coconut, the vanilla and salt on medium speed until smooth. Beat in powdered sugar. If frosting is too thick, beat in additional coconut cream, 1 teaspoon at a time, until frosting is smooth spreading consistency. Spread frosting on bars. Sprinkle with additional cinnamon and turmeric. For bars, cut into 8 rows by 5 rows.

how to store: Store these bars covered in the refrigerator. Let stand at room temperature 15 minutes before serving.

1 Bar: Calories 140; Total Fat 5g (Saturated Fat 4.5g, Trans Fat 0g); Cholesterol 15mg; Sodium 90mg; Total Carbohydrate 22g (Dietary Fiber 0g); Protein 1g
Exchanges: ½ Starch, 1 Other Carbohydrate, 1 Fat
Carbohydrate Choices: 1½

ingredient info:
What is cream of coconut? It is made from coconut cream and sugar. Cans can be found where drink mixers are stocked or in the baking aisle. Mostly known as a key ingredient in piña coladas, this decadent ingredient makes a great base for our coconut frosting, adding both sweetness and flavor. It separates during storage, so whisk it before measuring.

ingredient info:
Crazy for coconut? Either refined or unrefined coconut oil can be used in this recipe, with the unrefined version offering more coconut flavor. Depending on the room temperature, small flakes of fat may be visible after mixing, but they melt into the dough during baking.

ingredient info:
Turmeric is a member of the ginger family and is grown in warm climates in Asia. It is a common ingredient in Indian curries, adding a deep orange color to food. Find turmeric, which has been dried and ground, in the spice aisle. Here, it's peppery, mustard taste adds another layer of flavor to traditional pumpkin bars.

Peanut Butter Cookie Candy Bars

PREP TIME: 45 Minutes • **START TO FINISH:** 2 Hours • **36 bars**

COOKIE BASE
- 1 pouch Betty Crocker peanut butter cookie mix
- 3 tablespoons vegetable oil
- 1 tablespoon water
- 1 egg

FILLING
- ⅓ cup light corn syrup
- 3 tablespoons butter, softened
- 3 tablespoons peanut butter
- 1 tablespoon plus 1½ teaspoons water
- 1¼ teaspoons vanilla
- Dash salt
- 3½ cups powdered sugar

CARAMEL LAYER
- 1 bag (14 oz) caramels, unwrapped
- 2 tablespoons water
- 1½ cups unsalted dry-roasted peanuts

TOPPING
- 1 bag (11.5 oz) milk chocolate chips (2 cups)

1 Heat oven to 350°F. Spray bottom only of 13x9-inch pan with cooking spray.

2 In large bowl, stir Cookie Base ingredients until soft dough forms. Press dough in bottom of pan.

3 Bake 12 to 15 minutes or until light golden brown. Cool completely in pan on cooling rack, about 30 minutes.

4 Meanwhile, in large bowl, beat all Filling ingredients except powdered sugar with electric mixer on medium speed until creamy and smooth. Gradually beat in powdered sugar until well blended (filling will be thick). Press filling over cookie base. Refrigerate while preparing Caramel Layer.

5 In 2-quart saucepan, heat caramels and water over low heat, stirring constantly, until caramels are melted. Stir in peanuts. Spread evenly over filling. Refrigerate about 15 minutes or until firm.

6 In small microwavable bowl, microwave chocolate chips uncovered on High 1 to 2 minutes, stirring once, until chips are softened and can be stirred smooth. Spread evenly over caramel layer. Refrigerate about 1 hour or until chocolate is set. For bars, cut into 9 rows by 4 rows.

why it works:

Refrigerating, or cooling, the separate layers is important to the success of these bars. Refrigerating the filling (on the cookie base) firms up the layer before adding warm caramel to the bars. Chilling the caramel before spreading with melted chocolate makes it easier to spread the chocolate.

how to store:

Store these ooey-gooey bars covered at room temperature.

1 Bar: Calories 280; Total Fat 12g (Saturated Fat 4g, Trans Fat 0g); Cholesterol 10mg; Sodium 125mg; Total Carbohydrate 39g (Dietary Fiber 1g, Sugars 28g); Protein 4g
Exchanges: 1 Starch, 1½ Other Carbohydrate, 2½ Fat
Carbohydrate Choices: 2½

253

TOTABLE
TREATS

Monster Cookie Bars

PREP TIME: **10 Minutes** • START TO FINISH: **1 Hour 30 Minutes** • **24 bars**

1 pouch Betty Crocker peanut butter cookie mix
1 cup old-fashioned oats
⅔ cup creamy peanut butter
3 tablespoons vegetable oil
1 tablespoon water

1 egg
½ cup candy-coated chocolate candies
½ cup semisweet chocolate chips
⅓ cup finely chopped cocktail peanuts

1 Heat oven to 350°F. Spray bottom and sides of 13x9-inch pan with cooking spray.

2 In large bowl, mix cookie mix, oats, peanut butter, oil, water and egg with spoon until mixture comes together. Stir in candies, chocolate chips and peanuts. Press dough in bottom of pan.

3 Bake 16 to 20 minutes or until light golden brown. Cool completely in pan on cooling rack, about 1 hour. For bars, cut into 6 rows by 4 rows.

ingredient info:
Try adding ¼ cup raisins or dried sweetened cranberries for a bit of sweetness.

kitchen secret:
One secret to cutting bars easily is to line the pan with heavy-duty (spray if indicated in recipe) or nonstick foil. When it is time to cut the bars, just lift the foil out of the pan and cut the bar. It also makes cleanup extra easy.

how to store:
Store these bars in a tightly covered container.

1 Bar: Calories 220; Total Fat 11g (Saturated Fat 3g, Trans Fat 0g); Cholesterol 10mg; Sodium 160mg; Total Carbohydrate 25g (Dietary Fiber 1g, Sugars 15g); Protein 4g
Exchanges: 1½ Starch, 2 Fat
Carbohydrate Choices: 1½

254

TOTABLE
TREATS

Ultimate Turtle Cookie Bars

PREP TIME: **40 Minutes** • START TO FINISH: **2 Hours 10 Minutes** • **16 bars**

COOKIE BASE
- 1 pouch Betty Crocker chocolate chip cookie mix
- ½ cup butter, softened
- 1 egg
- ½ cup coarsely chopped pecans

CARAMEL LAYER
- 24 caramels, unwrapped
- 1 tablespoon milk
- ¾ cup pecan halves

TOPPING
- 3 tablespoons semisweet chocolate chips
- 1 teaspoon shortening

1 Heat oven to 350°F. In medium bowl, stir together Cookie Base ingredients until soft dough forms. Press evenly in ungreased 8-inch square pan. Bake 28 to 33 minutes or until golden brown.

2 Meanwhile, in 1-quart saucepan, heat caramels and milk over low heat, stirring frequently, until melted and smooth. Remove from heat.

3 Carefully spread melted caramels evenly over warm base; sprinkle with pecan halves. Cool completely in pan on cooling rack, about 1 hour.

4 In small microwavable bowl, microwave Topping ingredients uncovered on High 30 to 60 seconds, stirring once, until chips are softened and can be stirred smooth. Drizzle over pan. Let stand about 30 minutes or until chocolate is set. For bars, cut into 4 rows by 4 rows.

256

TOTABLE
TREATS

kitchen secret:
You can melt caramels in a saucepan or in the microwave. To microwave caramels (for step 2), place caramels and milk in 2-cup microwavable measuring cup, microwave uncovered on Medium-High (70%) 2 minutes; stir. Microwave 30 to 60 seconds longer, stirring every 15 seconds, until melted and smooth.

kitchen secret:
Use a wet, sharp knife to cut the gooey bars easily.

how to store:
Store these decadent bars in a covered container at room temperature.

1 Bar: Calories 320; Total Fat 18g (Saturated Fat 7g, Trans Fat 0g); Cholesterol 30mg; Sodium 210mg; Total Carbohydrate 38g (Dietary Fiber 1g, Sugars 27g); Protein 3g
Exchanges: 1 Starch, 1½ Other Carbohydrate, 3½ Fat
Carbohydrate Choices: 2½

Delicious Cookie Dips

Just when you thought cookies were yummy enough on their own . . . we bring you cookie dips! Super-simple to make, these dips take your cookies from mmm to mmm-marvelous. It just may be hard to eat a plain cookie again.

They're not only great with homemade cookies but can be used to dress up store-bought cookies as well. (And they'll make you forget they aren't homemade.) The dips can also be a fun change of pace with crackers or pretzels. Use the Citrusy or Mango Cookie Dips as dips for fruit or as the dressing for a fruit salad.

Our Monster Cookie Dip is a sure hit with kids and adults alike. Check the tips section of the recipe to find the surprise way we discovered to serve it!

(Continued on page 260.)

Clockwise from top right:
Citrusy Cookie Dip (page 261),
Mango Cookie Dip (page 261),
Monster Cookie Dip (page 260).

Betty Crocker Cookies

Monster Cookie Dip

PREP TIME: 15 Minutes
START TO FINISH: 1 Hour 15 Minutes
About 2 cups dip

4	oz (half of an 8-oz package) cream cheese, softened
4	teaspoons milk
½	cup creamy peanut butter
2	tablespoons butter, softened
3	tablespoons packed brown sugar
½	teaspoon vanilla
¾	cup powdered sugar
½	cup mini candy-coated chocolate candies (from a 10-oz bag)
¼	cup miniature semisweet chocolate chips
	Additional mini candy-coated chocolate candies, if desired

ingredient info: Try stirring in ¼ cup old-fashioned oats or chopped peanuts for added texture and crunch.

kitchen secret: For a fun twist, dollop teaspoonfuls of dip onto a parchment-lined cookie sheet and freeze to make frozen "cookie dough" bites that can be stirred into ice cream or eaten right out of the freezer. Store frozen bites in covered container for up to a week.

how to store: Store this dip covered in the refrigerator for up to 5 days. Let stand for 15 minutes before serving.

260

1 In medium bowl, beat cream cheese and milk with electric mixer on medium speed, scraping the bowl occasionally, until well mixed. Add peanut butter, butter, brown sugar and vanilla; beat until smooth and creamy. Gradually beat in powdered sugar, scraping the bowl occasionally, until well mixed.

2 Stir in chocolate candies and chocolate chips. Cover and refrigerate for 1 hour before serving. Garnish with additional mini chocolate-covered candies.

1 Tablespoon: Calories 90; Total Fat 5g (Saturated Fat 2.5g, Trans Fat 0g); Cholesterol 5mg; Sodium 35mg; Total Carbohydrate 8g (Dietary Fiber 0g); Protein 1g
Exchanges: ½ Starch, 1 Fat
Carbohydrate Choices: ½

Citrusy Cookie Dip

PREP TIME: **10 Minutes**
START TO FINISH: **10 Minutes**
2 cups dip

- ½ cup heavy whipping cream
- 1 package (8 oz) cream cheese, softened
- ¼ cup lemon curd (from 10 oz jar)
- ¼ cup orange marmalade (from 12 oz jar)
  Additional orange marmalade, if desired

1 In chilled medium bowl, beat whipping cream with electric mixer on high speed until soft peaks form. (Do not overbeat.) Set aside.

2 In medium bowl, beat cream cheese with electric mixer on low speed until smooth. Add lemon curd and orange marmalade; beat on low speed 30 to 60 seconds or until well blended. Fold whipped cream into cream cheese mixture. Serve immediately or cover and refrigerate until serving time. Garnish with additional orange marmalade.

ingredient info: Lemon curd is a thick preserve made from lemons, butter, eggs and sugar. You can find it with other jams, jellies and preserves. It's often served on scones or biscuits, but it can also be stirred into yogurt or ice cream or use as filling between cake layers.

why this works: Beating the whipped cream first saves you from cleaning the beaters twice! Just move them the whipped cream to beating the cream cheese.

how to store: Store this creamy dip in a covered container in the refrigerator.

1 Tablespoon: Calories 50; Total Fat 4g (Saturated Fat 2.5g, Trans Fat 0g); Cholesterol 15mg; Sodium 25mg; Total Carbohydrate 4g (Dietary Fiber 0g); Protein 0g
Exchanges: ½ Starch, ½ Fat,
Carbohydrate Choices: 0

Mango Cookie Dip

PREP TIME: **15 Minutes**
START TO FINISH: **1 Hour 15 Minutes**
About 2 cups dip

- 1 jar (7 oz) marshmallow creme
- 1 package (8 oz) cream cheese, softened
- 2 teaspoons grated lime zest
- 2 tablespoons fresh lime juice
- 1 teaspoon ground ginger
- 1 cup finely chopped fresh mango
  Additional finely chopped mango, if desired

1 In medium bowl, beat all ingredients except mango with electric mixer on high speed until mixed.

2 Cover; refrigerate 1 hour to blend flavors. Stir in 1 cup mango just before serving. Top with additional mango.

ingredient info: Look for mangoes that are primarily red and yellow in color and yield to gentle pressure.

why it works: Some mangoes will be juicier than others. Gently pat chopped mango with paper towels to remove some of the juice. Stir mango into the dip just before serving to prevent the dip from becoming too watery.

how to store: This dip is best used immediately after stirring in mango, but leftovers may be stored in a covered container in the refrigerator. The dip may be thinner as the mango will continue to water out.

1 Tablespoon: Calories 50; Total Fat 2.5g (Saturated Fat 1.5g, Trans Fat 0g); Cholesterol 5mg; Sodium 25mg; Total Carbohydrate 6g (Dietary Fiber 0g); Protein 0g
Exchanges: ½ Other Carbohydrate, ½ Fat
Carbohydrate Choices: ½

Thumbprint Cookie Bars

PREP TIME: 25 Minutes • **START TO FINISH: 1 Hour 45 Minutes** • **40 bars**

1 pouch (17.5 oz) Betty Crocker sugar cookie mix
½ cup butter, softened
4 oz (half of 8-oz package) cream cheese, softened
1 egg
3 tablespoons coarse white sparkling sugar
3 tablespoons plus 1 teaspoon apricot, blueberry, seedless raspberry or strawberry jam

1 Heat oven to 350°F. Spray 13x9-inch pan with cooking spray.

2 In large bowl, mix cookie mix, butter, cream cheese and egg with spoon until soft dough forms. Spread dough evenly in bottom of pan; sprinkle sugar over top.

3 Bake 19 to 23 minutes or until light golden brown. Using end of wooden spoon, immediately make 40 (½-inch) indentations in baked bar (8 rows by 5 rows) without going through to bottom of pan. Clean off end of wooden spoon with paper towel as needed. Fill each opening with ¼ teaspoon jam. Cool completely in pan on cooling rack, about 1 hour.

4 For bars, cut into 8 rows by 5 rows so jam is in center of each piece.

ingredient info:
Coarse sparkling sugar adds extra sparkle to holiday cookies and can be found in the cake decorating section at most grocery stores.

kitchen secret:
Cutting the bars while still warm will give a more polished look.

how to store:
To store these bars, remove them from the pan and store covered in a tightly covered container in single layer.

1 Bar: Calories 90; Total Fat 4g (Saturated Fat 2g, Trans Fat 0g); Cholesterol 15mg; Sodium 65mg; Total Carbohydrate 13g (Dietary Fiber 0g, Sugars 8g); Protein 0g **Exchanges:** 1 Other Carbohydrate, 1 Fat **Carbohydrate Choices:** 1

263

TOTABLE
TREATS

Snickerdoodle Bars

PREP TIME: 20 Minutes • **START TO FINISH:** 1 Hour 45 Minutes • 24 bars

BARS

2⅓	cups all-purpose flour
1¼	teaspoons baking powder
½	teaspoon salt
¾	cup butter, softened
1¼	cups granulated sugar
½	cup packed brown sugar
3	eggs
1	teaspoon vanilla

CINNAMON FILLING

1	tablespoon granulated sugar
1	tablespoon ground cinnamon

GLAZE

1	cup powdered sugar
1	to 2 tablespoons milk
¼	teaspoon vanilla

1 Heat oven to 350°F. Spray bottom only of 13x9-inch pan with cooking spray. In small bowl, mix flour, baking powder and salt; set aside.

2 In large bowl, beat butter with electric mixer on high speed until creamy. Beat in granulated sugar and brown sugar. Gradually beat in eggs and vanilla until well mixed. On low speed, beat in flour mixture until well mixed.

3 Spoon half the batter into pan; spread evenly. In small bowl, mix Cinnamon Filling ingredients; sprinkle evenly over batter. Drop teaspoon-size amounts of remaining batter evenly over cinnamon filling mixture.

4 Bake 20 to 25 minutes or until golden brown and toothpick inserted in center comes out clean. Cool completely in pan on cooling rack, about 1 hour.

5 In small bowl, stir Glaze ingredients until smooth and thin enough to drizzle. Drizzle over bars. For bars, cut into 6 rows by 4 rows.

264

TOTABLE TREATS

ingredient info:

If desired, sprinkle ⅓ cup cinnamon chips or chopped toasted pecans over cinnamon-sugar filling in center of bars.

how to store:

Store these bars in a covered container at room temperature, if you are packing for a picnic or for traveling, cut into bars and pack between sheets of waxed paper in sealed plastic food containers. For optimum packing of bars, wrap each individual brownie or bar in plastic wrap.

1 Bar: Calories 190; Total Fat 7g (Saturated Fat 4g, Trans Fat 0g); Cholesterol 40mg; Sodium 125mg; Total Carbohydrate 30g (Dietary Fiber 0g, Sugars 20g); Protein 2g **Exchanges:** ½ Starch, 1½ Other Carbohydrate, 1½ Fat **Carbohydrate Choices:** 2

Confetti Crunch Cookie Bars

PREP TIME: 20 Minutes • **START TO FINISH:** 2 Hours 45 Minutes • **42 bars**

COOKIE BASE

- 1½ cups sugar
- ½ cup butter, softened
- 1 package (8 oz) cream cheese, softened
- 1 egg
- 2 teaspoons vanilla
- 2½ cups all-purpose flour
- 1 teaspoon baking powder
- ½ teaspoon baking soda
- ½ teaspoon salt

- ½ cup plus 3 tablespoons rainbow sprinkles
- 1 tablespoon plus 2 teaspoons rainbow nonpareils

CEREAL TOPPING

- 1 bag (11.5 oz) milk chocolate chips (2 cups)
- 3 cups chocolate-flavored O-shaped toasted whole-grain oat cereal
- ¼ cup vanilla baking chips

1 Heat oven to 350°F. Line 13x9-inch pan with foil, leaving 2-inch overhang on sides; spray bottom with cooking spray.

2 In large bowl, beat sugar, butter and cream cheese with electric mixer on medium speed until fluffy. Beat in egg and vanilla until smooth. Add flour, baking powder, baking soda and salt, and beat on low speed until well blended. Stir in ¼ cup of the sprinkles and 1 tablespoon of the nonpareils. With floured hands, press mixture into bottom of pan (mixture will be sticky).

3 Bake 23 to 27 minutes, until edges are set, and top is light golden brown. Place pan on cooling rack; cool completely, about 1 hour.

4 In large microwavable bowl, microwave chocolate chips on High for 1 to 1½ minutes, stirring once, until chips are softened and can be stirred smooth. Stir in cereal until well coated. Add ¼ cup of the sprinkles and mix well. Spread on top of cooled bars.

5 In small microwavable bowl, microwave vanilla chips on 50% power for 30 to 45 seconds, stirring once, until chips are softened and can be stirred smooth. Drizzle over cereal; sprinkle with remaining 3 tablespoons sprinkles and 2 teaspoons nonpareils. Refrigerate 1 hour or until chilled and drizzle is set. Remove foil. For bars, cut into 7 rows by 6 rows.

ingredient info:

Switch up your sprinkles by using different colors to customize for a holiday occasion.

why it works:

For easy drizzling, transfer melted chip mixture into small, resealable food-storage plastic bag. Snip very small corner off one end, and drizzle lightly onto bars. Be sure to add sprinkles immediately after spreading the cereal mixture so the chocolate doesn't set up before sprinkles can attach to the topping.

how to store:

Store these bars loosely covered at room temperature.

267

TOTABLE TREATS

1 Bar: Calories 170; Total Fat 8g (Saturated Fat 5g, Trans Fat 0g); Cholesterol 20mg; Sodium 115mg; Total Carbohydrate 23g (Dietary Fiber 0g); Protein 2g
Exchanges: 1 Starch, ½ Other Carbohydrate, 1½ Fat
Carbohydrate Choices: 1½

Mango Raspberry Bars

PREP TIME: 15 Minutes • **START TO FINISH: 2 Hours 5 Minutes** • **24 bars**

BARS

- 1 cup plus 2 tablespoons all-purpose flour
- ½ cup plus 2 tablespoons butter, softened
- ¼ cup powdered sugar
- ½ cup slivered almonds
- ½ cup granulated sugar
- 1 egg
- ¾ cup fresh raspberries
- ½ cup chopped drained sliced mango (from 1-lb jar)

WHITE CHOCOLATE DRIZZLE

- 3 tablespoons white vanilla baking chips
- 1 teaspoon vegetable oil

1 Heat oven to 350°F. In medium bowl, mix 1 cup of the flour, ½ cup of the butter and the powdered sugar. Using floured fingers, press in ungreased 8-inch square pan building up ½-inch edges.

2 Bake 10 minutes.

3 Place almonds in blender or food processor; cover and blend until finely chopped. Add the granulated sugar and the remaining 2 tablespoons each flour and butter; cover and process until blended. Add egg; cover and process until smooth. Spread almond mixture over partially baked crust. Sprinkle with raspberries and mango.

4 Bake 35 to 40 minutes or until edges of crust are golden brown and top is very light brown and set. Cool completely in pan on cooling rack, about 1 hour.

5 In 1-quart saucepan, heat White Chocolate Drizzle ingredients over low heat, stirring constantly, until chips are melted and mixture is smooth. Drizzle over bars; let stand until drizzle is firm. For bars, cut into 6 rows by 4 rows.

268

TOTABLE TREATS

ingredient info:

Mangoes are a seasonal fruit, so we've used jarred mango slices in this recipe, but chopped peeled fresh mango can be used as well when available.

kitchen secret:

Let the fruit shine! Skip the White Chocolate Drizzle and the fruit can take center stage.

how to store:

Store these bars in a tightly covered container at room temperature.

1 Bar: Calories 120; Total Fat 7g (Saturated Fat 4g, Trans Fat 0g); Cholesterol 20mg; Sodium 40mg; Total Carbohydrate 12g (Dietary Fiber 1g, Sugars 7g); Protein 1g **Exchanges:** 1 Other Carbohydrate, 1½ Fat **Carbohydrate Choices:** 1

Photo appears in the chapter opener on page 224.

Chocolate-Frosted Mint Bars

PREP TIME: **25 Minutes** • START TO FINISH: **2 Hours 45 Minutes** • **36 bars**

CREAM CHEESE MIXTURE

1	package (8 oz) cream cheese, softened
¼	cup granulated sugar
1	egg
1	teaspoon mint extract
4	drops green food color

CHOCOLATE MIXTURE

1	cup butter
4	oz unsweetened baking chocolate, cut into pieces
2	cups granulated sugar

2	teaspoons vanilla
4	eggs
1	cup all-purpose flour

CHOCOLATE FROSTING

2	tablespoons butter
2	tablespoons corn syrup
2	tablespoons water
2	oz unsweetened baking chocolate, cut into pieces
1	teaspoon vanilla
1	cup powdered sugar

1 Heat oven to 350°F. Spray bottom and sides of 13x9-inch pan with cooking spray; lightly flour. In small bowl, beat cream cheese and ¼ cup granulated sugar with spoon until smooth. Stir in 1 egg, mint extract and food color until well mixed; set aside.

2 In 3-quart saucepan, melt 1 cup butter and 4 oz chocolate over very low heat, stirring constantly; remove from heat. Cool slightly, about 15 minutes.

3 Stir 2 cups sugar and 2 teaspoons vanilla into chocolate mixture. Add 4 eggs, one at a time, beating well with spoon after each addition. Stir in flour. Spread in pan. Carefully spoon cream cheese mixture over brownie mixture. Lightly swirl cream cheese mixture into brownie mixture with knife for marbled design.

4 Bake 45 to 50 minutes or until set. Cool in pan on cooling rack, about 30 minutes. Refrigerate 1 hour.

5 In 2-quart saucepan, heat 2 tablespoons butter, the corn syrup and water to rolling boil, stirring frequently; remove from heat. Stir in 2 oz chocolate until melted. Stir in 1 teaspoon vanilla and the powdered sugar; beat with spoon until smooth. Spread frosting over brownies. For bars, cut into 6 rows by 6 rows.

ingredient info:

If you're searching for mint extract, you will find both mint and peppermint extract available. We've called for mint extract in this recipe, which is actually a blend of spearmint and peppermint. Peppermint is a more intense mint flavor with a hint of the chemical menthol, which provides a cooling sensation. Either can be used in the recipe; it's personal preference and what you have on hand!

how to store:

Store these bars covered in the refrigerator.

269

TOTABLE TREATS

1 Bar: Calories 200; Total Fat 11g (Saturated Fat 7g, Trans Fat 0g); Cholesterol 50mg; Sodium 70mg; Total Carbohydrate 21g (Dietary Fiber 1g, Sugars 16g); Protein 2g
Exchanges: ½ Starch, 1 Other Carbohydrate, 2 Fat
Carbohydrate Choices: 1½

Caramel–Peanut Butter Bars

PREP TIME: 50 Minutes • **START TO FINISH: 4 Hours 50 Minutes** • **36 bars**

COOKIE BASE
- 1 pouch (17.5 oz) Betty Crocker sugar cookie mix
- ½ cup butter, softened
- 1 egg
- 15 miniature chocolate-covered peanut butter cup candies, unwrapped and coarsely chopped

FILLING
- 36 caramels (from 14-oz bag), unwrapped
- 1 can (14 oz) sweetened condensed milk (not evaporated)
- ¼ cup creamy peanut butter
- ½ cup peanuts

TOPPING
- 1 container milk chocolate creamy ready-to-spread frosting
- ½ cup chopped peanuts

kitchen secret:
Skip the cooking spray, and instead line the pan with quick-release foil for easy cleanup and removal of bars from the pan.

how to store:
Store these bars covered in the refrigerator.

1 Bar: Calories 260; Total Fat 11g (Saturated Fat 4g, Trans Fat 0g); Cholesterol 15mg; Sodium 160mg; Total Carbohydrate 36g (Dietary Fiber 1g, Sugars 28g); Protein 4g
Exchanges: 1 Starch, 1½ Other Carbohydrate, 2 Fat
Carbohydrate Choices: 2½

271

TOTABLE
TREATS

1 Heat oven to 350°F. Spray bottom and sides of 13x9-inch pan with cooking spray.

2 In large bowl, stir cookie mix, butter and egg until soft dough forms. Stir in candies. Press dough in bottom of pan.

3 Bake 18 to 20 minutes or until light golden brown.

4 Meanwhile, in 2-quart saucepan, heat caramels and milk over medium heat, stirring constantly, until caramels are melted. Stir in peanut butter; heat to boiling. Cook 2 minutes, stirring frequently. Remove from heat; stir in ½ cup peanuts. Spread over warm cookie base. Cool completely in pan on cooling rack, about 2 hours.

5 Spread frosting evenly over filling. Sprinkle with chopped peanuts. Refrigerate about 2 hours or until chilled. For bars, cut 9 rows by 4 rows.

Chocolate Chip Dream Bars

PREP TIME: 15 Minutes • **START TO FINISH:** 2 Hours 45 Minutes • 32 bars

BARS
1½	cups packed brown sugar
⅓	cup butter, softened
1	cup plus 2 tablespoons all-purpose flour
1	teaspoon vanilla
2	eggs
1	teaspoon baking powder
½	teaspoon salt
1	bag (6 oz) semisweet chocolate chips (1 cup)
1	cup milk chocolate chips

CHOCOLATE GLAZE
¾	cup milk chocolate chips
2	teaspoons vegetable oil

1 Heat oven to 350°F. In medium bowl, mix ½ cup of the brown sugar and the butter. Stir in 1 cup of the flour. Press in ungreased 13x9-inch pan.

2 Bake 10 minutes.

3 Meanwhile, in medium bowl, mix the remaining 1 cup brown sugar, the vanilla and eggs. Stir in the remaining 2 tablespoons flour, the baking powder and salt. Stir in semisweet and milk chocolate chips. Spread over crust.

4 Bake bars 15 to 20 minutes or until golden brown. Cool completely in pan on cooling rack, about 1 hour.

5 In 1-quart saucepan, heat Chocolate Glaze ingredients over low heat, stirring constantly, until chocolate is melted. Drizzle glaze over cooled bars. Refrigerate at least 1 hour until firm. For bars, cut into 8 rows by 4 rows.

kitchen secret:
To ensure your bars don't overbake, always bake the minimum time given in a recipe; check for doneness and continue to bake a minute or two longer, if needed.

how to store:
Store these bars at room temperature.

1 Bar: Calories 160; Total Fat 7g (Saturated Fat 4g, Trans Fat 0g); Cholesterol 20mg; Sodium 80mg; Total Carbohydrate 22g (Dietary Fiber 0g, Sugars 18g); Protein 1g **Exchanges:** ½ Starch, 1 Other Carbohydrate, 1½ Fat **Carbohydrate Choices:** 1½

Chewy Cinnamon Dulce de Leche Bars

PREP TIME: 20 Minutes • **START TO FINISH: 1 Hour 55 Minutes** • **36 bars**

1 cup packed brown sugar
½ cup butter, melted
1 teaspoon vanilla
½ teaspoon ground cinnamon
⅛ teaspoon salt
1 egg
1 cup plus 2 tablespoons all-purpose flour

½ cup chocolate-coated toffee bits (from an 8-oz package)
½ cup chopped pecans, toasted
¾ cup dulce de leche (caramelized sweetened condensed milk) (from 13.4-oz can)
1 teaspoon cinnamon-sugar

1 Heat oven to 350°F. Line 9-inch or 8-inch square pan with foil, extending foil 2 inches over 2 opposite sides of pan. Spray foil lightly with cooking spray.

2 In medium bowl, mix brown sugar, butter, vanilla, cinnamon, salt and egg with spoon until well mixed. Stir in 1 cup of the flour, the toffee bits and ¼ cup of the pecans until well mixed.

3 Reserve ½ cup dough. Spread remaining dough evenly in bottom of pan. Bake 20 minutes or until edges are light brown.

4 In small microwavable bowl, stir dulce de leche and remaining 2 tablespoons flour until well mixed. Microwave on High 30 to 40 seconds or until of spreading consistency. Pour and evenly spread on hot crust to within ¼ inch from edges.

5 In small bowl, mix reserved ½ cup dough with the remaining ¼ cup of pecans; drop by ½ teaspoonfuls onto dulce de leche mixture. Sprinkle with cinnamon-sugar.

6 Bake 25 to 30 minutes or until golden brown. Cool completely in pan on cooling rack, about 1 hour. Remove foil and bars to cutting board; remove foil. For bars, cut into 6 rows by 6 rows.

ingredient info:
Dulce de leche is an Argentinian mixture made with milk and sugar cooked until thick and golden brown. It can be found in the baking or Hispanic aisle in your favorite grocery store or Hispanic market.

why it works:
Gooey, dense bars such as these come out easily from the pan when you line the pan with foil first. Turn the pan upside down and form the foil over the bottom and sides of the pan. Then flip the pan over and set the shaped foil into the pan.

how to store:
Store these bars in a tightly covered container at room temperature.

1 Bar: Calories 110; Total Fat 5g (Saturated Fat 2.5g, Trans Fat 0g); Cholesterol 15mg; Sodium 40mg; Total Carbohydrate 15g (Dietary Fiber 0g); Protein 1g
Exchanges: ½ Starch, ½ Other Carbohydrate, 1 Fat
Carbohydrate Choices: 1

Chocolate Pecan Pie Bars

PREP TIME: 15 Minutes • START TO FINISH: 2 Hours 15 Minutes • 48 bars

1½   cups all-purpose flour
½   cup packed brown sugar
½   cup butter, softened
1   cup chopped pecans
¾   cup granulated sugar
¾   cup corn syrup

2   tablespoons butter, melted
1   tablespoon bourbon, if desired
½   teaspoon vanilla
3   eggs, beaten
1   bag (6 oz) semisweet chocolate chips (1 cup)

kitchen secret:
A delicious pecan pie flavor with a twist. These bars are perfect for a crowd.

how to store:
Store these pecan-studded bars covered in the refrigerator.

1 Bar: Calories 110; Total Fat 5g (Saturated Fat 2g, Trans Fat 0g); Cholesterol 20mg; Sodium 25mg; Total Carbohydrate 15g (Dietary Fiber 0g, Sugars 9g); Protein 1g
Exchanges: ½ Starch, ½ Other Carbohydrate, 1 Fat
Carbohydrate Choices: 1

1 Heat oven to 350°F. In large bowl, beat flour, brown sugar and butter with electric mixer on medium speed or mix with spoon. Press in ungreased 13x9-inch pan, building up ½-inch edges.

2 Bake 15 to 20 minutes or until golden brown.

3 In medium bowl, stir together remaining ingredients until well mixed. Pour over partially baked crust.

4 Bake 30 to 35 minutes or until set. Cool in pan on cooling rack about 15 minutes. Refrigerate at least 1 hour until firm. For bars, cut into 8 rows by 6 rows.

276

TOTABLE
TREATS

Nutty Coconut Bars

PREP TIME: 25 Minutes • **START TO FINISH: 1 Hour 50 Minutes** • **36 bars**

2 cups all-purpose flour
½ teaspoon baking powder
½ teaspoon salt
1 cup flaked coconut
1 cup sugar
¾ cup butter, softened
¼ teaspoon coconut extract
1 egg

1 jar (12 oz) caramel topping
1 cup chopped macadamia nuts, toasted
½ cup unblanched whole almonds, toasted, chopped
1½ cups semisweet chocolate chunks

1 Heat oven to 375°F. Line bottom and sides of 13x9-inch pan with foil, leaving foil overhanging at 2 opposite sides of pan; spray foil with cooking spray.

2 In medium bowl, mix flour, baking powder, salt and ½ cup of the coconut; set aside. In large bowl, beat sugar and butter with electric mixer on medium speed until light and fluffy. Add coconut extract and egg; beat 30 seconds. Add flour mixture; beat on medium speed 1 minute. Press in bottom of pan.

3 Bake 20 minutes or until edges are golden brown. Pour caramel topping over baked crust. Sprinkle with macadamia nuts, almonds, remaining ½ cup coconut and the chocolate chunks. Bake 2 minutes longer. Cool completely in pan on cooling rack, about 1 hour. Use foil to lift out of pan. For bars, cut into 9 rows by 4 rows.

ingredient info:

Macadamia nuts are native to Australia but are now grown primarily in Hawaii. These buttery nuts have a mild flavor, making them perfect in baking. If you don't have macadamia nuts, substitute almonds or cashews.

how to store:

These bars can be stored covered at room temperature.

1 Bar: Calories 188; Total Fat 11g (Saturated Fat 5g, Trans Fat 0g); Cholesterol 0mg; Sodium 96mg; Total Carbohydrate 23g (Dietary Fiber 1g, Sugars 0g); Protein 2g
Exchanges: ½ Starch, 1 Other Carbohydrate, 2 Fat
Carbohydrate Choices: 1½

279

TOTABLE TREATS

Oatmeal Brownies

PREP TIME: 25 Minutes • **START TO FINISH: 3 Hours 10 Minutes** • **48 brownies**

CRUST AND TOPPING

- 2½ cups quick-cooking or old-fashioned oats
- ¾ cup all-purpose flour
- ¾ cup packed brown sugar
- ½ teaspoon baking soda
- ¾ cup butter, melted

FILLING

- ⅔ cup butter, cut into pieces
- 4 oz unsweetened baking chocolate, cut into pieces
- 2 cups granulated sugar
- 1 teaspoon vanilla
- 4 eggs
- 1¼ cups all-purpose flour
- 1 teaspoon baking powder
- 1 teaspoon salt

why it works:

The crust is partially baked before adding the filling so that when the bars have baked, it will be perfectly done!

how to store:

Store these brownies covered at room temperature.

1 Brownie: Calories 150; Total Fat 7g (Saturated Fat 4g, Trans Fat 0g); Cholesterol 30mg; Sodium 120mg; Total Carbohydrate 20g (Dietary Fiber 1g, Sugars 12g); Protein 2g
Exchanges: 1½ Other Carbohydrate, 1½ Fat
Carbohydrate Choices: 1

1 Heat oven to 350°F. Spray 13x9-inch pan with cooking spray.

2 In large bowl, mix Crust and Topping ingredients except butter. Stir in melted butter. Reserve ¾ cup mixture for topping. Press remaining mixture in bottom of pan.

280

TOTABLE TREATS

3 Bake 10 minutes. Cool 5 minutes.

4 Meanwhile, in 3-quart saucepan, heat ⅔ cup butter and chocolate over low heat, stirring occasionally, until melted; remove from heat. Stir in granulated sugar, vanilla and eggs. Stir in flour, baking powder and salt.

5 Spread filling over partially baked crust. Sprinkle with reserved oat mixture.

6 Bake about 30 minutes or until center is set and topping is golden brown (do not overbake). Cool completely in pan on cooling rack, about 2 hours. For brownies, cut into 8 rows by 6 rows.

Mocha Toffee Truffle Bars

PREP TIME: **30 Minutes** • START TO FINISH: **3 Hours** • **36 bars**

- 1 pouch (17.5 oz) Betty Crocker sugar cookie mix
- ½ cup butter, melted
- 1 egg, slightly beaten
- 1 can (14 oz) sweetened condensed milk (not evaporated)

- 1 teaspoon instant coffee granules or crystals
- 1 bag (11.5 oz) milk chocolate chips (2 cups)
- 1 bag (8 oz) toffee bits (1½ cups)
- 1 cup chopped pecans

1 Heat oven to 350°F. In large bowl, stir cookie mix, butter and egg until soft dough forms. Spread in bottom of ungreased 13x9-inch pan.

2 Bake 12 to 15 minutes or until light golden brown.

3 Meanwhile, in small microwavable bowl, microwave condensed milk uncovered on High 1 minute. Stir in coffee granules until mostly dissolved; set aside. Sprinkle warm crust with chocolate chips, toffee bits and pecans. Drizzle condensed milk mixture evenly over pecans.

4 Bake 23 to 27 minutes or until top is golden brown and bubbly in center. Cool completely in pan on cooling rack, about 2 hours. For bars, cut into 9 rows by 4 rows.

ingredient info:
The coffee granules give these bars a subtle coffee flavor, but they can also be omitted, or you can add 1 teaspoon vanilla as a substitute.

how to store:
Store these coffee-flavored bars covered at room temperature.

1 Bar: Calories 220; Total Fat 12g (Saturated Fat 6g, Trans Fat 0g); Cholesterol 20mg; Sodium 100mg; Total Carbohydrate 26g (Dietary Fiber 0g, Sugars 21g); Protein 2g
Exchanges: ½ Starch, 1 Other Carbohydrate, 2½ Fat
Carbohydrate Choices: 2

283

TOTABLE
TREATS

Chewy Chocolate-Drizzled Granola Bars

PREP TIME: 20 Minutes • **START TO FINISH: 2 Hours 40 Minutes** • **24 bars**

BARS

- 1 cup packed brown sugar
- ⅔ cup creamy peanut butter
- ½ cup agave syrup or honey
- ½ cup butter, melted
- 2 teaspoons vanilla
- 3 cups quick-cooking oats
- ½ cup roasted and salted pistachio nuts, chopped
- ½ cup roasted and salted sunflower nuts
- ½ cup flaked coconut
- 2 tablespoons sesame seed
- ½ cup golden raisins
- ½ cup sweetened dried cranberries

CHOCOLATE DRIZZLE

- ½ cup dark chocolate chips
- 2 teaspoons shortening

1 Heat oven to 350°F. Line 13x9-inch pan with foil, leaving 2 inches overhanging on short sides of pan; spray with cooking spray.

2 In large bowl, mix brown sugar, peanut butter, agave syrup, butter and vanilla with a spoon. Stir in remaining bar ingredients. Press mixture evenly in pan (dough will be sticky).

3 Bake 27 to 30 minutes or until golden brown and center is set. Cool completely in pan on cooling rack, about 1 hour. Refrigerate 30 minutes.

4 Lift bars from pan using foil; peel back foil from sides of bars. To make rectangle-shaped bars, using sharp knife, cut bars into 6 rows (from the short side) by 4 rows (from the long side). Place bars on cookie sheet.

5 In small microwavable bowl, microwave chocolate chips and shortening uncovered on High 30 to 60 seconds, stirring once, until chips are softened and can be stirred smooth. Spoon melted chocolate into small resealable food-storage plastic bag; seal bag. Cut off tiny corner of bag; squeeze bag to drizzle chocolate over each bar. Refrigerate 15 minutes until chocolate is set.

ingredient info:

Customize these chewy granola bars! Substitute the golden raisins and cranberries with your favorite dried fruit. Try chopped dried apricots, mixed dried berries or a mix of chopped dried fruits. Milk or semisweet chocolate can be used in place of the dark chocolate.

why it works:

Lining the pan with foil makes it easy to cut the bars for grab-and-go snacking or breakfast. After chocolate is set, individually wrap bars in plastic wrap and store in the refrigerator. Or, omit lining pan with foil, leave bars in pan, drizzle with chocolate and bring whole pan to your next casual get-together.

how to store:

Store bars tightly covered in the refrigerator.

1 Bar: Calories 270; Total Fat 13g (Saturated Fat 5g Trans Fat 0g); Cholesterol 10mg; Sodium 100mg; Total Carbohydrate 32g (Dietary Fiber 2g); Protein 4g **Exchanges:** 1½ Starch, ½ Other Carbohydrate, 2½ Fat **Carbohydrate Choices:** 2

Cake Batter Cookie Bars

PREP TIME: **20 Minutes** • START TO FINISH: **2 Hours 20 Minutes** • **24 bars**

BARS
- 1 pouch (17.5 oz) Betty Crocker sugar cookie mix
- 1 box white cake mix with pudding
- 1 cup butter, melted and slightly cooled
- 3 eggs
- 1 teaspoon vanilla
- 3 tablespoons rainbow mix decorating decors

FROSTING
- 1 cup butter, softened
- 3 cups powdered sugar
- 2 to 3 tablespoons milk
- 1 teaspoon vanilla
   Assorted candy sprinkles

1 Heat oven to 350°F. Spray bottom of 13x9-inch pan with cooking spray.

2 In large bowl, beat Bar ingredients except decorating decors with electric mixer on low speed 30 seconds. Beat on medium speed about 1 minute or until blended. Stir in decorating decors. Spread in pan.

3 Bake 32 to 34 minutes or until golden brown. Cool completely in pan on cooling rack, about 1½ hours.

4 In large bowl, beat Frosting ingredients except sprinkles until combined. If necessary, add more milk, 1 teaspoon at a time, until spreading consistency. Spread frosting over bars. Sprinkle with candy sprinkles. For bars, cut into 6 rows by 4 rows.

ingredient info:
Using candy sprinkles of different shapes, sizes and colors gives these bars a different look every time!

how to store:
Store these soft bars in a tightly covered container.

1 Bar: Calories 370; Total Fat 18g (Saturated Fat 11g, Trans Fat 0g); Cholesterol 65mg; Sodium 320mg; Total Carbohydrate 49g (Dietary Fiber 0g, Sugars 33g); Protein 2g
Exchanges: 1 Starch, 2 Other Carbohydrate, 3½ Fat
Carbohydrate Choices: 3

287

TOTABLE
TREATS

Cookies-and-Milk Cheesecake Brownie Bars

PREP TIME: **30 Minutes** • START TO FINISH: **5 Hours 30 Minutes** • **30 bars**

BROWNIES

- 1 box (1 lb 2.3 oz) Betty Crocker fudge brownie mix
- ½ cup vegetable oil
- 3 tablespoons water
- 2 eggs

CHEESECAKE LAYER

- 2 packages (8 oz each) cream cheese, softened
- ¾ cup sugar
- 2 eggs
- 1 teaspoon vanilla

CHOCOLATE CHIP COOKIE LAYER

- 1 pouch Betty Crocker chocolate chip cookie mix
- 1 tablespoon all-purpose flour
- ½ cup butter, softened
- 1 egg

why it works:

Flour is added to the cookie dough to make it a little stiffer, so it will hold its shape within the cheesecake mixture.

how to store:

Be sure these cream cheese-filled bars are covered and stored in the refrigerator.

1 Bar: Calories 240; Total Fat 14g (Saturated Fat 6g, Trans Fat 0g); Cholesterol 55mg; Sodium 170mg; Total Carbohydrate 26g (Dietary Fiber 0g, Sugars 20g); Protein 2g
Exchanges: 1 Starch, 1 Other Carbohydrate, 2½ Fat
Carbohydrate Choices: 2

1 Heat oven to 350°F. Spray bottom only of 13x9-inch pan with cooking spray.

2 In large bowl, mix Brownie ingredients until well blended. Spread in pan.

3 Bake 20 minutes. Meanwhile, in large bowl, beat cream cheese with electric mixer on medium speed until smooth. Add sugar; beat until blended. Add 2 eggs and vanilla; beat just until blended. In medium bowl, stir together chocolate chip cookie mix and flour. Add butter and 1 egg; stir until soft dough forms.

4 Spread cheesecake layer mixture over hot brownie base. Drop teaspoonfuls of chocolate chip cookie dough over cheesecake layer.

5 Bake 35 to 40 minutes or until cookie is golden brown. Cool in pan on cooling rack for 1 hour. Refrigerate at least 3 hours. For bars, cut into 6 rows by 5 rows.

Peanut Butter Truffle Brownies

PREP TIME: 20 Minutes • **START TO FINISH:** 2 Hours 35 Minutes • **36 brownies**

BROWNIE BASE
- 1 box (1 lb 6.25 oz) Betty Crocker Supreme brownie mix
- ½ cup vegetable oil
- ¼ cup water
- 2 eggs

FILLING
- 2 cups powdered sugar
- ½ cup creamy peanut butter
- ½ cup butter, softened
- 2 teaspoons milk

TOPPING
- 1 cup semisweet chocolate chips
- ¼ cup butter

1 Heat oven to 350°F. Spray bottom only of 13x9-inch pan with cooking spray. Make brownies as directed on box for 13x9-inch pan using oil, water and eggs. Cool completely in pan on cooling rack, about 1 hour.

2 In medium bowl, beat Filling ingredients with electric mixer on medium speed until smooth. Spread evenly over brownie base.

3 In small microwavable bowl, microwave Topping ingredients uncovered on High 30 to 60 seconds, stirring once, until chips are softened and can be stirred smooth. Cool 10 minutes; spread over filling. Refrigerate about 30 minutes or until set. For brownies, cut into 9 rows by 4 rows.

kitchen secret:

These brownies are quite rich and decadent. If you are looking for just a bit of something sweet or want to serve them on a buffet, cut brownies diagonally or crosswise in half for smaller bite-size treats.

how to store:

Store these brownies in a tightly covered container in the refrigerator.

1 Brownie: Calories 210; Total Fat 11g (Saturated Fat 4g, Trans Fat 0g); Cholesterol 20mg; Sodium 115mg; Total Carbohydrate 25g (Dietary Fiber 0g, Sugars 19g); Protein 2g **Exchanges:** 1 Starch, ½ Other Carbohydrate, 2 Fat **Carbohydrate Choices:** 1½

291

TOTABLE
TREATS

Brownie Goody Bars

PREP TIME: 30 Minutes • START TO FINISH: 3 Hours 10 Minutes • 24 bars

1   box (1 lb 6.25 oz) Betty
    Crocker Supreme brownie
    mix
½   cup vegetable oil
¼   cup water
2   eggs
1   container vanilla creamy
    ready-to-spread frosting

¾   cup salted peanuts,
    coarsely chopped
3   cups crisp rice cereal
1   cup creamy peanut butter
1   bag (12 oz) semisweet
    chocolate chips (2 cups)

kitchen secret:

If you'd like to start with scratch brownies for these bars, you can use Double Chocolate Brownies, page 33. Then continue as directed in step 2 of this recipe.

how to store:

Store these bars tightly covered in the refrigerator.

1 Bar: Calories 390; Total Fat 19g (Saturated Fat 6g, Trans Fat 0g); Cholesterol 15mg; Sodium 200mg; Total Carbohydrate 49g (Dietary Fiber 2g, Sugars 34g); Protein 5g
Exchanges: ½ Starch, 3 Other Carbohydrate, ½ High-Fat Meat, 3 Fat
Carbohydrate Choices: 3

1   Heat oven to 350°F. Spray bottom only of 13x9-inch pan with cooking spray. Make brownies as directed on box for 13x9-inch pan using oil, water and eggs. Cool completely in pan on cooling rack, about 1 hour.

2   Spread brownies with frosting. Sprinkle with peanuts; refrigerate while making cereal mixture.

3   In large bowl, measure cereal; set aside. In 1-quart saucepan, melt peanut butter and chocolate chips over low heat, stirring constantly. Pour over cereal in bowl, stirring until evenly coated. Spread over frosted brownies. Refrigerate about 1 hour or until set. For bars, cut into 6 rows by 4 rows.

292

TOTABLE
TREATS

Decadent Cherry Mousse Brownies

PREP TIME: 35 Minutes • **START TO FINISH: 3 Hours 5 Minutes** • **24 brownies**

1   box (1 lb 2.3 oz) Betty Crocker fudge brownie mix
½   cup vegetable oil
3   tablespoons water
2   eggs
3   oz white chocolate baking bars (from 6-oz package)
⅓   cup whipping cream
1   cup cream cheese creamy ready-to-spread frosting (from 16-oz container)

¼   cup chopped well-drained maraschino cherries
1   to 2 drops red food color
1½   cups semisweet chocolate chips
¼   cup butter

how to store:
Store these fudgy cherry brownies in a tightly covered container at room temperature.

1 Brownie: Calories 280; Total Fat 15g (Saturated Fat 6g, Trans Fat 0.5g); Cholesterol 25mg; Sodium 120mg; Total Carbohydrate 36g (Dietary Fiber 1g); Protein 1g
Exchanges: ½ Starch, 2 Other Carbohydrate, 3 Fat
Carbohydrate Choices: 2½

1   Heat oven to 350°F. Spray bottom of 13x9-inch pan with cooking spray. Bake brownies as directed on box using oil, water and eggs. Spread into pan.

2   Bake for 24 to 26 minutes or until toothpick inserted 2 inches from side of pan comes out almost clean. Cool completely in pan on cooling rack, about 1 hour.

3   In medium microwavable bowl, microwave 3 oz white baking chocolate and whipping cream uncovered on High 1 to 2 minutes, stirring once, until chocolate is melted. Refrigerate 30 minutes or until slightly thickened.

4   Stir frosting, maraschino cherries and food color into chocolate mixture until well blended. Spread evenly over cooled brownies.

5   In small microwavable bowl, microwave chocolate chips and butter uncovered on High 1 to 2 minutes, stirring once until smooth. Carefully spread over mousse. Refrigerate 30 minutes or until set. Cut into 6 rows by 4 rows.

295

TOTABLE
TREATS

Peanut Butter Brownies

PREP TIME: **15 Minutes** • START TO FINISH: **2 Hours 25 Minutes** • **30 brownies**

BROWNIES

1	box (1 lb 6.25 oz) Betty Crocker Supreme brownie mix
½	cup vegetable oil
¼	cup water
3	eggs
½	cup packed brown sugar
½	cup crunchy peanut butter

PEANUT BUTTER FROSTING

1	container vanilla creamy ready-to-spread frosting
½	cup creamy peanut butter
2	to 3 teaspoons milk

ingredient info:

For extra peanutty taste, stir ⅓ cup peanut butter chips into the brownie batter. You can also use creamy peanut butter in place of the crunchy peanut butter.

how to store:

Store these brownies tightly covered at room temperature.

1 Brownie: Calories 250; Total Fat 11g (Saturated Fat 3g, Trans Fat 0g); Cholesterol 20mg; Sodium 150mg; Total Carbohydrate 34g (Dietary Fiber 0g, Sugars 25g); Protein 3g
Exchanges: 1 Starch, 1½ Other Carbohydrate, 2 Fat
Carbohydrate Choices: 2

1 Heat oven to 325°F. Spray bottom only of 13x9-inch pan with cooking spray. Make brownie batter as directed on box using oil, water and 2 of the eggs. Spread three-fourths of brownie batter in pan. Set remaining batter aside.

2 In small bowl, mix brown sugar, ½ cup crunchy peanut butter and the remaining 1 egg. Evenly spoon peanut butter mixture by tablespoonfuls onto brownie batter. Top with random tablespoonfuls of remaining brownie batter. Cut through batter several times with knife for marbled design.

3 Bake 33 to 38 minutes or until toothpick inserted 2 inches from side of pan comes out clean or almost clean. Cool completely in pan on cooling rack, about 1½ hours.

4 In medium bowl, mix Peanut Butter Frosting ingredients until smooth and spreadable. Spread frosting over brownies. For brownies, cut into 6 rows by 5 rows.

296

TOTABLE
TREATS

Chocolate Cashew Brownies

PREP TIME: **45 Minutes** • START TO FINISH: **2 Hours 40 Minutes** • **24 brownies**

BROWNIES

1	cup butter, softened
¾	cup granulated sugar
½	cup packed brown sugar
1	teaspoon vanilla
2	eggs
1¾	cups all-purpose flour
¾	cup unsweetened baking cocoa
1	teaspoon salt
½	teaspoon baking soda
1	cup semisweet chocolate chips (6 oz)
¾	cup miniature marshmallows
½	cup chopped cashews

FROSTING

3	cups powdered sugar
¼	cup butter, softened
½	teaspoon vanilla
3	to 4 tablespoons half-and-half or milk
¼	teaspoon unsweetened baking cocoa
	Additional cashew halves, if desired

kitchen secret:

To sprinkle the cocoa evenly, place the cocoa in a spoon and tap the edge of the spoon gently over the bars.

how to store:

Store these brownies covered at room temperature.

1 Brownie: Calories 300; Total Fat 14g (Saturated Fat 8g, Trans Fat 0g); Cholesterol 40mg; Sodium 150mg; Total Carbohydrate 41g (Dietary Fiber 1g, Sugars 30g); Protein 3g
Exchanges: 1 Starch, 1½ Other Carbohydrate, 2½ Fat
Carbohydrate Choices: 3

1. Heat oven to 350°F. Spray 13x9-inch pan with cooking spray.

2. In large bowl, beat 1 cup butter with electric mixer on medium speed until smooth and creamy. Beat in granulated sugar, brown sugar, 1 teaspoon vanilla and the eggs until smooth. On low speed, beat in flour, ¾ cup cocoa, the salt and baking soda until soft dough forms. Stir in chocolate chips, marshmallows and chopped cashews. Spread mixture in pan.

3. Bake 15 to 20 minutes or until set. Cool completely in pan on cooling rack, about 1 hour.

4. In small bowl, mix all Frosting ingredients except cocoa and cashews, adding enough of the half-and-half until frosting is smooth and spreadable. Frost brownies. Sprinkle with ¼ teaspoon cocoa and cashew halves. Let stand about 30 minutes or until frosting is set. For brownies, cut into 6 rows by 4 rows.

Milk Chocolate–Malt Brownies

PREP TIME: 15 Minutes • **START TO FINISH: 1 Hour 50 Minutes** • **48 brownies**

½ cup butter

1 bag (11.5 oz) milk chocolate chips (2 cups)

¾ cup sugar

1 teaspoon vanilla

3 eggs

1¾ cups all-purpose flour

½ cup chocolate-flavor malted milk powder

½ teaspoon baking powder

¼ teaspoon salt

1 cup chocolate-covered malted milk balls, coarsely chopped

1 Heat oven to 350°F. Spray bottom and sides of 13x9-inch pan with cooking spray.

2 In 3-quart saucepan, melt butter and chocolate chips over low heat, stirring frequently. Remove from heat; cool slightly.

3 Stir in sugar, vanilla and eggs. Stir in flour, malted milk powder, baking powder and salt. Spread batter in pan. Sprinkle with malted milk balls.

4 Bake 30 to 35 minutes or until toothpick inserted in center comes out clean. Cool completely in pan on cooling rack, about 1 hour. For brownies, cut into 8 rows by 6 rows.

why it works:
Be sure to just coarsely chop the malted milk balls so that you'll have pieces you can bite into when enjoying these lunchbox favorites.

how to store:
Store these brownies covered at room temperature.

1 Brownie: Calories 100; Total Fat 4g (Saturated Fat 3g, Trans Fat 0g); Cholesterol 20mg; Sodium 55mg; Total Carbohydrate 13g (Dietary Fiber 0g, Sugars 9g); Protein 1g
Exchanges: ½ Starch, ½ Other Carbohydrate, 1 Fat
Carbohydrate Choices: 1

300

TOTABLE
TREATS

Pictured clockwise from top left are Chocolate Coconut Cookie Tots, page 307; Blueberry-Apricot Balls, page 323; and Chocolate-Covered Toffee Grahams, page 304.

Too Hot to Bake

Chocolate-Covered Toffee Grahams

PREP TIME: 20 Minutes • START TO FINISH: **1 Hour** • **About 3 dozen cookies**

12	oz vanilla-flavored candy coating (almond bark), chopped	36	graham cracker squares
4	oz white chocolate baking bars or squares, chopped	12	oz chocolate-flavored candy coating, chopped
4	tablespoons shortening	4	oz semisweet baking chocolate, chopped
		½	cup toffee bits

1 Line two cookie sheets with cooking parchment paper. In medium microwavable bowl, microwave vanilla candy coating, white chocolate and 2 tablespoons of the shortening uncovered on High 1 to 2 minutes or until melted and mixture can be stirred smooth.

2 Dip 18 of the graham cracker squares in mixture, coating both sides; tap off excess. Place on one cookie sheet. Refrigerate 20 minutes or until coating is firm.

3 Meanwhile, in another medium microwavable bowl, microwave chocolate candy coating, semisweet chocolate and remaining 2 tablespoons shortening uncovered on High 1 to 2 minutes or until melted and mixture can be stirred smooth.

4 Dip remaining 18 graham cracker squares in mixture, coating both sides; tap off excess. Place on the remaining cookie sheet. Refrigerate about 20 minutes or until coating is firm.

5 Drizzle any remaining white chocolate mixture and semisweet chocolate mixture over dipped grahams; sprinkle with toffee bits. Refrigerate until firm.

why it works:

Dipping graham crackers in candy coating can be a bit messy. Dip the top of the cracker in the mixture and turn over with a fork. Carefully remove cracker, gently tapping the fork to remove excess coating. Place bottom side down on the cookie sheet.

how to store:

Store these cookies in a tightly covered container at room temperature.

1 Cookie: Calories 190; Total Fat 10g (Saturated Fat 7g, Trans Fat 0g); Cholesterol 0mg; Sodium 70mg; Total Carbohydrate 24g (Dietary Fiber 0g, Sugars 0g); Protein 0g
Exchanges: ½ Starch, 1 Other Carbohydrate, 2 Fat
Carbohydrate Choices: 1½

Photo appears in the chapter opener on page 302.

Cranberry Granola Cookies

PREP TIME: 20 Minutes • **START TO FINISH: 50 Minutes** • **About 2 dozen cookies**

1 bag (11 oz) oats 'n dark chocolate protein granola
1 cup chopped sweetened dried cranberries
1 cup pistachio nuts
¾ cup packed brown sugar
½ cup corn syrup
¼ cup creamy peanut butter
1 teaspoon vanilla

1 Line cookie sheets with waxed paper. In large bowl, mix granola, cranberries and pistachio nuts.

2 In 2-quart saucepan, mix brown sugar, corn syrup and peanut butter. Heat to boiling over medium-high heat, stirring constantly. Boil and stir 1 minute. Remove from heat; stir in vanilla.

3 Pour syrup over granola mixture, stirring until evenly coated. Drop mixture by scant ¼ cupfuls onto waxed paper. Cool completely, about 30 minutes.

ingredient info:
Substitute walnuts or cashews for the pistachio nuts if you like. Bits of any dried fruit can be substituted for the dried cranberries.

how to store: Store these cookies loosely covered at room temperature.

1 Cookie: Calories 170 (Calories from Fat 45); Total Fat 5g (Saturated Fat 1g, Trans Fat 0g); Cholesterol 0mg; Sodium 55mg; Total Carbohydrate 27g (Dietary Fiber 1g, Sugars 12g); Protein 4g
Exchanges: 1 Starch, 1 Other Carbohydrate, 1 Fat
Carbohydrate Choices: 2

Chocolate Coconut Cookie Tots

PREP TIME: 30 Minutes • **START TO FINISH: 1 Hour** • **About 3 dozen cookies**

2 cups shredded coconut, toasted (see below)
½ cup creamy peanut butter
⅓ cup honey
1 cup quick-cooking rolled oats
¼ cup unsweetened baking cocoa
¼ cup chia seeds

1 Line trays with cooking parchment paper. Reserve ½ cup of the toasted coconut; set aside.

2 In medium bowl, stir together peanut butter and honey until smooth. Stir in 1½ cups of the coconut, the oats, cocoa and chia seeds until well mixed.

3 Divide dough in half. Shape each half into 18-inch log (dough will be sticky). Cut into 1-inch pieces. Roll tots in remaining ½ cup toasted coconut, pressing coconut into dough on all sides and forming into "tot" shape. On trays, place cookie tots. Cover loosely and refrigerate 30 minutes or until firm.

Toasting Coconut

This is the perfect way to add color and an extra level of flavor to your coconut. You can toast coconut on the stovetop or in the oven. Immediately after cooking, spread on waxed or cooking parchment paper to cool and stop the coconut from getting too dark. To have on hand, make extra ahead and store in freezer in resealable food-storage plastic bag. To toast coconut, spread in ungreased shallow pan and bake at 350°F for 5 to 7 minutes, stirring occasionally, until golden brown, or sprinkle in ungreased skillet. Cook over medium-low heat 6 to 14 minutes, stirring frequently until coconut begins to brown, then stirring constantly until golden brown.

why it works:

This recipe uses quick-cooking rolled oats because they are cut into smaller pieces than old-fashioned oats. This provides more cut surfaces for the peanut butter-honey mixture to adhere and makes them easier to chew.

how to store:

Store these cookies tightly covered in the refrigerator. Remove cookies 10 to 15 minutes before serving.

1 Cookie: Calories 80; Total Fat 4g (Saturated Fat 2g, Trans Fat 0g); Cholesterol 0mg; Sodium 30mg; Total Carbohydrate 8g (Dietary Fiber 1g); Protein 1g
Exchanges: ½ Starch, ½ Fat
Carbohydrate Choices: ½

307

TOO
HOT
TO
BAKE

Peanut Butter Kiss Cookies

PREP TIME: 35 Minutes • **START TO FINISH: 35 Minutes** • **About 3½ dozen cookies**

4 cups bite-size squares
oven-toasted corn cereal

½ cup chopped
cocktail peanuts

½ cup creamy peanut butter

2 tablespoons butter

1 bag (10 oz) miniature
marshmallows (5½ cups)

About 44 milk chocolate
candy drops or pieces,
unwrapped

1 Line cookie sheets with waxed paper or cooking parchment paper. Spray large bowl with cooking spray; mix cereal and peanuts in bowl.

2 Spray medium microwavable bowl with cooking spray; add peanut butter, butter and marshmallows. Microwave uncovered on High 2 to 3 minutes, stirring after each minute, until mixture can be stirred smooth.

3 Pour hot marshmallow mixture over cereal and peanuts; stir until well coated. To form each cookie, drop mixture by tablespoonful onto waxed paper; place 1 milk chocolate drop in center of each, and slightly press down. Repeat with remaining cereal mixture and chocolates. If mixture begins to harden, reheat in microwave on High 30 to 60 seconds.

4 Cool completely, at least 1 hour.

ingredient info:
Try a drizzle of melted semisweet chocolate chips to decorate these no-bake treats.

why it works:
For best results, work quickly while scooping cereal mixture from bowl. Reheat the cereal mixture in the microwave if needed.

how to store:
Store these cookies in a tightly covered container at room temperature.

1 Cookie: Calories 70; Total Fat 4g (Saturated Fat 2g, Trans Fat 0g); Cholesterol 0mg; Sodium 45mg; Total Carbohydrate 6g (Dietary Fiber 0g, Sugars 3g); Protein 1g **Exchanges:** ½ Starch, 1 Fat **Carbohydrate Choices:** ½

Honeyed Peanut Butter and Jelly Cookies

PREP TIME: 15 Minutes • **START TO FINISH: 1 Hour 15 Minutes** • **About 3 dozen cookies**

4 cups honey graham cereal squares

⅓ cup honey-roasted peanuts

½ cup sweetened dried cranberries

½ cup creamy peanut butter

2 tablespoons butter, cut into pieces

1 bag (10 oz) miniature marshmallows (5½ cups)

1 Line cookie sheets with waxed paper or cooking parchment paper. Spray large bowl with cooking spray; place cereal, peanuts and cranberries in bowl.

2 Spray medium microwavable bowl with cooking spray; add peanut butter, butter and marshmallows. Microwave uncovered on High 2 to 3 minutes or until smooth, stirring after each minute.

3 Pour hot marshmallow mixture over cereal mixture; stir until cereal is well coated. Drop mixture by rounded tablespoonfuls onto waxed paper. If mixture becomes hard to scoop, reheat in microwave 1 minute. Cool completely, at least 1 hour.

why it works:

It is important to work quickly while scooping out the cereal mixture so it won't become too hard to scoop. If this happens anyway, reheating the cereal mixture will help make scooping easier.

why it works:

Spraying the tablespoon with cooking spray will help cereal mixture not stick while scooping.

how to store:

Store these cookies in a tightly covered container at room temperature.

1 Cookie: Calories 90; Total Fat 3g (Saturated Fat 1g, Trans Fat 0g); Cholesterol 0mg; Sodium 65mg; Total Carbohydrate 13g (Dietary Fiber 0g, Sugars 8g); Protein 1g
Exchanges: ½ Starch, ½ Other Carbohydrate, ½ Fat
Carbohydrate Choices: 1

Granola Jam Thumbprint Cookies

PREP TIME: **20 Minutes** • START TO FINISH: **1 Hour** • **About 14 cookies**

3 cups cranberry almond protein granola
½ cup packed brown sugar
½ cup light corn syrup
½ cup creamy peanut butter or creamy no-stir almond butter

½ teaspoon vanilla
¼ cup red raspberry, grape or strawberry jam
About 12 almond slices, if desired

1 Line cookie sheet with cooking parchment paper. In food processor, place granola. Cover; process until granola is finely ground. Place in medium bowl; set aside.

2 In 2-quart heavy saucepan, mix brown sugar, corn syrup and peanut butter. Heat to boiling over medium-high heat, stirring constantly. Remove from heat; stir in vanilla.

3 Pour syrup mixture over granola. Stir until well combined. Let cool 5 minutes. Shape mixture into 14 balls. Place balls on cookie sheet. Flatten ball slightly and press thumb into center of each ball to make indentation. Spoon jam in indentation of each cookie. Top each with almond slice.

ingredient info:
There are so many types of granola. If you prefer, substitute the cranberry almond protein granola with your favorite type. For an extra-fancy touch, drizzle the tops of the cookies with melted white chocolate.

why it works:
Spray hands with cooking spray while shaping the cookies to prevent sticking.

how to store:
Store these cookies covered at room temperature.

1 Cookie: Calories 230; Total Fat 7g (Saturated Fat 2g, Trans Fat 0g); Cholesterol 0mg; Sodium 115mg; Total Carbohydrate 37g (Dietary Fiber 1g, Sugars 21g); Protein 6g
Exchanges: 1½ Starch, 1 Other Carbohydrate, 1 Fat
Carbohydrate Choices: 2½

Chewy Protein Cookies

PREP TIME: **15 Minutes** • START TO FINISH: **30 Minutes** • **About 1 dozen cookies**

¼ cup butter
⅓ cup packed brown sugar
⅓ cup honey
2 cups protein cranberry
  almond bran cereal

½ cup sweetened
  dried cranberries
½ cup sliced almonds,
  chopped

1 Line cookie sheet with cooking parchment paper. In 2-quart saucepan, melt butter over medium heat. Add brown sugar and honey; stir until well combined. Cook over medium heat 2 to 3 minutes or until sugar is dissolved. Remove from heat.

2 Add cereal, cranberries and almonds; fold in to coat evenly. Place 2½-inch round biscuit cutter on cookie sheet. Spoon 3 rounded tablespoonfuls cereal mixture in center of cookie cutter; press firmly. Remove cutter. Repeat with remaining cereal mixture. Refrigerate 15 minutes or until set.

ingredient info:

It's easy to personalize these cookies. Use raisins, currents, or dried blueberries in place of the cranberries, and choose your favorite nut in place of the almonds.

how to store:

Store these cookies in a resealable food-storage plastic bag, and eat within 5 days.

1 Cookie: Calories 220; Total Fat 9g (Saturated Fat 4g, Trans Fat 0g); Cholesterol 10mg; Sodium 55mg; Total Carbohydrate 31g (Dietary Fiber 2g, Sugars 24g); Protein 2g
Exchanges: 1½ Starch, ½ Other Carbohydrate, 1½ Fat
Carbohydrate Choices: 2

Cranberry Nut Cookies

PREP TIME: 15 Minutes • **START TO FINISH: 45 Minutes** • **About 2 dozen cookies**

4	cups honey cluster original bran flake cereal
1	cup chopped sweetened dried cranberries
½	cup roasted unsalted sunflower nuts
⅓	cup cashew pieces
¾	cup packed brown sugar
½	cup corn syrup
¼	cup creamy peanut butter
1	teaspoon vanilla

1 In large bowl, mix cereal, cranberries, sunflower nuts and cashews.

2 In 2-quart saucepan, mix brown sugar, corn syrup and peanut butter. Heat to boiling over medium-high heat, stirring constantly. Boil and stir 1 minute. Remove from heat; stir in vanilla.

3 Pour syrup over cereal mixture, stirring until evenly coated. Drop mixture by slightly less than ¼ cupfuls onto waxed paper. Cool completely, about 30 minutes.

ingredient info:
Substitute walnuts or peanuts for the cashews if you like. Bits of any dried fruit can be substituted for the dried cranberries.

how to store:
Store these cookies in a tightly covered container at room temperature.

1 Cookie: Calories 150; Total Fat 4g (Saturated Fat 0g, Trans Fat 0g); Cholesterol 0mg; Sodium 65mg; Total Carbohydrate 27g (Dietary Fiber 2g, Sugars 15g); Protein 2g
Exchanges: 1 Starch, 1 Other Carbohydrate, ½ Fat
Carbohydrate Choices: 2

TOO
HOT
TO
BAKE

Seed-Packed Power Bites

PREP TIME: **20 Minutes** • START TO FINISH: **1 Hour 20 Minutes** • **About 24 bites**

¼ cup toasted sesame seed
3 tablespoons poppy seed
¼ cup quick-cooking oats
¼ cup sweetened dried cranberries or raisins

¼ cup whole flaxseed (any variety)
¼ cup miniature semisweet chocolate chips
¼ cup almond or peanut butter
2 tablespoons honey

1 On small plate, stir together 2 tablespoons of the sesame seed and 2 teaspoons of the poppy seed; set aside.

2 In food processor bowl with metal blade, place remaining ingredients. Cover; process with on-and-off pulses until fruit is finely chopped and mixture holds together.

3 Shape tablespoonfuls of dough into 1-inch balls; roll in reserved sesame-poppy seed mixture. Place in plastic storage container. Cover and refrigerate until firm, about 30 minutes. Serve cold or at room temperature.

1 Bite: Calories 70; Total Fat 4g (Saturated Fat 0g, Trans Fat 0g); Cholesterol 0mg; Sodium 10mg; Total Carbohydrate 6g (Dietary Fiber 1g, Sugars 4g); Protein 1g
Exchanges: ½ Other Carbohydrate, 1 Fat
Carbohydrate Choices: ½

kitchen secret:
Toasted sesame seed can be purchased in the Asian section of the grocery store. To toast at home, sprinkle sesame seed in ungreased heavy skillet. Cook over medium-low heat 5 to 7 minutes, stirring frequently until browning begins, then stirring constantly until golden brown. Cool before using.

why it works:
Lightly wet hands with water or spray with cooking spray to keep dough from sticking to hands while shaping.

how to store:
Store these cookies in a tightly covered container in the refrigerator.

Unexpected Ways to Use Cookies

Can you really ever get enough cookies? We think not! Here are some fun ways to use them as a garnish for other foods, so the love affair with cookies can continue:

WHOLE COOKIES

- Use semi-soft cookies between the soft layers (such as whipped cream or pudding) in your favorite trifle.
- Press cookies into the side of a frosted cake or on top of a frosted cupcake.
- Use small cookies to press into the whipped cream on top of desserts such as pies, ice cream pies or cheesecakes.
- Garnish smoothies, whipped cream-topped milkshakes or coffee drinks with a cookie
- Use sturdy, unfrosted cookies in place of graham crackers for s'mores.
- Line small, unfrosted cookies in serving bowl before adding cut-up fruit.

CRUSHED COOKIES

- Fold crushed cookies into ice cream or pudding just before serving.
- Use cookie crumbs between layers of yogurt or pudding for parfaits.
- Dip the sides of ice cream sandwiches into crushed cookies; freeze until firm.
- Dip chocolate-covered bananas in crushed cookie crumbs and sprinkles before freezing for frozen bananas.

Blueberry-Apricot Balls

PREP TIME: 45 Minutes • **START TO FINISH: 1 Hour 45 Minutes** • **About 3½ dozen cookies**

1	cup quick-cooking oats	2	tablespoons fresh orange juice
½	cup coconut		
2	teaspoons grated orange zest	½	cup roasted cashew butter
		2	tablespoons honey
½	cup chopped dried apricots	½	cup coarsely chopped dried blueberries
½	cup chopped toasted cashews		

1 In large bowl, mix oats, coconut and orange zest; set aside.

2 In food processor bowl with metal blade, place apricots, cashews and orange juice. Cover; process with on-and-off pulses about 45 seconds or until finely chopped. Add cashew butter and honey; process until well blended and mixture comes together in a ball. Add apricot mixture and blueberries to oat mixture; stir until well mixed.

3 Firmly shape 1 tablespoonful of apricot mixture into 1-inch balls. Cover loosely and refrigerate about 1 hour before serving.

1 Cookie: Calories 60; Total Fat 2g (Saturated Fat 1g, Trans Fat 0g); Cholesterol 0mg; Sodium 10mg; Total Carbohydrate 7g (Dietary Fiber 0g, Sugars 4g); Protein 1g
Exchanges: ½ Starch, ½ Fat
Carbohydrate Choices: ½

why it works:

Finely chopping the cashews and apricots with the orange juice in the food processor makes it easier to make a more uniform mixture.

kitchen secret:

Place these cookies on a serving plate before refrigerating. Or, you can place balls directly in a storage container before chilling if you plan to serve them later. Stash a few cookies in a snack-size resealable food-storage plastic bag for a quick school or work snack.

how to store:

Store these balls in a tightly covered container in the refrigerator.

TOO
HOT
TO
BAKE

Oatmeal Chocolate Chip Cookie Bars

PREP TIME: 15 Minutes • **START TO FINISH: 1 Hour 15 Minutes** • **16 bars**

4 cups chocolate O-shaped toasted whole-grain oat cereal
1 cup old-fashioned or quick-cooking oats
½ cup creamy cookie butter or cookie spread

½ cup honey
¼ cup packed brown sugar
½ cup miniature semisweet chocolate chips

ingredient info:

Cookie butter is very much akin to peanut butter—similar consistency and color. The rich gingerbread flavor actually comes from the so-called "Speculoos cookie," a crunchy Belgian cookie that has a hint of caramel.

how to store:

Store these bars covered at room temperature up to 1 week.

1 Bar: Calories 180; Total Fat 5g (Saturated Fat 2g, Trans Fat 0g); Cholesterol 0mg; Sodium 60mg; Total Carbohydrate 30g (Dietary Fiber 1g, Sugars 20g); Protein 1g
Exchanges: ½ Starch, 1½ Other Carbohydrate, 1 Fat
Carbohydrate Choices: 2

1 Line bottom and sides of 8-inch square pan with foil or cooking parchment paper. Spray foil with cooking spray.

2 In large bowl, mix cereal and oats; set aside.

3 In large microwavable bowl, microwave cookie butter, honey and brown sugar uncovered on High 2 to 3 minutes, stirring every 30 seconds, until mixture is boiling and slightly thickened.

4 Pour over cereal mixture in bowl; stir until evenly coated. Gently stir in chocolate chips. Using buttered back of spoon, press mixture very firmly in pan. Refrigerate about 1 hour or until firm enough to cut. For bars, cut into 4 rows by 4 rows.

TOO HOT TO BAKE

Chocolate Mint Bars

PREP TIME: 30 Minutes • **START TO FINISH: 45 Minutes** • **25 bars**

½   cup butter
1   bag (10 oz) mint-flavored semisweet chocolate chips (1 ⅔ cups)
2   cups chocolate wafer cookie crumbs
¼   cup butter, softened

1   tablespoon milk
½   teaspoon peppermint extract
½   teaspoon vanilla
1   drop green food color
2   cups powdered sugar
⅓   cup butter

1   Spray 9-inch square pan with cooking spray. In 2-quart saucepan, melt ½ cup butter and ¼ cup of the chocolate chips over low heat, stirring constantly. Remove from heat. Stir in cookie crumbs until well mixed; press evenly in pan. Refrigerate until firm, about 10 minutes.

2   Meanwhile, in small bowl, beat ¼ cup butter, the milk, peppermint extract, vanilla and food color with electric mixer on medium speed until well mixed. Gradually beat in powdered sugar on low speed until smooth.

3   Spread peppermint mixture evenly over crumb mixture. In 1-quart saucepan, melt remaining chocolate chips and ⅓ cup butter over low heat, stirring constantly; spread evenly over peppermint mixture. Refrigerate about 15 minutes or until chocolate is set. For bars, cut into 5 rows by 5 rows.

ingredient info:

To ease preparation, purchase prepared chocolate crumbs. Otherwise, place about 45 chocolate cookies in a plastic bag and press with a rolling pin until finely crushed, or crush in a food processor.

how to store:

Store these bars in a tightly covered container in the refrigerator.

1 Bar: Calories 210; Total Fat 13g (Saturated Fat 7g, Trans Fat 0g); Cholesterol 20mg; Sodium 115mg; Total Carbohydrate 23g (Dietary Fiber 1g, Sugars 19g); Protein 1g
Exchanges: ½ Starch, 1 Other Carbohydrate, 2½ Fat
Carbohydrate Choices: 1½

Brown Butter–Peanut Bars

PREP TIME: 30 Minutes • **START TO FINISH: 1 Hour 30 Minutes** • **18 bars**

¾ cup butter
1 bag (16 oz) miniature marshmallows (8 cups)
10 cups bite-size squares oven-toasted rice cereal
¾ cup chopped peanuts

2 tablespoons dark chocolate chips
½ teaspoon vegetable oil
  A pinch of sea salt flakes or coarse kosher salt

1 Spray 13x9-inch pan with cooking spray.

2 In 6-quart Dutch oven, melt butter over medium heat. Cook 6 to 8 minutes, stirring constantly, until butter turns deep golden brown.

3 Add marshmallows; stir until completely melted and mixture is well blended, 1 to 2 minutes. Remove from heat. Add cereal and peanuts; mix well. Using a spatula sprayed with cooking spray, press mixture evenly into pan. Cool 15 minutes.

4 In small microwavable bowl, microwave chocolate chips and oil uncovered on High 30 to 60 seconds. Stir until smooth. Drizzle over bars. Sprinkle with salt. Refrigerate about 45 minutes or until chocolate is set. For bars, cut into 6 rows by 3 rows.

ingredient info:

Here are two helpful tips for browning butter:

Using a pan with a light-colored interior will help you to see the butter change color.

After the butter melts, it will begin to foam. Don't rush the process. The color will change slowly at the beginning of cooking and then quickly in the last 2 minutes.

why it works:

For easy cutting and cleanup, line the bottom and sides of the pan with foil or cooking parchment paper, before spraying with cooking spray.

how to store:

Store these bars in a tightly covered container at room temperature.

1 Bar: Calories 260; Total Fat 11g (Saturated Fat 6g, Trans Fat 0g); Cholesterol 20mg; Sodium 210mg; Total Carbohydrate 35g (Dietary Fiber 1g, Sugars 16g); Protein 3g
Exchanges: 1 Starch, 1½ Other Carbohydrate, 2 Fat
Carbohydrate Choices: 2

Fruity Trail Mix Bites

PREP TIME: 10 Minutes • **START TO FINISH: 1 Hour 15 Minutes** • **24 bites**

¼ cup butter
¼ cup packed brown sugar
¼ cup agave syrup
1½ cups old-fashioned or quick-cooking oats

½ cup chopped walnuts
½ cup dried apricots, chopped
¼ cup roasted salted hulled pumpkin seeds (pepitas)
1 package (5 oz) cranberry and chocolate trail mix

1 Spray 9-inch square pan with cooking spray.

2 In 2-quart saucepan, melt butter over medium heat. Stir in brown sugar and agave syrup. Heat to boiling over medium heat, stirring constantly. Boil and stir 1 minute. Remove from heat.

3 Add oats, walnuts, apricots and pepitas; stir well to coat evenly. Stir in trail mix just until mixed.

4 Spread into pan, pressing firmly into bottom. Refrigerate about 1 hour or until set. For bites, cut into 6 rows by 4 rows.

1 Bite: Calories 120; Total Fat 6g (Saturated Fat 2g, Trans Fat 0g); Cholesterol 5mg; Sodium 25mg; Total Carbohydrate 13g (Dietary Fiber 1g); Protein 2g
Exchanges: ½ Starch, ½ Other Carbohydrate, 1 Fat
Carbohydrate Choices: 1

330

TOO
HOT
TO
BAKE

kitchen secret:
If your apricots are very dry, place them in a small bowl and cover with hot water. Let stand 5 minutes; drain well and chop as directed.

ingredient info:
We've used a trail mix with chocolate chips, but you can use 1 cup of your favorite trail mix. If there is chocolate in the mix, stir in at the end as we have done in this recipe so the chocolate doesn't melt. If your trail mix does not have chocolate, you can just stir in with the oats.

how to store:
Store these bites in a tightly covered container in the refrigerator. If you like, let stand at room temperature a few minutes before serving.

Peanutty Candy Bars

PREP TIME: **25 Minutes** • START TO FINISH: **2 Hours 25 Minutes** • **24 bars**

BARS

- 8 cups bite-size squares oven-toasted rice cereal
- 1 package (10 oz) peanut butter chips (about 1⅔ cups)
- ¼ cup chopped cocktail peanuts
- ¼ cup butter, cut into pieces
- 1 bag (10 oz) miniature marshmallows (5½ cups)
- ½ cup caramel bits

TOPPING

- 1 package (12 oz) semisweet chocolate chips (about 2 cups)
- 1 bar (1.86 oz) milk chocolate-covered peanut, caramel and nougat candy, unwrapped, chopped (about ½ cup)
- ¼ cup finely chopped cocktail peanuts

ingredient info:
Caramel bits are small unwrapped caramel pieces that can be found in the baking aisle.

how to store:
Store these bars in a tightly covered container at room temperature.

1 Bar: Calories 220; Total Fat 9g (Saturated Fat 4g, Trans Fat 0g); Cholesterol 5mg; Sodium 115mg; Total Carbohydrate 31g (Dietary Fiber 1g, Sugars 19g); Protein 2g
Exchanges: 1 Starch, 1 Other Carbohydrate, 1½ Fat
Carbohydrate Choices: 2

1 Spray 13x9-inch pan with cooking spray. Spray large bowl with cooking spray. In bowl, stir together cereal, ⅔ cup of the peanut butter chips and ¼ cup peanuts.

2 Spray medium microwavable bowl with cooking spray; add butter and marshmallows. Microwave uncovered on High 1 minute 30 seconds to 2 minutes or until smooth, stirring after each minute. Stir in caramel bits; microwave 30 seconds. Stir well to blend (a few caramel bits may remain unmelted).

3 Pour hot marshmallow mixture over cereal mixture in bowl; stir until cereal is well coated. Press firmly in pan.

4 In medium microwavable bowl, microwave chocolate chips and remaining 1 cup peanut butter chips uncovered on High 1 to 2 minutes, stirring every 30 seconds, until smooth. Spread over bars. Sprinkle chopped candy and ¼ cup peanuts over top. Let stand about 2 hours or until set. For bars, cut into 6 rows by 4 rows.

TOO
HOT
TO
BAKE

Caramel Corn Scotcheroos

PREP TIME: 20 Minutes • **START TO FINISH:** 2 Hours 20 Minutes • **24 bars**

8 cups bite-size squares oven-toasted corn cereal

1½ cups creamy peanut butter

¾ cup honey

½ cup caramel topping

3 tablespoons butter, cut into pieces

1 package (12 oz) semisweet chocolate chips (about 2 cups)

1 cup butterscotch chips

1 Spray 13x9-inch pan with cooking spray. Place cereal in large bowl; set aside.

2 In 3-quart saucepan, heat 1 cup of the peanut butter, the honey, caramel sauce and butter just to boiling over medium heat, stirring constantly.

3 Pour hot mixture over cereal in bowl; stir until evenly coated. Spray back of spoon with cooking spray. Using back of spoon, press mixture firmly into pan.

4 In medium microwavable bowl, microwave chocolate chips, butterscotch chips and remaining ½ cup peanut butter uncovered on High 1 to 2 minutes, stirring every 30 seconds until smooth. Spread over bars. Refrigerate about 2 hours or until set. For bars, cut into 6 rows by 4 rows.

ingredient info:

Semisweet chips are used in these bars, but dark chocolate chips or milk chocolate chips can be used instead of semisweet.

how to store:

Store these bars in a tightly covered container at room temperature.

1 Bar: Calories 320; Total Fat 16g (Saturated Fat 7g, Trans Fat 0g); Cholesterol 0mg; Sodium 190mg; Total Carbohydrate 39g (Dietary Fiber 2g, Sugars 27g); Protein 5g
Exchanges: 1½ Starch, 1 Other Carbohydrate, 3 Fat
Carbohydrate Choices: 2½

TOO
HOT
TO
BAKE

Peanut Butter *and* Jelly Pinwheels

PREP TIME: 20 Minutes • **START TO FINISH: 1 Hour 10 Minutes** • **About 2½ dozen cookies**

3	tablespoons butter
1	bag (10 oz) marshmallows or 4 cups miniature marshmallows

7	cups crushed cinnamon toast flavor cereal (about 4½ cups)
½	cup creamy peanut butter
½	cup raspberry or strawberry preserves

1 Line a 15x10x1-inch baking pan with waxed paper or cooking parchment paper, leaving 1 inch waxed paper overhanging short sides of pan; spray with cooking spray.

2 In large microwavable bowl, microwave butter uncovered on High about 45 seconds or until melted. Add marshmallows; toss to coat. Microwave 1 to 1½ minutes longer. Stir until marshmallows are completely melted and mixture is well mixed.

3 Add cereal; stir until well mixed. Spoon into baking pan, pressing gently with hands lightly moistened with water. Remove waxed paper with cereal mixture to work surface. Spread peanut butter over cereal mixture; spread with preserves. Tightly roll up cereal mixture, starting with a long end; peeling away the paper as you roll. Place roll on cutting board.

4 Using serrated knife, cut roll crosswise into ¾-inch slices.

1 Cookie: Calories 130; Total Fat 4.5g (Saturated Fat 1.5g, Trans Fat 0g); Cholesterol 0mg; Sodium 95mg; Total Carbohydrate 20g (Dietary Fiber 1g); Protein 1g
Exchanges: ½ Starch, 1 Other Carbohydrate, 1 Fat
Carbohydrate Choices: 1

why it works:

You want the cereal crushed enough so it's easy to cut through when done but not so finely crushed that it's like crumbs. Place cereal in a gallon-size plastic bag, and crush it with a rolling pin.

why it works:

The cereal mixture is sticky and needs to be spread thinly. Pressing the mixture with hands moistened lightly does the trick.

how to store:

For best results, wrap the roll with cooking parchment paper or plastic wrap and store in the refrigerator to keep the roll from drying out. If you have leftover slices, store them in a tightly covered container in single layers with pieces of waxed paper between the layers in the refrigerator.

337

TOO
HOT
TO
BAKE

3-Ingredient Cereal Bars

PREP TIME: **5 Minutes** • START TO FINISH: **15 Minutes** • **24 bars**

3   tablespoons butter
1   bag (10 oz) miniature
    marshmallows (5½ cups)

5   cups O-shaped whole-grain
    oat cereal

1 Spray bottom and sides of 13x9-inch pan with cooking spray. In large microwavable bowl, microwave butter and marshmallows uncovered on High about 2 minutes, stirring after each minute, until mixture is smooth.

2 Immediately stir in cereal until evenly coated. Pour cereal mixture into pan. Spray back of spoon with cooking spray. Using back of spoon, press mixture firmly into pan until even. Cool at least 10 minutes. For bars, cut into 6 rows by 4 rows.

Party Cereal Bars

Cut bars with any simple-shaped cookie cutter and sprinkle bars with sprinkles.

why it works:

No need for a sharp knife for these bars, which makes them kid friendly. They are pliable but firm enough so that we recommend using a table knife for a clean cut.

how to store:

Store these cereal bars in a loosely covered container.

1 Bar: Calories 80; Total Fat 2g (Saturated Fat 1g, Trans Fat 0g); Cholesterol 0mg; Sodium 40mg; Total Carbohydrate 15g (Dietary Fiber 3g, Sugars 7g); Protein 0g
Exchanges: 1 Other Carbohydrate, ½ Fat
Carbohydrate Choices: 1

Sweet-and-Salty Cereal Bars

PREP TIME: **15 Minutes** • START TO FINISH: **1 Hour 15 Minutes** • **16 bars**

4 cups honey nut O-shaped whole-grain oat cereal
1 cup dry-roasted peanuts
1 cup candy-coated chocolate candies
1 cup pretzel sticks, coarsely broken
⅓ cup packed brown sugar
⅓ cup light corn syrup
1 tablespoon butter

1 Line bottom and sides of 8-inch square pan with foil or cooking parchment paper. Spray foil with cooking spray.

2 In large bowl, mix cereal, peanuts, chocolate candies and pretzels; set aside.

3 In large microwavable bowl, microwave brown sugar, corn syrup and butter uncovered on High 2 to 3 minutes, stirring every 30 seconds, until mixture is boiling. Microwave an additional 1 minute, allowing mixture to boil and thicken slightly. Let stand 3 minutes to cool slightly.

4 Pour over cereal mixture in bowl; stir until evenly coated. Spray back of spoon with cooking spray. Using back of spoon, press mixture very firmly into pan. Refrigerate about 1 hour or until firm enough to cut. For bars, cut into 4 rows by 4 rows.

why it works:

Lining a pan with foil or cooking parchment paper provides for easy cleanup as well as ease in removing the bars from the pan for cutting. Simply remove the foil from the pan, peel foil from sides and cut bars.

how to store:

Store these bars covered at room temperature up to 1 week.

1 Bar: Calories 220; Total Fat 9g (Saturated Fat 3g, Trans Fat 0g); Cholesterol 0mg; Sodium 150mg; Total Carbohydrate 31g (Dietary Fiber 2g, Sugars 18g); Protein 3g
Exchanges: 1 Starch, 1 Other Carbohydrate, 1½ Fat
Carbohydrate Choices: 2

Chocolate–Peanut Butter Candy Bars

PREP TIME: **15 Minutes** • START TO FINISH: **45 Minutes** • **32 bars**

24	creme-filled chocolate sandwich cookies
4	cups miniature marshmallows
¼	cup butter
1	cup semisweet chocolate chips
1	can (14 oz) sweetened condensed milk (not evaporated)

1⅔	cups peanut butter chips
¼	cup creamy peanut butter
1	cup coarsely chopped honey-roasted peanuts
4	peanut butter crunchy granola bars (2 pouches from 8.9-oz box), crushed
1	teaspoon vegetable oil

kitchen secret:

To easily crush granola bars, leave them in the pouches. Gently pound with meat mallet or rolling pin to break them up.

how to store:

Store these bars loosely covered at room temperature.

1 Bar: Calories 240; Total Fat 12g (Saturated Fat 4g, Trans Fat 0g); Cholesterol 10mg; Sodium 130mg; Total Carbohydrate 29g (Dietary Fiber 1g, Sugars 21g); Protein 5g
Exchanges: 2 Starch, 2 Fat
Carbohydrate Choices: 2

1 Line 13x9-inch pan with foil, leaving foil overhanging at 2 opposite sides of pan. In food processor, process cookies until finely chopped; set aside.

2 In 2-quart saucepan, heat marshmallows and butter over low heat, stirring constantly, until melted and smooth. Stir in chopped cookies and ¾ cup of the chocolate chips until well mixed. Press in bottom of pan.

3 In medium microwavable bowl, microwave condensed milk and peanut butter chips uncovered on High 60 seconds, stirring once, until smooth. Stir in peanut butter. Stir in peanuts and crushed granola bars. Spread over chocolate layer.

4 In small microwavable bowl, microwave remaining ¼ cup chocolate chips and the oil uncovered on High 30 seconds or until chips are softened and can be stirred smooth. Drizzle chocolate diagonally over peanut butter layer.

5 Refrigerate 30 minutes or until set. Use foil to lift bars from pan. For bars, cut into 8 rows by 4 rows.

Gluten-Free Cereal Bars

PREP TIME: 5 Minutes • **START TO FINISH: 20 Minutes** • **18 bars**

¼ cup butter
1 bag (10 oz) large
   marshmallows or 4 cups
   miniature marshmallows

8 cups bite-size squares
   oven-toasted rice cereal

1 Spray 13x9-inch (3-quart) baking dish or pan with cooking spray.

2 In large microwavable bowl, microwave butter uncovered on High about 45 seconds or until melted. Add marshmallows; toss to coat. Microwave 1 to 1½ minutes longer. Stir until marshmallows are completely melted and mixture is well blended.

3 Add cereal; mix well. Using waxed paper or spatula sprayed with cooking spray, press mixture evenly into baking dish. Cool 15 minutes. For bars, cut into 6 rows by 3 rows.

kitchen secret:

If the mixture is difficult to press into pan, slightly dampen fingers with water.

how to store:

Store these bars in a loosely-covered container at room temperature.

1 Bar: Calories 130; Total Fat 4g (Saturated Fat 1g, Trans Fat 0g); Cholesterol 0mg; Sodium 170mg; Total Carbohydrate 23g (Dietary Fiber 0g, Sugars 10g); Protein 1g **Exchanges:** ½ Starch, 1 Other Carbohydrate, ½ Fat **Carbohydrate Choices:** 1½

Good Morning Breakfast Bars

PREP TIME: 15 Minutes • START TO FINISH: 1 Hour 15 Minutes • 12 bars

½ cup packed brown sugar
⅓ cup light corn syrup
   or honey
¼ cup peanut butter
½ teaspoon ground cinnamon

4 cups whole-grain wheat and
   bran flakes and raisins
   multivitamin cereal
½ cup chopped peanuts or
   sliced almonds

1 Butter 8-inch square pan. In 3-quart saucepan, heat brown sugar and corn syrup just to boiling over medium heat, stirring frequently. Remove from heat; stir in peanut butter and cinnamon until smooth.

2 Stir in cereal and peanuts until evenly coated. Press firmly in pan. Let stand about 1 hour or until set. For bars, cut into 4 rows by 3 rows.

why it works:

These cereal and nut breakfast bars are easy to make and portable. Wrap individual bars in plastic wrap, and take on the go—on the bus, in the car or to work—for a midmorning snack.

how to store:

Store these breakfast bars loosely covered at room temperature.

1 Bar: Calories 210; Total Fat 6g (Saturated Fat 1g, Trans Fat 0g); Cholesterol 0mg; Sodium 120mg; Total Carbohydrate 34g (Dietary Fiber 3g, Sugars 18g); Protein 4g **Exchanges:** 1½ Starch, 1 Other Carbohydrate, 1 Fat **Carbohydrate Choices:** 2

TOO
HOT
TO
BAKE

Metric Conversion Guide

VOLUME

U.S. UNITS	CANADIAN METRIC	AUSTRALIAN METRIC
¼ teaspoon	1 mL	1 ml
½ teaspooon	2 mL	2 ml
1 teaspoon	5 mL	5 ml
1 tablespoon	15 mL	20 ml
¼ cup	50 mL	60 ml
⅓ cup	75 mL	80 ml
½ cup	125 mL	125 ml
⅔ cup	150 mL	170 ml
¾ cup	175 mL	190 ml
1 cup	250 mL	250 ml
1 quart	1 liter	1 liter
1½ quarts	1.5 liters	1.5 liters
2 quarts	2 liters	2 liters
2½ quarts	2.5 liters	2.5 liters
3 quarts	3 liters	3 liters
4 quarts	4 liters	4 liters

WEIGHT

US. UNITS	CANADIAN METRIC	AUSTRALIAN METRIC
1 ounce	30 grams	30 grams
2 ounces	55 grams	60 grams
3 ounces	85 grams	90 grams
4 ounces (¼ pound)	115 grams	125 grams
8 ounces (½ pound)	225 grams	225 grams
16 ounces (1 pound)	455 grams	500 grams
1 pound	455 grams	0.5 kilogram

NOTE: The recipes in this cookbook have not been developed or tested using metric measures. When converting recipes to metric, some variations in quality may be noted.

MEASUREMENTS

INCHES	CENTIMETERS
1	2.5
2	5.0
3	7.5
4	10.0
5	12.5
6	15.0
7	17.5
8	20.5
9	23.0
10	25.5
11	28.0
12	30.5
13	33.0

TEMPERATURES

FAHRENHEIT	CELSIUS
32°	0°
212°	100°
250°	120°
275°	140°
300°	150°
325°	160°
350°	180°
375°	190°
400°	200°
425°	220°
450°	230°
475°	240°
500°	260°

INDEX

RECIPE TESTING AND CALCULATING NUTRITION INFORMATION

RECIPE TESTING:

- Large eggs and 2% milk were used unless otherwise indicated.

- Fat-free, low-fat, low-sodium or lite products were not used unless indicated.

- No nonstick cookware and bakeware were used unless otherwise indicated. No dark-colored, black or insulated bakeware was used.

- When a pan is specified, a metal pan was used; a baking dish or pie plate means ovenproof glass was used.

- An electric hand mixer was used for mixing only when mixer speeds are specified.

CALCULATING NUTRITION:

- The first ingredient was used wherever a choice is given, such as ⅓ cup sour cream or plain yogurt.

- The first amount was used wherever a range is given, such as 3- to 3½-pound whole chicken.

- The first serving number was used wherever a range is given, such as 4 to 6 servings.

- "If desired" ingredients were not included.

- Only the amount of a marinade or frying oil that is absorbed was included.

- Diabetic exchanges are not calculated in recipes containing uncooked alcohol, due to its effect on blood sugar levels.